AUTOPHOBIA

AUTOPHOBIA

Love and Hate in the Automotive Age

BRIAN LADD

University of Chicago Press CHICAGO AND LONDON

BRIAN LADD is a research associate in the history department at the University at Albany, State University of New York. He is the author of *The Ghosts of Berlin: Confronting German History in the Urban Landscape*, also published by the University of Chicago Press.

The University of Chicago Press, Chicago 60637
The University of Chicago Press, Ltd., London
© 2008 by The University of Chicago
All rights reserved. Published 2008
Printed in the United States of America

17 16 15 14 13 12 11 10 09 08   1 2 3 4 5

ISBN-13: 978-0-226-46741-2 (cloth)
ISBN-10: 0-226-46741-4 (cloth)

Library of Congress Cataloging-in-Publication Data

Ladd, Brian, 1957–
    Authophobia : love and hate in the automotive age / Brian Ladd.
      p. cm.
    Includes bibliographical references and index.
    ISBN-13: 978-0-226-46741-2 (cloth : alk. paper)
    ISBN-10: 0-226-46741-4 (cloth : alk. paper) 1. Automobiles—Social aspects.
2. Automotive ownership—Social aspects. 3. Transportation, Automotive—
Social aspects. 4. Environmental degradation. I. Title.
    HE5611.L26 2008
    303.48'32—dc22

                                                          2008014520

∞ The paper used in this publication meets the minimum requirements of the American National Standard for Information Sciences—Permanence of Paper for Printed Library Materials, ANSI z39.48-1992.

Contents

Illustrations

Dream Machines

Where would we be without cars? Stuck in the mud, or in the nineteenth century, we are told. Cars have been the basic tools and the great glories of the modern age. They liberated the farmer from isolation and ignorance. They helped lift millions out of poverty: remote country dwellers, stranded ghetto residents, American auto workers, and then the entire working class of the industrial world. Cars bring people together. They permit ordinary folk to go places once reserved for the exclusive few. Even today, in poorer lands, an automobile can transform lives, not only providing a family—or perhaps a whole clan—with convenient transportation, not only making it possible to reach a new job, but often itself becoming a source of employment—as a taxi, as a jitney, as a carrier of commercial goods around a city or across the countryside. But those are not the only reasons poor people dream of the car in their future. They, too, yearn to sit proudly behind the wheel of a gleaming machine, and to floor its accelerator—to feel, for a moment, that they are leaving the world behind. The car combines the promise of thrills with the sovereign assurance of mobility. Mobility is freedom—freedom is mobility—and before the car, mobility was unavailable, or slow, or (as with trains) dependent on the whim or goodwill of others. No wonder cars have the power to stir the blood like no other modern invention.

And yet the contrarians have never been silenced. Where indeed, they ask, would we be without cars? Liberated, in a word. Cars are the scourge of civilization. They make us fat and lazy, unfeeling and selfish, prisoners in our steel cages. They poison the air and change the climate. Their voracious appetite for natural resources yokes us to the whims of distant dictators with oil wells. They kill the equivalent of a dozen jumbo-jet crashes every day, and cripple and sicken far more. They devour the land, forcing us apart until we are helpless without them, stuck on clogged roads and hardly able to get around at all. When we lament suburban sprawl and the decline of community, we are looking at the handiwork of the automobile.

Few of us identify wholeheartedly with one side or the other, with either the industry shills and radical libertarians who offer paeans to the car, or the technophobes, tree huggers, and killjoys who curse it. From time to time we worry about our personal contribution to energy shortages and air pollution and global warming. Yet few of us ever cancel a journey, or go on foot or by bicycle or train, merely to reduce our carbon footprint. In fact, the idea of taking away our cars, or forcing us into smaller vehicles, or charging us fees to drive or park, or closing streets to cars, makes many of us indignant in defense of our right to drive. But then: one frantic errand too many, plus a traffic jam, and a flash of road rage—and the convenience of driving, much less the thrill of it, pales in the face of an uneasy realization that we are not really our best selves behind the wheel, and that there ought to be a better way.

A rational discussion about the merits of automobiles is scarcely possible. It is too hard to imagine our lives apart from our driving. Nor can we picture our cities and suburbs arranged around anything but highways and parking lots. Cars have fundamentally shaped our age—in the thoroughly car-centered United States, and no less profoundly in the clogged lanes of Europe and the exhaust-choked chaos of the world's largest and fast-growing metropolises, from squalid Lagos to splendid (if smoggy) Shanghai. Once we have cars—and especially once there are nearly as many cars as drivers—we can fully benefit from the great convenience they offer. Yet as we organize our lives around their needs, the freedom they bring can begin to feel more like slavery. Certainly they have come to dictate our living arrangements. Cities in the automobile age have been shaped by a search for space to drive cars and to park them, along with the countervailing desire to escape their dangers and their noise—but to escape by car. The sinews of city and country are highways where pedestrians and bicyclists are out of place and in peril. Homes present just a garage door to the street. Indeed, new houses often look like garages with drivers' quarters attached, much as early garages were converted stables with chauffeurs' quarters above.

Figure 1. Refusing to face the problems of the automobile. Tom Toles cartoon. © 1989 The Washington Post. Reprinted with permission of Universal Press Syndicate.

After a century at the wheel, have we—and our planet—had enough? Could we be reaching the end of the automotive age? Car critics tout revived mass transit, renewed possibilities for bicycling, and newly designed walkable communities. These glimmers of hope, they believe, may soon become indispensable models for people forced to cease taking their cars for granted. Cars are the largest contributor to what we are told is our "unsustainable" lifestyle. Volatile gasoline prices go up much more than they go down, and it seems clear that oil supplies will only get tighter. One in eight barrels of the world's oil production is burned on American highways alone, with the rest of the world's automotive share growing rapidly. That means our driving becomes ever costlier. It means helpless dependence on unstable regions of the world. It means continued air pollution. It means that Americans' per capita contribution to global warming dwarfs that of other countries (and the total U.S. share was by far the largest until China began its rapid motorization), because the automobile's contribution exceeds that of any other source except electrical power generation.

Add the astonishing price in human lives that we pay for our automobility: thirty million dead in the twentieth century and 1.2 million more every year since, most of them young and healthy. Plus all the hassles of the three-car suburban family: the utter dependence on automobiles to get everywhere; the hours spent commuting to work, running errands, transporting the kids to every single activity—even to school, and certainly to friends' houses that cannot be reached any other way. Add the longing for a friendly neighborhood amid the reality of closed garage doors and, at best, a quick wave to a neighbor through the windshield.

Something has to change. Clearly the end is near. Or is it? Many of us remember hearing, and perhaps saying, similar things during the 1970s, when acute if brief fuel shortages awakened a more universal awareness of our precarious dependence on cars, just as a new and robust environmental movement demanded action against the choking clouds of urban smog. Wise critics predicted the imminent end of the automobile age. Since then, however, the number of cars on the road has more than doubled. That was an end that never came.

Even when worries about oil supplies were new, the cry to abandon our cars was not. The years before the oil crisis, the late 1960s and early 1970s, may have been the golden age of car-bashing in the U.S. and Europe, when exposés of the freeway-industrial "road gang" such as Helen Leavitt's *Superhighway—Superhoax* jostled for attention alongside manifestos of revolt like Kenneth R. Schneider's *Autokind vs. Mankind*. Western Europe was quickly catching up to the United States in the size of its car fleet and in its collective outrage at the destruction of cities by noise, fumes, blood, and pavement. Public outcry was finally demanding action against the huge and growing death toll from traffic accidents. Yet that revolution, too, faded to a whimper and vanished out the rearview mirror, along with books like *Dead End* and *Road to Ruin*. People kept buying cars and driving them.

For that matter, those militant car critics seemed to be recycling objections that perceptive intellectuals had been raising for years. There are many reasons to think of the 1950s as the pinnacle of the car culture, at least in the United States. The era's paramount symbol of prosperity was the gigantic chrome-laden sedan. It was the golden age of drive-in restaurants and drive-in movies. Certainly it was the high-water mark of Detroit's role in the American economy. Yet by the time the postwar auto boom was a decade old, the carmakers were under fire for their high-handed disregard for the needs of ordinary Americans—for their inefficient, oversized, overpriced, shoddy, and downright unsafe cars. The writer John Keats declared that 1957 marked "the end of an era" of automotive excess, the unmistakable mark of that end being the Ford Motor Company's ridiculous Edsel. And in a sense Keats was right: his attacks on 1950s suburban conformity opened the way for other condemnations of car culture and the auto industry. The most sensational was that of young Ralph Nader, who captured the nation's attention with his 1965 book, *Unsafe at Any Speed*, which revealed Detroit's willful inattention to its customers' safety. Yet the carmakers absorbed the embarrassment, made adjustments, and kept selling cars. When we hear that the Detroit automakers are doomed, it is worth remembering that for half a century they have appeared to be lumbering dinosaurs on the verge of extinction, and despite one screwup after another—Edsels, death traps, gas-guzzlers, and so on—they still loom large in the American economy and culture—and so, by now, do Toyota and its Japanese rivals.

An English observer seems to sum up a century of disquiet: "It began by being a scientific experiment, went on to become the instrument of the adventurous, then became the toy of the rich, then the ambition of the poor, and finally the servant of everyone. . . . From being the plaything of society it has come to dominate society. It is now our tyrant, so that at last we have turned in revolt against it, and begun to protest against its arrogant ways."[1] These words could have been written in 2001, or 1971, but in fact they date to 1911. Many criticisms of the automobile have been around as long as there have been cars. They were always dangerous, noisy, and polluting; they have always disrupted families and communities. Somehow we have managed to endure their tyranny for a century. Perhaps they're really not so bad. Perhaps they're one of those indispensable things we love to hate. But why do the same complaints keep coming back, again and again? Is it that some Luddites just can't accept reality? Is this a history of pessimists, of losers, of contrarians? Or have we really fallen into the clutches of a dreadful monster?

There are two ways to read the evidence of this century of Cassandras. The obvious approach is to take note of how wrong the naysayers have been, how often they have recycled the same false assumptions about technology and change and human nature, how they have persisted in their disdain for ordinary people, how they have refused to acknowledge the ways people adapted automotive technology to their benefit. That kind of analysis is useful for making sense of the car haters' motives and logic, and, often, for understanding how they have been so prejudiced, narrow-minded, and wrong. But sometimes it is also worth recalling that the mythical Cassandra was right. History, it is said, is written by the winners, and for the past century motorists have clearly been the winners. The losers—those who have suffered the very real distress caused by the automobile—have a different story to tell. The fact that much has been done to mitigate the problems of air pollution, accident fatalities, and traffic congestion makes it easy for boosters to assure themselves that any remaining flaws are just as ephemeral. Certainly some are. Yet there is also little doubt that human beings' reliance on this particular bit of machinery is not a permanent characteristic of our world. Someday we will, eagerly or reluctantly, choose another path. Many of the automobile's critics have claimed to glimpse our car-free future. Up to now, these critics have been mostly (if perhaps not entirely) wrong. Probably some of them have made accurate predictions of the future yet to come. Even if we doubt their predictions, though, we should acknowledge their grievances.

The problem with the car haters' view of the world is not just that their predictions have been so wrong. They have underestimated the automobile's staying power because, too often, they have persisted in denying its attractions. They often insist that if all the stupidity, corruption, and special interests were removed from transportation planning, all the unfair subsidies to automobiles would vanish, and people would gladly abandon their cars in favor of trains or bicycles or walking shoes. Their single-minded focus on the outrageous inefficiency of a two-ton gas-guzzler transporting a single person (probably to the gym, to get some exercise) blinds them to the ways in which cars are in fact remarkably effective tools to provide the individual mobility around which modern lives are organized—in many ways far more efficient than, say, trains. It is still possible to make a compelling case that our dependence on our cars has become a liability, in view of urban decay, dwindling energy supplies, environmental devastation, and climate change. Yet such arguments, important as they are, may ultimately carry little weight. Whether or not cars are a wise choice, people love them, and cannot imagine life without them.

There have been many attempts to impose a rational calculus on automotive desires. This book is not one of them. Nor does it propose to settle the disputed question of whether or how much cars in any or all lands benefit from government subsidies. Since a great deal of money is at stake just in taxes, fees, and public expenditures related to automobiles, there is an understandable need to evaluate the wisdom of spending public money to promote (or discourage) their use. However, there are many different ways of measuring the costs and benefits of driving, since auto use is so embedded in people's lives and in government finances around the world. The only consensus in the heated debates about automotive subsidies is that everything is being done wrong. Those who believe the automobile is a boon to civilization, worthy of universal support, argue that it is paying its own way, while governments burden motorists with exorbitant taxes and fees (and waste money on mass-transit systems hardly anybody wants). The automobile's opponents insist that this bane of civilization is massively subsidized (and many academic experts agree). There is little doubt that governments, for most of the twentieth century, looked favorably upon automobiles—particularly in the United States, which has historically taxed them lightly, but in most other lands as well. One response, during the late twentieth century, was for many governments to add new subsidies to rail and bus transit. The wisdom of any of these subsidies can be questioned; their removal has rarely been contemplated. They are hostage to politics, as perhaps they should be.[2] Although many car critics believe that a definitive calculation of the costs and benefits of auto use would settle the issue in their favor, these costs and benefits are too pervasive (and shot through with questions of equity, justice, and communal well-being) to lend themselves to a definitive measurement. Nor is it clear that the removal of all automotive subsidies, if it were possible, would draw many people out of their cars. Too many other bonds of habit, affection, need, and fear bind people to their prized possessions.

The hostility to cars, in all its phases, has provoked a pro-auto response that often successfully punctured the illogic of the car haters and revealed the implausibility of their visions of a car-free future. The motley band of propagandists for the automobile eagerly remind you that the critics are still on the wrong side of history, as more and more people embrace the freedom offered by the automobile, and worldwide car use continues to grow—most dramatically in a land such as China, where millions of people are only now getting a chance to experience the comfort and mobility a car can provide. The problem with these boosters' claims is their complacent embrace of the car. Having satisfied themselves that particular alternatives to our car-centered existence are not practical, the car's defenders rest their case. Too often, they dismiss or belittle all the harm said to be caused by automobiles—pollution, climate change, obesity, urban decay, social isolation, antisocial behavior, carnage on the roads. These problems, they argue, are either unimportant, or easily solved, or the inevitable price of the marvelously free and prosperous lives we live, lives made possible by our cars.

A history of the advocacy and promotion of automobiles would thus be a colorful story of success, but also a fascinating history of denial. Another way to understand that denial—the approach taken in this book— is to trace the triumph of the automobile through the eyes of those who hated or resisted it. This history of hostility to the automobile is inevitably also a history of its appeal, as seen through the (admittedly distorted) lens of those who spurned it.

Cars are often credited with many of the changes in people's lives during the twentieth century. Ironically, the same claim is made by both car lovers and car haters. From one side, we hear that the mobility offered by cars has been our greatest fount of freedom. Critics respond that automobiles have shattered our cities, polluted the countryside, and poisoned social interaction. Both sides are giving cars too much credit. Historians of technology warn against the fallacy of believing that our machines change our lives all by themselves, and that we simply accept what they bring to us. Technology, they argue, is always "socially constructed": cars, like all machines, were invented, sold, and adapted to suit needs and desires that either already existed or were already changing for many reasons. Automotive technology is also politically constructed: powerful interests have made their influence felt in lasting ways, notably in the construction of roads.

Still, it would be wrong to deny that cars have made a difference: their availability at certain times, in certain forms, has clearly reshaped lives, homes, and landscapes. Their existence, their capabilities, and their technological limitations have shaped modern cities in particular. Historians of technology have another theory that applies here: the idea of "path dependence" suggests that once cars began to reshape cities (or rather, once people began to reshape cities to fit their cars) later decisions were constrained by the earlier ones. Once you choose to buy a car, for example, you have a reason to live in a place where it is easy and cheap to park that car—even if you end up with no other way to get to work. You might start shopping at stores that were previously inaccessible. And as others make the same decisions, as your suburban home, office park, and shopping mall become organized entirely around automotive access, it becomes difficult, costly, and unappealing to reorganize your life (and your neighbors') to eliminate or even reduce your driving. In a more profound way, once you get used to cruising around town encased in a glass-and-steel bubble, your perception of town changes fundamentally, along with the demands you make on it. The result can be (and clearly in some cases has been) a growing dependence on cars that is not inspired by any love for them. People just get used to their cars: as has been said many times, the love affair turns into a marriage. If prosperous Westerners no longer exclaim over the benefits of electricity or central heating, so, too, is it with automobiles.

A striking fact about the automobile as a technological artifact—one that makes possible the generalizations in this book—is how little it has really changed in the course of a century and more, for all its hyped and often useful technological refinements. A wide variety of motorized and wheeled vehicles have clattered and dashed across the surface of the earth, but the great majority of them are recognizably of a single type: a metal (or at any rate a rigid) box, mounted on four wheels, powered by a petroleum-burning engine, capable of carrying a few people rapidly through town or country, constrained mainly by the limits imposed by external obstructions in the vehicle's path. The motor vehicle has taken other forms, some of them of great significance—motorcycles, trucks, and buses—but variations on the basic passenger car have shaped most people's experiences. (Although these vehicles have been adapted in endlessly varied ways, there is also a standard model of ownership: taxis and collectively owned cars are the exception; the norm is ownership and exclusive use by an individual or family.) It took a few years after 1900 for the gasoline-powered internal-combustion engine to drive its steam and electric rivals from the field, but even they were in most respects not too different. Most car books celebrate the uniqueness of one or another particular automotive type: the Ford Thunderbird, Jaguar XJ, or East German Trabant; the V-8 or the Wankel engine; the station wagon or the coupe; General Motors or Toyota. This book takes the opposite tack, assuming the fundamental similarity of all these machines.

This technological uniformity helps explain the consistency in reactions to the car, favorable and hostile. Part of the story of the automobile is the sometimes astonishing continuity in the ways people have beheld, welcomed, and despised it. Certainly there are differences between the experiences of driving or riding in slow or fast cars, open or closed ones, crank-started or computerized ones. Still, the visceral thrill of speed has been shared across the century, as have the convenience of getting places and the inconvenience of parking your car when you arrive. The sense of control, the liberation from social constraints, the impetus to aggression—all have been felt, celebrated, and lamented again and again. This similarity of experience can be—and often is—offered as evidence of the brilliance of the machine and the perfection with which it suits our nature and our needs. Such an explanation is too simple. We also must also consider the stubborn "path dependence" of our reliance on this device. The combination of established habits and entrenched interests, for example, has impeded even the relatively modest switch to electric cars: the unaccustomed need to plug them in to recharge, and to be aware of their limited range, weighs more heavily on motorists than the welcome quiet and cleanliness or the freedom from petroleum and filling stations.

Among the many studies of the ways people have coped with automobiles, few venture across national borders. Most writers treat their own countries alone.[3] There are sound scholarly reasons for their limited horizons: the car culture has left behind an overwhelming amount of material in many nations and languages, and there are bound to be questionable generalizations in a book that claims to cover the entire world, by an author who (like everyone) knows some parts of it better than others. But national studies fall back too readily either on supposedly universal desires or on national peculiarities—a German love of technology, Italian mistrust of government, American intoxication with freedom, Japanese submissiveness. The sale and promotion of automobiles has long been a transnational endeavor, as cars have been adapted to the geography, culture, and economies of all nations. Car critics in different lands have also studied and echoed one another. The nation that looms largest in this book is, appropriately, the United States, which has dominated car culture since its early years. Outside the U.S., the largest concentration of cars has long been in western Europe (along with Japan), and the struggles with the automobile there are my secondary focus. Other nations also put in an appearance to illustrate the varied contexts in which cars have operated.

The automotive history in this book is not about the machines, but rather about the world in which they have been bought, driven, parked, and crashed. Even if the machines themselves are recognizably the same as a century ago, the context in which they operate has changed profoundly. When cars were rich men's toys, just an occasional roaring nuisance on the city street or country lane, they meant something very different from the floods of vehicles packed onto suburban freeways and parking lots.

Through the eyes of the car's critics, we can understand how automobiles have disrupted lives in different times and places.

The most important of the changing contexts is the other technological artifact (in addition to the automobile) that this book is about: the city. Cities are large, complex, and fairly permanent entities, certainly more so than automobiles. Yet in the past century they have changed more than cars, and the automobile may be the single most important cause of that change. Cities all over the world have been rebuilt to accommodate growing populations, but also to a great extent to make room for their cars. This painful reconstruction is a large part of the story of people's discontent with the automobile. Its promoters have typically been people who happily turn their backs on the cities of slums and teeming streets, while car critics have fought a rearguard action to defend old cities and neighborhoods against the damage wrought by the car.

This history tries to capture the voices of some of the snobs, romantics, iconoclasts, and passionate idealists who denounced the plague of automobiles. Where possible, the merits of their claims are measured against facts, as is the resonance or (more typically) failure of their appeals. The book proceeds more thematically than chronologically, in view of the recurrence of attitudes across the century. The first chapter, on early critiques of motorists' arrogance and aggression, is separated from the second partly by World War II and partly by the arrival of mass automobility, first in the U.S. and then in Europe, which dampened the criticism even as it magnified the threat. The third chapter frames the book's central conflict, between cars that demanded space and mobility, and cities organized around proximity and stability. Chapter 4 focuses more narrowly on urban and transportation policies in the 1960s and 1970s, when opposition to urban freeways around the world grew into a fundamental critique of car use and of the economic interests and professional blinders that perpetuated car-centered policies. The fifth chapter addresses the question of why car use and automotive polemics have changed so little since the 1970s, despite all the critics' cultural, urban, and environmental grievances.

"Autophobia" is an obscure psychiatric diagnosis of "fear of oneself." Fear, or hatred, of automobiles is quite a different thing. Yet the automobile has become such a central tool (and toy) of modern life that it might make sense to claim that fear of cars is tantamount to fear of being human in the automobile age. For hundreds of millions of people around the world, cars offer cherished mobility as well as the chance for aggressive self-assertion, enhanced by the thrills that come with the feeling of risking one's life (along with others'). Qualms about these blessings of automobility leave automotive skeptics open to charges of misanthropy and blindness to human nature as well as timorousness in the face of basic human pleasures. Autophobes know all too well that their contempt, hatred, or fear of cars puts them at odds with their own societies, and often with themselves. But they have honorable reasons for their discomfort with a machine that sometimes seems to transform us into pure id, or at least into heedless teenagers. The fact that many of us have chosen to become virtual centaurs attached to our four-wheeled prosthetic bodies does not mean that we are wise to rely on these vehicles for our transportation, our self-esteem, or our tokens of success.

CHAPTER ONE

Roadkill: The New Machine Flattens Its Critics

"Roadkill" is the popular American term for the hundreds of millions of animals that fall victim to automobiles every year, their carcasses—large and small, furry or not (in the case of Texas armadillos)—littering the roads, glimpsed by speeding motorists but rarely eliciting even a wince, except when the beast in question is an aromatic skunk. In the American ideology of heedless progress, "roadkill" has also become a label for anything and anyone standing in the way of the relentless march of destiny. The fate of these obstructionists is unvarying: the speeding locomotive—or rather, the speeding car—of progress will flatten them. The automobile, our great vehicle of progress, demands its tribute, whether the hapless cats and deer on the road, the houses and neighborhoods swept away for new roads, or the shattered rural idylls. It is considered good form to dispatch all "roadkill" without any lingering sentimentality—although of course the human bodies crushed by speeding cars are generally granted a little more respect. We hope the grieving survivors of automotive casualties will appreciate the necessity of their sacrifice, and we certainly expect them to get over it.

Although the automobile's conquest of public opinion has never been complete, it is astonishing how quickly cars became both fashionable and ubiquitous. The early motorists' confidence was not misplaced. They knew the future was theirs, and the following century seems to have proved them right. But historians, like moralists, sometimes like to point out that might does not always make right. What if we look at the early history of the automobile from the roadkill's point of view?

In many places the first motorcar appeared suddenly, roaring or clattering down the road and drawing hungry stares even as it shattered the peace forever. As a machine, however, the modern automobile emerged gradually, an amalgam of many technologies cobbled together to serve a variety of purposes. From the perspective of the automobile-centered late twentieth century, it was easy to believe that human beings had finally perfected the machine they had always desired. Although we have yet to discover any prehistoric cave paintings of cars, the thirteenth-century philosopher Roger Bacon is credited with predicting the possibility of them, and Renaissance drawings by Leonardo da Vinci and Albrecht Dürer depict what have been interpreted as prototype automobiles. Even as an actual machine, the self-propelled road vehicle has a long if slim history. In the decades after the invention of the steam engine in the eighteenth century, various French, British, and American entrepreneurs experimented with "road engines." Innovation sputtered to a halt, however, after the rapid development of mobile steam engines riding on rails rather than roads. Not only did steam engines prove to be well suited to rails; the newly powerful railway interests pressed their advantage by demanding that restrictions be placed on their road-based rivals. The decisive phase of automotive development came much later in the nineteenth century, in the form of several technological breakthroughs shared among the industrialized nations of Europe and North America.

This innovation was driven less by the skill of inventors than by a growing demand for mobility—that is, a large base of potential customers. These were the prosperous middle classes of the industrial lands, far more numerous than any wealthy class ever before, and possessed of a desire and often a need to be mobile. Their appetite for travel had been whetted by transportation innovations of the previous decades, above all the railways. Since railroads usually operated on their own rights of way, they had not brought their speed to the existing network of country roads and city streets (until electric street railways appeared, just before automobiles did), nor could they satisfy a demand for small, maneuverable vehicles or for individual mobility. Numerous technologies competed to fill those needs: improved horse-drawn carriages; that new sensation, the remarkably efficient human-powered bicycle; and various motorized vehicles.

At the turn of the nineteenth century there were in fact three competing automotive technologies to choose from. Of the three, the gasoline-fueled internal-combustion engine gained a reputation as safer, faster, and more reliable, but that reputation was not entirely deserved, and it was by no means inevitable that both steam and electric automobiles would pass from the scene (or that the rival petroleum engine invented by Rudolf Diesel would be relegated to a secondary role). The invention of the internal-combustion automobile took place, like most inventions, in many steps, but is usually dated to the 1880s in southwestern Germany. The stationary four-stroke internal-combustion engine built by Nicolaus Otto in 1876 was installed in a carriage by his former assistants Gottlieb Daimler and Wilhelm Maybach in their workshop in Cannstatt, while, in Mannheim, Carl Benz modified a bicycle to create a three-wheeled, self-propelled vehicle. (Many of the early cars could accurately be described as "horseless carriages," but others more resembled motorized bicycles.)

Popular histories of technology typically tell the stories of intrepid inventors whose clever machines changed the world by dint of their manifest usefulness or their inherent fascination. But no machine, no matter how clever, can conquer the world by itself. It needs promoters and enthusiasts. As it turned out, there was a vast market for automobiles as practical vehicles for transporting people and goods, but that market did not exist at the outset of the automobile age. The machines were too inefficient, unreliable, and expensive, and, more important, the established vectors of transportation had to be rearranged before the new machines could take control. Above all, this meant that roads—and ultimately cities—had to be rebuilt to accommodate the new vehicles.

What bridged the gap between the invention and its practical use were the enthusiasts. They appeared during the 1890s, especially in France, where the firm of Panhard & Levassor licensed Daimler's engine. Paris and the French Riviera were the first places where cars became fashionable. (The French influence is apparent in the fact that many languages have adopted the French word "automobile," not to mention "chauffeur" and "garage"—although speakers of other tongues stopped short of calling their motor fuel "essence." In the early years, there also seems to have been less opposition to car use in France than in neighboring lands.) As the first cars wheezed down city streets, they drew crowds of the curious and the enthralled, and early auto races demonstrated the thrilling possibilities of road travel at breathtaking speeds—as fast as a train, but free of tracks, locomotives, and engineers. Wealthy and adventurous men (and a few women) in many lands began to acquire their own automobiles and to venture around town and across the countryside in them.

For the early enthusiasts, speed was the key attraction, coupled with the sense of individual mastery that came with driving. The railroad had long given people the chance to move across the earth at breathtaking speeds, but its path was restricted to its rails and its control to a professional engineer, with passengers confined to a passive role. Cars promised a different experience—not, for many years to come, a more comfortable journey, but rather a more exhilarating one. In the 1890s, when most people were no more likely to drive a car than to ride a racehorse, auto races promised thrills for a few drivers as well as crowds of onlookers. Crashes were common, often fatal, and part of the excitement of the race. The machine's power—the power of life and death—depended on an individual driver, a role to which anyone could aspire. Soon the airplane would come along to offer some of the same thrills, but only for a select few, and not in the narrow confines of city streets or country lanes. The automobile, by contrast, let ordinary people (or at least ordinary people with money) take control of a speeding vehicle on familiar roads, with exciting and often disastrous results.

Speed was never the only reason to drive, of course, and in 1902 an automotive writer was confident that "in time the intoxication of the rapid motion of the automobile will wear off, and the pleasure of using such machines will be found in the opportunity that it gives to enjoy fresh air, change of scene and the beauties of nature, with the sense of freedom and independence that cannot be enjoyed in railroad trains."[1] Certainly some motorists came to prefer these gentler pursuits, but many others have shared the spirit of the thrill-seeking English writer Aldous Huxley (famous, ironically, for the dystopian Fordist future portrayed in his novel Brave New World), who was still insisting years later that the best modern intoxicant was "the drug of speed," which "provides the one genuinely modern pleasure," a feeling only available in a car going upwards of seventy miles per hour.[2]

In the beginning the automobile was a toy, suitable for racing, thrills, and leisure outings. Perhaps someday it will again be mainly a toy, but for now, millions of people across the world have come to see it as a necessity. Although they may explain that necessity in terms of rationally defensible needs of daily life, many of them still rely on their cars to satisfy thoroughly irrational passions: for speed, thrills, and aggression, or for a sense of autonomy and individuality. For most of its users, a car is many things at once, and therefore not easily replaced.

In 1900 car owners were almost by definition wealthy, especially since they often employed chauffeurs: many wouldn't have dreamed of trying to operate their own vehicles. Automobiles became the most visible intrusion of city life into the countryside—noisier, dirtier, and more dangerous variations on the bicycles that had been all the rage a few years before. When Edith Wharton exclaimed that "the motor-car has restored the romance of travel," in 1908, she meant that her car and chauffeur could carry her to the most picturesque towns in France.[3] In rural Europe, cars remained a sign of wealthy urban invaders into the 1930s. Farmers and villagers watched them roar (or splutter) by, get stuck, or run off the road, and they reacted with amusement, contempt, fear, hatred, envy, or perhaps admiration.

The emblematic English motorist was, curiously enough, an amphibian: the character of Mr. Toad in Kenneth Grahame's popular 1908 children's story, *The Wind in the Willows*, embodies the heedless, thrill-seeking, upper-class motorist, intoxicated by speed and completely helpless against his own irresistible urge to race and crash motorcars, until his reckless ways land him in prison. Still, Toad was ultimately a harmless and even lovable eccentric. The prolific English philosopher C. E. M. Joad could not bring himself to see real human motorists as anything less than mortal threats to all civilized refinement. In a 1927 book (whose subject was, significantly, the pernicious influence of everything American) he came straight to the point: "motoring is one of the most contemptible soul-destroying and devitalizing pursuits that the ill-fortune of misguided humanity has ever imposed upon its credulity." The motorist was nothing but an obnoxious showoff: he "desires to advertise to the world at large that he has amassed enough money to hurl himself over its surface as often and as fast as it pleases him."[4]

It was usually the machines' noise that announced their arrival in the countryside. Many early drivers, inspired by racers, wanted their vehicles to roar (much as many motorcyclists do today) and thereby made themselves very unpopular, at least until mufflers became obligatory. Joad likened the noise of cars sputtering down country roads to "a regiment of soldiers" who "had begun to suffer simultaneously from flatulence." Motorists also liked to announce their presence (as if that were necessary) by blowing their horns in a cacophony like "a pack of fiends released from the nethermost pit."[5] The eminent German sociologist Werner Sombart complained bitterly of a world in which "*one* person was permitted to spoil thousands of walkers' enjoyment of nature."[6] Joad raged at the "Babbitts" who claimed they could enjoy the countryside while racing across it, filling it with fumes and an infernal din: "Everyone knows that the only way to see the country is to walk in it."[7] (Joad's translation of good taste into groupthink—"everyone knows"—is all the more astonishing when, two pages later, he projects the same arrogance onto the motorist: "Like everyone of vulgar tastes, he thinks that all men share them.")

In England and Germany, the heartlands of Romanticism, movements to protect the endangered countryside from the ravages of modernity had arisen before the automobile age, but it was in the decades after 1900 that they acquired a sense of urgency. As an English observer lamented in 1937, "the car, unlike the train, does not clot its horrors at the journey's end but smears them along the way."[8] In the United States, where greater numbers of cars made the threat more acute, the wilderness-preservation movement was almost entirely a product of the automobile age, and its leaders' paramount goal, during the 1930s in particular, was to cordon off pristine areas from the automobile. Vast and remote Yellowstone and Yosemite may have been very different places from the South Downs or the Black Forest, but in every case their defenders feared that the automobile would upset a precarious balance, bringing too many people, too quickly, and perhaps the wrong sort of people. The automobile's critics scoffed at the claim that motorists had a right to bring their noisy vehicles with them. After all, as Joad observed, they gained nothing from the experience: "From the country they are completely cut off; they cannot see its sights, hear its sounds, smell its smells, or enjoy its silence."[9]

Joad was just as certain that motoring was bad for the motorist. "At the end of the journey he descends cold and irritable, with a sick headache born of rush and racks. He clamours for tea or dinner, but, lacking both bodily exercise and mental stimulus, he eats without appetite, and only continues to eat because at a motoring hotel there is nothing else to do. It is at such places that the modern fat man is made."[10] Some might think Joad was prescient here; but this is snobbery rather than analysis. Still, in his defense we might take note of the fatuous claims being made for the physical and psychic benefits of motoring. Many a car-loving physician praised the invigorating effects of swift movement through fresh air. New York City health commissioner Royal S. Copeland (later a U.S. senator) went further in 1922: "Most of us get enough exercise in the walking necessary, even to the most confined life, to keep the leg mus-

MEMBERS OF THE "GUILD OF NATURE-LOVERS" PASSING A PETROL-STATION.

Figure 2. Country hikers under siege. *Punch* cartoon by Charles Harrison, 1928. Reproduced with permission of Punch Ltd., www.punch.co.uk.

cles fairly fit. It is from the waist upward that flabbiness usually sets in. The slight, but purposeful effort demanded in swinging the steering wheel, reacts exactly where we need it most. Frankly I believe that steering a motor car is actually better exercise than walking, because it does react on the parts of the body least used in the ordinary man's routine existence."[11] The country walker Joad begged to differ: "Observe the bored and scowling couple lolling in this Daimler which is just about to drive you off the road into the ditch. The man is puny, and pot-bellied; the woman flabby, yellow and wrinkled. Their minds are vacant, their tempers irritable and their bodies idle and cold."[12] Soon the addition of quarreling children in the back seat would complete the picture of domestic automotive bliss.

No one claimed driving was healthy for pedestrians or bystanders. Apart from the danger to their lives and limbs, there was, first of all, the dust. Country dwellers wailed at the clouds of dust descending on their lungs, their homes, and their gardens. Unpaved country roads (that is, nearly all of them) had always been dusty, but the tires of speeding cars churned the dust faster and farther than horses, oxen, or wagons ever had. A statement from a 1909 British road-building handbook reveals the severity of the plague (if not necessarily an accurate diagnosis of it): "It is a matter of common knowledge that our great infantile mortality is largely attributable to dust."[13] The problem would eventually be solved by better road construction, and experiments with new pavements began early in the auto age. At first, however, it was hard to imagine that such expense could ever be justified, and discussion turned to speed limits and even to outright bans on automobiles.

As unpleasant as the newfangled machines themselves were, the atrocious behavior of their operators only began with horn honking. Unsuspecting farm dogs and fowl were slaughtered by the thousands as they wandered onto once-safe roads. Some drivers—perhaps not many, but enough to besmirch the reputation of all—made a sport of running them down. Many others simply couldn't understand what all the fuss was about—coming, as they did, from a class that did not have to count its chickens. Looking back from the calmer atmosphere of the 1920s, a German motor club official evoked an era of rural hysteria: "Naturally things were not as bad as they were portrayed in the village newspapers. Whenever a world-weary hen darted under a car, the Podunk Times could be counted on to publish an outraged philippic under the headline 'Automotive Mass Murder.'"[14] It is hardly surprising that motorists chose the ridiculous chicken as the symbol of rural resistance. In 1913 the Paris newspaper Le Figaro recounted the legend of the "automotive chicken": farmers, it was said, bred it especially for its ability to dash under the wheels of passing cars, thus enabling its owner to extract five francs in damages from the motorist.[15] (American rubes allegedly played for higher stakes: Long Island farmers were rumored to steer their worn-out horses into the path of William K. Vanderbilt's racing car, confident that the rich gentleman would pay handsomely for a slaughtered nag.)[16]

Even as rural folk complained about their endangered fowl, they embraced the nobler horse as the symbol of their threatened way of life. On roads that had long belonged to horses, motor cars were a terror to the beasts and their drivers alike, with spooked animals causing their share of calamities. Motorists were not always sympathetic, blaming hostility on the envy and sloth of the unmotorized masses. Most motorists had next to nothing in common with impoverished cart drivers, who often had to spend every daylight hour on the road, snoozing while their animals picked their way along. Auto clubs and magazines buzzed with bitter complaints about the rural conservatism that reflexively took the side of the dumb horse (and its dim driver) against the clever motorist. In 1904, a German motor journal deplored the press's reference to "automobile accidents" even when the automobile was not the cause: "The noble horse, despite all its virtues still stupider than a motorist, remains untouchable, although it has been proved a hundred times that horses and horse-drawn wagons cause more accidents that automobiles."[17] A similar lament appeared in an Italian auto magazine in 1912: "Horses, trams, trains can collide, smash, kill half the world, and nobody cares. But if an automobile leaves a scratch on an urchin who dances in front of it, or on a drunken carter who is driving without a light," then woe to the motorist.[18]

Nor did rural people adapt adroitly to the new dangers: with alarming frequency, speeding cars maimed and killed humans as well as chickens. Motorists fumed at the astonishing stubbornness of people who refused to recognize the new realities of the road: if pedestrians did not change their ways, they were to blame when calamity (in the form of a car) struck. As a contributor to a German motor magazine observed in 1909, more in sorrow than in anger, "A large proportion of accidents happen because the other users of the street refuse to acknowledge and adapt to the changed circumstances brought about by the appearance of the motor car. The heedlessness with which the public still crosses the busiest streets is beyond belief; and many parents let their children use the street as a playground, as if streetcars and automobiles simply don't exist."[19] Still, only the most callous expected to be able to kill or maim passersby without consequences—probably not even Colonel J. T. C. Brabazon, a Conservative

The Lady (to voluble casualty). "ONE WOULD THINK YOU HAD NEVER BEEN RUN OVER BEFORE."

Figure 3. The traffic accident as occasion for humor. *Punch* cartoon by Bert Thomas, 1928. Reproduced with permission of Punch Ltd., www.punch.co.uk.

MP (and later minister of transport), who, outraged by a 1934 proposal to impose speed limits in order to save lives, sputtered, "Over six thousand people commit suicide every year, and nobody makes a fuss about that."[20] (This callousness has always remained just beneath the veneer of civility, surfacing at the end of the century in fantasy video games like *Carmageddon*, which rewards "drivers" for killing pedestrians.)

The first traffic deaths in any town or village were shocking incidents, but as early as 1906, Prince Heinrich zu Schönaich-Carolath noted on the floor of the German parliament that car accidents, often deadly ones, "have unfortunately become a regular column in the daily press."[21] As the Russian writer Ilya Ehrenburg declared portentously in 1929, "At first such things were known as 'catastrophes.' Now people speak of 'accidents.' Soon they'll stop speaking altogether. Silently they'll haul away the victim and silently write down the number. Sentimental neighbors wipe their noses, of course, and philosophically minded people argue about the 'new peril.' Commissions discuss protective laws. But the automobile keeps right on doing its job. . . . It only fulfills its destiny: It is destined to wipe out the world."[22]

Ehrenburg's jaundiced view of the course of civilization was not widely shared. From the beginning, skeptics had to face the charge that they stood in the way of progress. As a German observer asked in 1906, "Who are these people who cry for government help against the motorists? They are the same ones who didn't want gas lighting half a century ago and who petitioned the King of Prussia to stop the railroad being built from Berlin to Potsdam." These "same people" think "the automobile is the personification of progress, and since they always fight that, they have to clamor against the petroleum-fueled monster."[23] The condemnation of car critics as enemies of progress has remained boosters' trump card for a century, apparent, for example, whenever commentators sneer at proposals to curb auto use by invoking the Duke of Wellington's apocryphal complaint that railroads would "only encourage the common people to move about needlessly." The reactionary duke's modern counterparts stand accused of wanting to return us to the unlamented "horse-and-buggy days." Yet already in 1908 the French writer and motorist Octave Mirbeau savored the irony of these claims: "How frustrating, how thoroughly disheartening it is that these pig-headed, obstructive villagers, whose hens, dogs and sometimes children I mow down, fail to appreciate that I represent Progress and universal happiness. I intend to bring them these benefits in spite of themselves, even if they don't live to enjoy them!"[24]

It was easy to dismiss passionate car critics as conservatives, snobs, or defenders of privilege. From the beginning we can distinguish two strands of rural complaint, both with a conservative tinge: the poor peasant's resentment of the highhanded rich motorist, and the outraged good taste of educated people who enjoyed their quiet sojourns in the countryside. They were horrified by the noisy machines and the crude behavior of their fellow visitors from the city: their reckless and sometimes deliberately dangerous driving, their condescension toward the rustics they encountered, or the litter they left behind for the country folk to clean up. What prosperous car critics shared with peasants was a revulsion at violence, boorishness, and ostentation and, at bottom, a perception of motorists as antisocial.

The articulate snobbery of Joad and Sombart should not blind us to the fact that cars were mainly toys of the well-to-do—at least briefly in the United States, for much longer in Europe, and still today in many lands—and a poor and carless majority has borne the brunt of what economists call the "negative externalities" of auto use. For example, by the 1920s rural English hospitals were staggering under the costs of treating auto accident victims—the motorists who careened off the roads as well as the locals who got in their way.[25] Poor country folk grumbled but saw little recourse against people of more wealth and influence. It is harder to know what these poor people thought, since they were less likely to explain themselves in writing. What we do have is evidence of the actions some people took to defend roads they saw as theirs.

Stone throwing was common. There are many recorded examples from Germany and Switzerland, but things were worse in the Netherlands, according to a pioneering German woman motorist, who recorded in her diary in 1905 that "a journey by automobile through Holland is dangerous, since most of the rural population hates motorists fanatically. We even encountered older men, their faces contorted with anger, who, without any provocation, threw fist-sized stones at us."[26] The more typical culprits were boys, but the fact that their misbehavior was so common suggests that parents chose not to discourage their escapades. Angry young farmers sometimes deployed another readily available weapon: a bucket of fresh dung. Or they strewed nails and broken glass on roads. Between 1904 and 1906, farmers around Rochester, Minnesota, plowed up roads to prevent cars from passing. Farmers near Sacramento, California, dug ditches across roads in 1909 and actually trapped thirteen cars.[27] Worse yet were ropes and wires tied between trees to block roads. If firmly attached, they could do great damage. A shocking case occurred in the Prussian countryside outside Berlin in 1913, when a wire strung across a highway by unknown assailants struck a couple speeding back to the city after a Sunday drive, beheading them.[28]

Direct confrontations between motorists and angry peasants were common enough, as the American millionaire and motor enthusiast William K. Vanderbilt II could attest. Even as he personally popularized the automobile in some circles, he seems to have single-handedly provoked international hostility to it as well. He has been credited with enraging the local populace enough to inspire the first speed limits near his homes in Newport, Rhode Island, in 1900, and on Long Island in 1902. Nor did he have an easy time on his European motor tours. In Pau, France, in 1899, after he killed two dogs that were attacking his tires, he had to race away from an angry mob. A few years later, also in France, he fired warning shots after being threatened with whips and rocks. Faced with another irate mob after his car struck and injured a Tuscan child in 1906, he drew his revolver again, but several men seized it and proceeded to hit and kick him until police intervened. Three years later, it was Swiss farmers who beat him up and threatened to burn his car.[29]

Even if motorists had reason to be fearful, they kept venturing into the countryside, often taking precautions to protect themselves. Both sides made regular use of whips. Recommendations that farmers be prepared to use their guns against cars made it into print in several midwestern U.S. states, while German motorists' handbooks before World War I routinely advised drivers to carry weapons for their protection.[30] Some motorists also thought it prudent to flee the scene of an accident, for fear of worse things being done to them by enraged peasants—who would of course be all the more incensed at the hit-and-run drivers' arrogance. A 1909 German law even permitted drivers to abscond from the scene of an accident, as long as they reported to the police the next day.[31] Still, it made for a bit of an uproar when, in 1910, a member of the German parliament from an anti-Semitic splinter party wrote a newspaper article blasting the "completely or half drunk" speeding road devils who threatened honest rural workers, and urging every wagon driver to get a revolver "so that you can defend yourself when the modern vermin attacks you."[32]

He was not the only rural politician who exploited anti-auto sentiments to rally his constituents against the rich urban interlopers. Nor is the anti-Semitic connection surprising, since it was common to blame Jews both for "nomadic" mobility and for urban influences, especially in central Europe. The stereotype could signal vicious prejudice but might also be dismissed with humor. Even a German motoring magazine joked that the answer to the question "Who was the first German motorist?" was "Jakob Israel from Berlin."[33] Politicians from mainstream parties often abhorred motorists, too. That became clear in a session of the Prussian parliament in 1908, in which Baron von Eynatten mocked a brochure published by the Imperial Automobile Club, an organization enthusiastically supported by the emperor himself. To laughter and applause from his colleagues, Eynatten read out lines from the brochure in a scornful tone—assertions, for example, that "panic on the part of the public" caused most accidents, that coachmen must be made to realize that "quiet times on country roads are a thing of the past," and that "the road is for vehicles, not for pedestrians" to linger and make conversation.[34] England, meanwhile, echoed with scorn for the "road hogs." In a 1903 parliamentary debate, Sir Brampton Gurdon demanded an end to leniency: "I would almost consent in some cases to the punishment of flogging."[35]

Rarely, however, did this kind of rhetoric spur any political action, not even in Europe, where the era of rural opposition to automobiles lasted much longer than in the United States. There were, of course, economic interests at stake as well. Soon the auto industry and related services would become an economic force that few politicians dared to defy. At first, however, they felt the pressure of existing interests threatened by the automobile. We can, for example, detect the hand of the horse-and-cart lobby in a 1908 English poster that lamented the loss of 100,000 jobs in that industry only after capturing the attention of passersby with an attack on the "reckless motorists" who "kill your children," dogs, and chickens, "fill your house with dust" as well as "spoil your clothes with dust" and "poison the air we breathe."[36]

The resort to weapons grew out of anger over real confrontations, but was also fueled by an inchoate fear of the other side. As long as motorists were strangers, and often rude ones, they represented the front rank of a frightening invasion of alien mores and technology. In 1903, a rural Michigan newspaper slyly played on its readers' presumed equation of automobiles with uncivilized savagery: "A Crow chief has discarded the tomahawk for an automobile. The cunning old murderer!"[37] Automobiles represent the more abstract threat of modern technology in Hermann Hesse's cantankerous 1927 novel *Steppenwolf*, in which "the struggle between humans and machines"[38] takes the form of a fantasy scene of snipers gleefully shooting down passing cars and drivers—a preview of later video games, perhaps, except that the latter invariably take the motorists' side.

For a few years, some jurisdictions were willing to entertain the idea of banning cars. In the late 1890s, when the citizens of Mitchell, South Dakota, heard that someone in the state capital, Pierre, over a hundred miles away, had built a motor vehicle, they prohibited its use on their streets. Most such attempts to ban cars were short-lived or unenforced, gone by about 1905 in some West Virginia counties, for example. Even the exclusive New England island resorts of Mount Desert, Maine, and Nantucket, Massachusetts, relented within a few years.[39] (The exception is Mackinac Island, Michigan—ironically, a traditional summer playground of Detroit's elite—which has held to its ban for more than a century.) The sanctity of the Sunday stroll inspired Sunday driving bans in parts of Germany and Switzerland before and during World War I. The most notorious ban was imposed by the impoverished Swiss alpine canton of Graubünden, home of such famous resort towns as Davos and St. Moritz. Its total prohibition of cars began in 1900 and was repeatedly reaffirmed by popular referendums (albeit also granted some exceptions) until it was finally repealed in 1925. It was easy to caricature these mountain men (women could not vote) as dull-witted peasant reactionaries, but their resentment was grounded in the solidarity of villages hugging narrow mountain roads and in cold calculations of the costs of road maintenance, the viability of their newly completed mountain railway, and even the preference of spa owners for the more reliable paying visitors who arrived by train and who came expressly to enjoy the peace and quiet now threatened by automobiles.[40]

Meanwhile, severe restrictions that amounted to a virtual ban were disappearing. Fearing that mobile steam engines might explode, the British parliament passed the notorious Red Flag law in 1865. Until motorists got it repealed in 1896, it limited the speed of a "road locomotive" to two miles per hour in town and four in the country, and required that it be preceded by a man on foot carrying a red flag to warn passersby. The state of Vermont kept a similar law for several more years; Iowa tried one that required motorists to telephone ahead to warn towns of their arrival.[41]

Hardly anyone outside of the Alps defended this kind of restriction much after 1900. In its place came more or less moderate speed limits set by local or national governments from the 1890s on, much disputed and frequently changed thereafter. The limit in town was typically equated to that of a trotting horse, about ten miles per hour, with rural limits varying much more widely if they existed at all. Even where the rules were clear, their enforcement furnished plenty of tinder for conflict. From the very first years of the twentieth century, drivers in many lands bewailed the small-town speed trap.[42] Police sometimes strung ropes across the road to stop scofflaws. In Chicago's North Shore suburbs, they soon switched to wire cables, since, as a motor magazine reported, "the more determined offenders . . . fitted scythelike cutters in front of their machines" to cut the ropes.[43] Auto clubs in Britain and the U.S. organized patrols and signals to warn their members of speed traps.[44] In the 1920s, while a German magazine maintained a list of offending localities, French auto clubs called for a boycott of "autophobic" towns, and the strict enforcement of speed limits prompted a British motor magazine to do the same in 1935.[45] The clubs also thought they should be given all responsibility for disciplining the few bad apples in their midst, although they made few moves to do so. Nor, for that matter, did many courts hand down severe penalties for traffic violations, in part because judges often saw motorists as respectable citizens from their own social circles.[46] In some places, motorists had more to fear from vigilante anti-speeding groups. But they have never ceased to resent speed traps, which reveal all too crassly the arbitrary limits of the independence and self-control on which drivers pride themselves.

Even if the small-town speed trap remained a sore point, in the U.S. the fundamental urban-rural tension dissipated by the 1910s, as the Ford Motor Company led the way in producing cars cheap enough for the masses. In a 1906 speech, Woodrow Wilson, then the president of Princeton University, put forth the critics' standard view, arguing that "nothing has spread socialistic feeling in this country more than the use of automobiles. To the countryman they are a picture of arrogance of wealth with all its independence and carelessness." Wilson's view was more typical of Europe than of America, and in later years, his words have frequently been mocked as evidence of the fatuousness of car critics. Even at the time, before Ford's Model T, American automobile proponents argued that he was out of touch with the contemporary countryside.[47] Soon, the roar of an approaching car no longer meant the arrival of strangers, since the Model T became an affordable and nearly indispensable tool of rural life. Even urban visitors were often welcomed for the dollars they brought. Things remained very different in most other places, although Canada and Australia, other prosperous and spacious lands dotted with isolated farms, began to follow the American lead. In Europe, only a few favored places attracted enough motoring tourists to boost the local economy, and up to the middle of the century few farmers could afford their own automobiles. By 1929, the U.S. had more than twenty motor vehicles for every hundred people, an average of nearly one per family (although a large minority of families had none). New Zealand, Australia, and Canada had about half as many. Britain and France led Europe with about four or five cars per hundred people.

The new mechanical contraptions themselves offered plenty to object to, and often their drivers and passengers only made matters worse. But the bigger threat came with the cars' invisible baggage: all the trappings of modern life. Such things nearly always came from the city. Perhaps the car merely sped their passage outward, or perhaps it bore some irresistible power—making it, for example, the catalyst of "Non-virtue" in William Faulkner's novel *The Reivers*. It was too easy to blame the car for all the woes of modernity, yet there were reasons to see it as a particular agent of moral laxity and other distressing modern maladies.

The biggest problem was simply that cars did exactly what they were designed to do: they moved people around freely and quickly. First they brought city people, and their city ways, into the countryside; then they carried country people to town, neighbors out of their neighborhoods, and family members out of their families—notably young people and, most alarmingly, young women. In much of this, the bicycle had been a precursor: by the 1880s, well-to-do city men in many countries were wheeling their way through the countryside, to the bemusement or alarm of the locals. The shock was all the greater when women started to appear on bicycles as well, sporting the lighter, looser clothing that cycling demanded. To a lesser extent, the automobile also entailed a reduction in the hitherto weighty attire expected of a lady: slimmer skirts to fit into car seats as well as shorter ones for drivers needing to manipulate foot pedals. A female cyclist was perhaps more ostentatiously athletic than a motorist, but the latter offered the disturbing specter of a woman either commanding a throbbing motor vehicle herself, or taking an unchaperoned ride beside a young man. Still, there seems to have been surprisingly little complaint about cars as feminist vehicles, although Virginia Scharff's study of American women motorists unearthed an obvious cautionary tale in the form of a serialized 1905 story of an upper-class woman dangerously inflamed by the combined influence of her fast car and her French chauffeur.[48]

The spread of the automobile was mostly celebrated, certainly by the 1920s, in Europe as well as America. Physicians, typically among the first to acquire automobiles, could persuasively argue that cars made them better able to reach sick patients. Some enthusiastic doctors also praised motor travel as a source of invigorating stimulation for tired nerves, muscles, and blood vessels. Less heard were the contrary voices of nerve specialists who lamented the sensory overstimulation and virtual intoxication brought on by speed.[49] For city dwellers, a car offered access to the healthful country air, whether for weekend outings or for suburban residence, and it gave commuters a pleasant alternative to crowded streetcars and sidewalks. Cars dramatically increased the mobility of country people, giving them access to a wider circle of neighbors as well as to town, its shops, and its culture. In line with widely shared scientific beliefs of the age, some American observers also foresaw eugenic benefits of the new mobility: since young men might range more widely in their courting, it would be possible to break dangerous patterns of rural inbreeding.[50]

Still, people in many lands shared the vague belief that the countryside was the repository of moral virtues under siege in the cities. Urban slums were reputed to be moral sinks that sucked downward the rural people who migrated there. The first cars, too, usually came from the city, and their role was very simple, in the view of some critics: they were getaway cars, carrying desperate criminals and their gangs to the countryside and enabling them to strike and escape quickly (the theme of early films as well as a 1929 American play). The venerable diplomat George Kennan, who would have heard this criticism of cars in the 1920s, was repeating it seventy years later.[51] The fact that real criminals used cars was mostly beside the point. What mattered was that cars carried not just criminals but an aura of vice.

Balancing this mistrust of the urban poor were many national variations on the belief that the upper classes were the greatest moral offenders. (Think of Henry Higgins's rebuke to Eliza Doolittle's protestations that "I'm a good girl, I am" in George Bernard Shaw's 1912 play and 1938 screenplay Pygmalion: "We want none of your slum prudery here, young woman. You've got to learn to behave like a duchess.") Rich young people had the means to escape the protective gaze of family and neighbors. That was the mobility they carried to the countryside, first on bicycles and then in cars; and that was what cars soon offered less wealthy people as well, particularly in the United States. By the 1920s, the widespread ownership of cars in the U.S., especially in rural areas, meant that the vices promoted by the automobile were now a widespread problem.

Robert and Helen Lynd's famous sociological study of Muncie, Indiana, in the mid-1920s ("Middletown," as they labeled it) portrayed the automobile as the agent of profound social transformation. The picture was by no means one-sidedly negative, in the view of either the investigators or their informants, but the book offered several examples of worrisome changes. Every outbreak of youth crime fanned fears of juvenile delinquency, and cars seemed to hasten these excesses of youthful freedom. Cars had long been linked to sex crimes in particular (including many acts that have long since ceased to be classified as crimes). Sexual innuendo accompanied the automobile all along, in ordinary conversation, in advertising, and most famously in popular songs ("You can go as far as you like with me, in my merry Oldsmobile"). Muncie's juvenile court judge complained that "the automobile has become a house of prostitution on wheels."[52] A similar tirade appeared in an Australian newspaper in 1924: "A Peter the Hermit is needed to preach a crusade against the unseemly uses to which motor cars are put at balls and dances in the city and in the country also. At a recent ball in a fashionable suburb nearly every motorcar was a miniature bar; all know with what result. These practices should be stopped in order to save our fine young women."[53] The same moral panic accompanied the later motorization of other lands, in 1950s Italy, for example, and 1960s Spain, where the Catholic Church pleaded with young people to resist the notorious nexus of cars and sin.[54]

Some people praised the automobile for bringing families together by popularizing the family outing, when everyone piled into the family car for an invigorating day in the country. But the growing use of the car by young people in order to escape the family home reinforced the Lynds' intimation that this family togetherness might be only a passing phase. And even family outings were not universally praised. They typically took place on Sundays, and often lasted all day. "Preaching to 200 people on a hot, sunny Sunday in midsummer on 'The Supreme Need of Today,' a leading Middletown minister denounced 'automobilitis—the thing those people have who go off motoring on Sunday instead of going to church.'"[55] Soon it became apparent how many small-town habits were under threat from the automobile. Motorists' wider social circles permitted them to neglect their neighbors, and as their shopping habits reached far beyond the crossroads store, it subsequently closed in many places, leaving everyone more dependent on their own car or someone else's.[56] This much-lamented loosening of community bonds has also been celebrated by those who were happy to flee their nosy neighbors or escape dependence on the miserable general store. For good or ill, nearly everyone agreed that the change wrought by the automobile was profound.

Next to housing, cars were the most expensive goods that tempted families to spend their money rather than save it. People who mortgaged their houses to buy cars were frowned on by neighbors who classified homes as necessities and cars as luxuries. But the belief that cars were necessities, too, had become even more firmly established by the time of the Lynds' follow-up study a decade later, when they found that despite the hardships of the Great Depression, cars were even more central to people's lives than they had been in the 1920s. "While some workers lost their cars in the depression, the local sentiment, as heard over and over again, is that 'People give up everything in the world but their car.'"[57] Outsiders' beliefs that a car ought to be seen as a luxury permitted them to tut-tut over poor people's eager embrace of the seductive machines. Innumerable commentators have quoted the rural woman who, when asked by a U.S. government interviewer in the 1920s why her family had acquired a car before installing indoor plumbing, supposedly replied, "You can't go to town in a bathtub!"[58] While her moralistic contemporaries valued hygiene over mobility, the prevailing view for the rest of the twentieth century was that the woman's indignant defense of her car had really been quite rational.

Enthusiasts for this new technology, and for technology in general, saw their detractors as Luddites—indeed, that label, or something like it, continues to dog the car's detractors. In the early twentieth century, technological optimists generally believed that life was getting better, thanks in large part to our new machines. Their argument remains the same a century later: to dwell on the auto's drawbacks is to miss the big picture—even if those drawbacks include a rising death toll.

DRIVING AND AGGRESSION

It was probably the excitement of auto racing that convinced the early British film director Cecil Hepworth that the automobile was ideally suited to bring thrills to motion pictures. Speed and danger are the appeal of his 1900 film *How It Feels to Be Run Over*, in which a horse and cart steer around a camera placed in the road before a heedless automobile races directly into it. Even without the speed, cars meant violence, as Hepworth showed in another short film from the same year, *Explosion of a Motor Car*, in which the event promised by the title is followed by a shower of body parts raining from the sky.

The very sensations that thrilled early motorists disquieted car skeptics, and even some enthusiasts. Not only did the automobile loosen social controls, it seemed to unleash primitive drives. In a 1906 parliamentary debate, the German vice-chancellor, Arthur von Posadowsky-Wehner, pondered the "peculiar psychological effect" that enticed drivers to excessive speed.[59] Octave Mirbeau described motoring as a disease and speed as an addiction. The result was megalomania: "When I am in the car, possessed by speed, humanitarian feelings drain away. I begin to feel obscure stirrings of hatred and an idiotic sense of pride. No longer am I a miserable specimen of humanity, but a prodigious being in whom are embodied—no, please don't laugh—Elemental Splendor and Power. And given I am the Wind, the Storm, the Thunderbolt, imagine with what contempt I view the rest of humanity from the vantage-point of my car."[60]

Already in 1900, the automotive writer Louis Baudry de Saunier, one of motoring's first and most ardent boosters, warned of the machine's disturbing power: "The automobile makes even the calmest man burn with an inextinguishable thirst for speed."[61] Another early enthusiast, the Austrian automotive journalist (and former Olympic cycling gold medalist) Adolf Schmal, reflected at greater length on this phenomenon in the 1913 edition of his handbook for motorists: "I know kind, well-bred, and considerate people who, as soon as they feel the steering wheel in their hands and the gas pedal under their foot, are seized by an automotive frenzy. It seems as if everything we normally call good breeding is suddenly extinguished in them. These otherwise kind, well-bred, and considerate people are capable of racing up to a tram stop at thirty kilometers per hour and sending a score of people into panicked flight, without being aware of the brutality of their conduct. I have often asked myself what might be hidden in an automobile that would, in an instant, turn a well-bred and considerate person into a lout."[62] A few years later, he was still puzzling over the fact that cars seemed to make fierce aggressors out of "even delicate female creatures who are otherwise the personification of sweetness": "People who otherwise have nothing belligerent about them will, in an automobile, suddenly be possessed of no other desire than to 'defeat' another motorist. Some of the overwhelming power of the machine must spill over into the brain of its occupant—this phenomenon can't be explained any other way."[63]

Most drivers may not recognize themselves in Schmal's portrait, but few rush-hour survivors would deny that "this phenomenon" has persisted. Although physicians and psychologists have long offered professional diagnoses of the fearful hold of the automobile over the human mind and body, that power has probably always been best grasped by marketers. Manufacturers and sellers of automobiles have long recognized the subversive thrill of speed. In addition to sponsoring auto racing, they have rarely hesitated to promote fast and aggressive driving. On display at the Henry Ford Museum in Dearborn, Michigan, is a remarkable fan letter written to Ford by the famous outlaw Clyde Barrow (of Bonnie and Clyde) in 1934. In it Barrow confesses that his line of work "hasent been strickly legal" but he adds that he wants to praise Mr. Ford's "dandy car," the powerful Ford V-8 always being his vehicle of choice "when I could get away with one. For sustained speed and freedom from trouble the Ford has got every other car skinned." The Ford Motor Company made no secret of this praise from a notorious criminal, later using it in advertising, despite the lack of any clear evidence that it was really sent by Barrow. (It appears not to be in his handwriting. A few weeks later, Ford received a similar mash note from the other celebrity outlaw of the day, the bank robber John Dillinger, but that letter is acknowledged to be a forgery.) A glance at more recent car ads will confirm that the language of naked aggression remains commonplace: a car is a "beast" or "brute" that "roars" or "growls"; it offers a "monster" engine and "brutal" speed that lets you "leave your neighbor in the dust," "blow off" other cars, and "obliterate traffic."[64]

It is easy to construct a simple historical dichotomy, associating automobiles with modernity, technological progress, economic growth, individualism, self-fulfillment, and freedom. Certainly many car haters were technopessimists and censorious moralists. At least in Europe, however, enthusiasm for technology and speed, and for cars in particular, often went hand in hand with opposition to liberal individualism. After all, there was something atavistic about the visceral thrill of speed. The liberating power of technology meant different things, depending on whether one was being liberated from the shackles of tradition or the anxieties of modernity. One might ask, for example, which is more in evidence in a 1906 article in an Italian motoring magazine praising the automobile as the great achievement of our "feverish" and "anxious" age: "The automobile is the modern symbol of fire, and fire creates and destroys."[65] This was the sentiment enshrined by some of the first intellectuals to embrace the automobile, the Italian futurist artists such as Filippo Marinetti, who exalted "the beauty of speed" and the leonine roar of the motor car, along with militarism, violence, danger, and death, while denouncing feminism, democracy, and other emasculating tendencies of modern life.

The First World War powerfully reinforced the association of automobiles with aggression, but in a largely positive way, as each of the major belligerents took pride in its effective mobilization of motor vehicles. The most famous incident came near the beginning, in September 1914, when Paris's new fleet of Renault taxis carried reinforcements thirty miles out to the valley of the Marne, to stop the German advance on their city. Later, trucks ferried soldiers and supplies to the French front, motor ambulances saved lives, and the emergence of the tank toward the end of the war heralded a new age of motorized combat. The horrors of World War I, we should recall, were mainly those of static warfare, while the mobility of trucks and tanks promised relief from the relentless slaughter in the trenches.

At least in Europe, the technological progress associated with the automobile was the same kind embraced by enthusiasts for war and authoritarian nationalism. The very first wave of automotive fervor, in belle epoque Paris, came as France was bitterly divided over the Dreyfus affair, and the anti-Dreyfusard opponents of the Republic, partisans of the army and of religious bigotry, apparently dominated the ranks of motoring enthusiasts.[66] A few years later, the Italian futurists embraced the Fascist Party of Benito Mussolini, who shared the futurist devotion to technological speed and militaristic display as well as to the subordination of the individual to the nation and of woman to man. Similar sentiments appeared in Germany among the war veterans and aviators who flocked to the Nazi party.

Indeed, one of the most famous auto enthusiasts (albeit one who never drove) was Adolf Hitler, who loved riding in his large Mercedes sedans. Apart from motorized war and genocide, in fact, Hitler may be best known for his regime's two celebrated automotive projects, the "people's car" (Volkswagen) and the autobahns. It is not surprising that later aficionados of both usually deny that they had any connection with the Third Reich's larger and more ominous designs. Just as predictably, many historians have asserted that these civilian projects were really part of Hitler's war machine. The arguments that the Volkswagen was just an excuse to build up a manufacturing infrastructure for tanks, and that the autobahns were built primarily to move armies, are exaggerated at best, but the promotion of automobiles and of mechanized warfare were both part of a technological optimism, tinged with aggression, that loomed large in the Third Reich. Even if the autobahns ultimately proved to be of little military value, the celebrated construction program was not only a source of jobs during the Depression but also a project designed to boost national pride and, in a literal sense, national unity, while exploiting the undeniable (if, for the majority, still unattainable) appeal of motor travel.

Hitler delighted the German auto industry with his enthusiastic embrace of it. Just days after becoming chancellor in 1933, he addressed the Berlin International Auto Show with a promise to reduce motor taxes in order to increase sales. A few months later, he broke ground on his first autobahn, and soon he began working with the automotive engineer Ferdinand Porsche on the design of an inexpensive "people's car," which would have gone into mass production had it not been derailed by that other Hitler project, World War II. Fundamental to the Nazi agenda was the desire to overcome bitter class divisions within Germany. Hitler's love of powerful sedans did not blind him to the fact that in Germany, as elsewhere in Europe, the automobile remained a token of wealth and privilege. The image of the motorist as a wealthy man, or indeed as a wealthy Jew, was now to be ruthlessly suppressed in favor of a unified nation of racially pure drivers. Hitler wanted his new people's car to give ordinary folks full access to the previously exclusive pleasures of automobility, just as had been accomplished in the United States, thanks to Henry Ford, a man Hitler greatly admired for his efficient organization of industrial production, his attention to the desires of ordinary people, and his outspoken anti-Semitism. Germany had fallen behind the U.S. in the 1920s, Hitler declared, because the republic had blocked the growth of motorization, a mistake the new Third Reich would not repeat.[67] In his speech at the 1934 Berlin auto show (an annual event for him) Hitler observed, "It is distressing to know that millions of honest, diligent, and able people, whose lives offer them limited opportunity, are denied the use of a mode of transportation that would, especially on Sundays and holidays, grant them a joy hitherto withheld from them." He demanded that "the automobile be stripped of its class-specific and therefore divisive character. It must cease to be a luxury and become a practical device!"[68]

If automobiles are to be equated with freedom, as they have been throughout the century, Hitler's endorsement of them ought to raise the question of what kind of freedom they bring. Car haters can take comfort in having Fascists and Nazis as their historical enemies. Not that antifascists or anti-Nazis were necessarily car haters, however: although the appeal of socialism depended partly on resentment of the rich, European socialist leaders and parties—the most consistent enemies of fascist and radical nationalist movements—were favorably inclined toward the automobile, as a source of industrial jobs and as a technology that promised a better future for the masses. Autophobia was a cause for reactionary peasants and aristocrats. Paradoxically, Nazism's intellectual and organizational roots lay partly in the anti-urban milieu most hostile to the automobile. Typical of the Nazis' intellectual supporters was the prominent architect and rural preservationist Paul Schulze-Naumburg, who denounced the pernicious influence of the motorcar long before he became a zealous promoter of Nazi cultural policies.[69] And any wish to denounce aggressive drivers as Nazis must take account of Hitler's condemnation of them. In a speech at the last peacetime Berlin auto show, in 1939, he lamented that people were driving unreasonably fast on the new autobahns. It was intolerable, he declared, that traffic deaths in the six years of his Third Reich had nearly matched the death toll of the Franco-Prussian war of 1870–71. Anyone who caused an accident was "an unscrupulous criminal" who shed the precious blood of the nation.[70]

The 1930s did in fact see major road safety initiatives in Britain and the United States, the leading automotive nations (along with France, where worries about safety seem to have taken hold more slowly). At first, the growing carnage on the roads often induced a helpless resignation. A 1931 article in the Atlantic Monthly lamented the "fundamental incompatibility of machines and men, steel and flesh" at high speeds, and concluded that "we may as well accept complacently an annual slaughter that will increase not only with the increase in the number of cars, but also with the rise in the kill per car—the inevitable penalty of greater congestion. Possibly this rise in the kill per car will become sufficiently alarming to change our views on the 'saturation point' of automobiles; but this effect on us is not likely."[71] J. C. Furnas sought a more tonic effect in his widely reprinted article "And Sudden Death," originally published in the August 1935 issue of the popular magazine Reader's Digest. He served up graphic descriptions of car-crash injuries: "If you customarily pass without clear vision a long way ahead, make sure that every member of the party carries identification papers—it's difficult to identify a body with its whole face bashed in or torn off. The driver is death's favorite target. If the steering wheel holds together, it ruptures his liver or spleen so he bleeds to death internally. Or, if the steering wheel breaks off, the matter is settled instantly by the steering column's plunging through his abdomen."[72] Furnas aimed not to improve car design—that movement would not come for decades—but to shock drivers into greater caution. That was also the goal of the newly established safety organizations, which were largely funded or manipulated by the auto industry. In addition to the education of drivers, they preached the need for police to enforce traffic laws and for owners to better maintain their cars.

Revulsion against the carnage on British roads kept motor safety in the public eye during the 1930s. There was, however, little agreement about the chief causes of the problem. As in the U.S., quasi-official safety campaigns were put in the hands of the motor clubs and the auto industry, which ignored hazardous car design, minimized the role of speed in crashes, and blamed cyclists and pedestrians for their failure to yield the road. The defensive pro-motorist impetus of the safety campaign was apparent in the 1939 report of a House of Lords Select Committee charged with investigating ways to reduce road casualties: "Propaganda should be employed for the purpose of making those who do not own motor-cars realise how much they owe to motor transport for the supply of their food, for passenger service and so on. There still remains in the public mind a prejudice against motor-cars, born no doubt in the old days when few people owned them, and when they were considered as luxuries rather than part of an essential and national service, as they are today."[73]

This bias attracted more criticism in Britain than in the U.S., thanks to the existence of the Pedestrians' Association, founded in 1929, a pressure group without an American equivalent. Just after World War II, the association's chairman, J. S. Dean, poured his accumulated indignation into a small book entitled *Murder Most Foul*. With obvious relish, Dean pointed out the manifest affinities between aggressive motorists and the recently defeated fascist enemy: "Never before in the history of civilization has it been so easy to kill and maim without incurring punishment or even censure. Never before in all history has it been a common custom to kill and maim people because they get in your way when you are in a hurry, or even when you are not in a hurry but merely wish to feel you are. It is a fantastic and unprecedented situation: a fit prelude to race extermination and Belsen. . . . Scratch a road hog and you'll find a Fascist."[74] He went on to explain that the "British motor propagandists," great admirers of recent German methods, perfected the "Big Lie" before Hitler and Goebbels, theirs being that "speed is not dangerous."[75] Small wonder that in their history of interwar Britain, Robert Graves and Alan Hodge contended that in these years, "A new division of Britain took place: Motorists and Pedestrians."[76] Dean would have bridled at the aircraft and

Pedestrian (to reckless driver). "D-DON'T KILL ME—I'M ON MY WAY—TO BUY A CAR—SO—I'LL SOON BE ON YOUR SIDE!"

Figure 4. A world divided between pedestrians and motorists. *Punch* cartoon by G. L. Stampa, 1927. Reproduced with permission of Punch Ltd., www.punch.co.uk.

auto manufacturer Sir Dennistoun Burney's more complacent belief that "people may be divided into those who possess cars and those who want to possess them."[77] Perhaps that characterization better fit the U.S., where the former category was so much larger. Yet in 1935 New Jersey's governor, Harold Hoffman, declared that his nation's division between "the drivers and the pedestrians" was as profound as that between North and South in the Civil War.[78]

GROWING PAINS?

A traditional history of the automobile's advance might chalk up everything in this chapter to "growing pains," as societies adjusted to the new technology, and the technology was adapted to people's needs and desires. Certainly many skeptics made peace with the automobile during these years, and many more people grew up with it, accepting its inescapable presence largely without question. Millions acquired cars in the United States, as did small but growing minorities elsewhere. Others came to know the benefits of automotive transport in other ways: not only by catching rides with motorized acquaintances, but also by traveling by motor coach or bus, or by seeing trucks bring goods to them. Not to be forgotten is the role of the motorcycle, which brought the speed and convenience of motor transport to many people without cars.

After some initial hesitation, most governments strongly promoted the automobile. Many of their efforts to encourage its wider use in the 1910s, 1920s, and 1930s also helped solve its early problems. Urged on by the increasingly influential national auto clubs, they oiled, tarred, or paved rural roads, and the horrendous clouds of dust largely disappeared (not, however, the exhaust fumes). Ambitious programs of road construction produced many more miles of suitable paved surfaces, and new taxes helped shift the costs to automobile owners and users. The mandatory use of mufflers reduced the noise of individual cars, although their growing numbers contributed to an incessant din, punctuated by the honking of horns. Insurance and liability laws began to hold motorists responsible for damage they inflicted, as did the licensing of cars and drivers. Driver training and, even more, the imposition and enforcement of speed limits and a thicket of other traffic regulations complicated motorists' journeys but reduced the rate at which they crashed.

It is easy enough to conclude that opponents of the automobile were misguided. Certainly they made many false predictions; certainly their words and actions reveal intellectual blinders and appalling prejudices. Their failure, however, was due not to their blinkered ideas but rather to their weakness, that is, their inability to slow the advance of the automobile. Motorists were a minority, but, as it turned out, a well-organized and influential one. As early as 1908, a member of the Prussian parliament seemed to recognize that he was fighting against the tide of history when he tried to insist that the automobile represented "not progress but rather the retrogression of civilization."[79] The history of automobiles has certainly been a story of growth. The organic metaphor of "growing pains" makes sense of that history by implying that the motorized society would be expected to reach a normal maturity. A good deal of evidence fits this story, and by the late 1930s, there were many reasons to be optimistic about the future of the automobile.

If most people were happy with the blessings of automobility, how do we characterize the remaining critics? Unhappy reactionaries, railing in vain against rapid change? Romantics pining for a vanished world? Simply the pathetic losers of history, the buggy manufacturers and general-store proprietors and rural sluggards? It is convenient to think of their suffering at the hands of motorists as the growing pains of automobility—unavoidable, regrettable, and ultimately forgettable—and to write them off as roadkill on the route to automotive maturity.

Yet the automobile's drawbacks were far from resolved, and even as some critics were won over, new ones emerged to take their place. If we focus on the lingering problems, we can recognize, with the benefit of hindsight, that solutions to many of them were not imminent. Could the automobile continue to be the great agent of individual freedom without bursting all bonds of civility? Would the virtues of the family or village community be wiped out by the new automobility? What would happen to cities as they filled up with cars? The great engine of individual mobility was disrupting, even destroying, old patterns of sociability and civility. Unless something new and better replaced the old ways, this could scarcely be called progress.

CHAPTER TWO

Buyer's Remorse:
The Tarnished Golden Age

At the end of World War II, Americans, 6 percent of the world's population, owned a full three-quarters of its cars. They, nearly alone in the world, had emerged from the war with their standard of living largely intact. The burden of paying for the war, on top of the staggering destruction of lives and property, had left victorious Britain in dire straits, yet it was better off than newly liberated France, which in turn had not suffered the degree of devastation in bombed, defeated, and occupied Germany and Japan. Even Canada, New Zealand, and Australia, although intact and prosperous, lagged far behind the U.S. in both wealth and automobile ownership. For a few years, car culture meant the United States, and the U.S. meant modernity, freedom, and self-expression.

THE AGE OF EXCESS

Wartime rationing of gasoline and rubber tires had curtailed driving and pushed many Americans back onto streetcars and buses, but with the return of peace, shortages quickly disappeared, old cars came down off blocks, and Detroit retooled its tank and aircraft assembly lines to satisfy the pent-up demand for new cars. Even at the time, the postwar years appeared to be a golden age of automobility, with the manufacturers churning out almost uniformly mammoth cars, varied only in the degree of excess lavished on their plush interiors and chrome-laden bodies. After the deprivation and immobility enforced by depression and war, car-centered recreation—whether Sunday drives or Saturday night courtship—returned with a vengeance. Automobile-oriented businesses such as motels and shopping strips sprang up all over the country, and "drive-in" restaurants and movie theaters brought commerce and entertainment into the car itself.

Detroit's Big Three auto manufacturers (General Motors, Ford, and Chrysler) had finally recognized the United Auto Workers union and negotiated contracts that enabled assembly-line workers to share fully in the postwar boom. By general consensus, the auto industry was the single most important motor of prosperity, both because of its enormous payroll and because of the stimulus it provided to other basic industries such as steel, petroleum, and rubber, and to businesses ranging from automotive sales and maintenance to the rapidly growing network of services provided to Americans on wheels, from the new motels and drive-ins to suburban housing developments and vacation resorts.

A car was, apart from a house, the largest item in consumers' budgets. It was their badge of prosperity, their most cherished possession, and the means to fulfill such other desires as outings and vacations. Since nearly every car on the market could hold several people comfortably, it also fit the prevailing ideal of the family as a consuming unit. Advertisers had little trouble persuading Americans of the splendor of automotive travel, and they were cheered on by enthusiasts like the landscape architect John R. Griffith: "The modern automobile and its highways are as integral to our lives as the marketplace, forum, or acropolis to the ancients." The well-designed highway, he added, "expresses an aspiration of mid-twentieth-century America, just as the functional structures of the ancient Greeks expressed their aspiration of beauty in everyday life."[1]

Times of abundance kindle anguished talk of the corrupting influence of wealth. The fifties have become enshrined as a decade of rampant consumerism because articulate contemporaries declared their disappointment with, or contempt for, the effects of its extraordinary prosperity. American anti-automobilism in particular had long since ceased to be the province of the resentful and carless poor. More than in the 1920s, intellectuals and arbiters of taste fretted about the moral fiber of a nation of drivers. If this era of unprecedented mass prosperity saw no fierce religious backlash against material excess, it did bring to the fore a generation of secular pessimists worried about a leveling of taste. The 1950s was the decade of *The Organization Man* and *The Lonely Crowd*, among other expressions of a fear that wealth was making Americans either crass or miserable.[2] A skeptical take on the automobile, the paramount symbol of mass consumption, became the token of a dissenting intellectual elite that would, over the next decades, become increasingly associated with that supposedly out-of-touch bastion of car-free America, the island of Manhattan.

Another theme of the decade was the disillusionment of the motorist. Driving had once been an adventure, a journey of discovery. Now a paved and homogenized landscape left nothing to discover. Decades before, some motorists were already complaining that the adventure was gone: the roads were crowded with other cars, and places were beginning to look all the same, with garish signs at every turn inviting motorists to leave their money in the hands of an enterprising rural pest with a souvenir shop, food stand, or row of ramshackle tourist cabins. By the 1950s, even the tacky American interwar landscape became bathed in nostalgia, as the rapid proliferation of roadside restaurant and motel chains such as Howard Johnson's and Holiday Inn, with their standardized gables, signs, and color schemes, made the landscape of California indistinguishable from that of Maine. Even Jack Kerouac's iconic novel *On the Road*, published in 1957, can be read as a wistful look back at the emptier highways of the 1940s, when Kerouac began his travels.[3] "It is difficult to say just when the last shred of fun disappeared from the American highway," mused the writer John Keats in 1958. "It is now possible to drive across the face of the nation without feeling you've been anywhere or that you've done anything."[4]

When recreational motoring was not fully absorbing, it often seemed a complete waste of time. Already in a 1903 novel, the German writer Heinrich Mann sent his characters on a car trip, "but when they reached their destination and sat peacefully in the village tavern, the outing was suddenly pointless."[5] In his 1934 "Choruses from the Rock," T. S. Eliot observed caustically that "all dash to and fro in motor cars":

I journeyed to the suburbs and there I was told:
We toil for six days, on the seventh we must motor,
To Hindhead or Maidenhead.

The Swiss writer Max Frisch offered a bemused portrait of American motorists' futile search for recreation in a description of New York summer weekends in his 1954 novel, *Stiller*: "On Sundays, hundreds of thousands of cars roll out across the Washington bridge, for example: three abreast, an army of city dwellers in an urgent search for nature. Nature is actually already there: lakes flash by, woods with green underbrush,

A CALIFORNIAN HOLIDAY

Figure 5. Car-centered recreation in Los Angeles, as portrayed by a visiting English couple in 1930. Sketch by Jan and Cora Gordon, from their book *Star-Dust in Hollywood* (London: George G. Harrap, 1930).

untamed woods, and then again open fields without a single house: a feast for the eyes, indeed, paradise. But they drive on by." After all, you can't just stop on the parkway. Three hours' drive brings the traffic to a spacious picnic ground where people sit in their cars for the afternoon before heading back into traffic.[6] The same phenomenon appalled Lewis Mumford, the self-taught American scholar of cities who emerged as midcentury's most prominent car critic. What angered him was the misguided assumption "that it is quite all right to make the city less and less habitable as long as enough roads are built to permit people to escape by car once a week—only to crowd back, worn and defeated, on Sunday evening."[7]

Detroit's eye-popping and ever-changing cars offered an inexhaustible topic of conversation. Modernist designers such as Raymond Loewy condemned the bloated shapes and chrome encrustations of 1950s cars (apart from his own designs for Studebaker). Modernism claimed to be grounded in the rational needs of the object: form follows function. This was the line taken by the writer E. B. White in lamenting the absence of an "honest" car: "A garbage scow carries a filthy load, but it has clean lines—cleaner by far than the lines of the 1958 automobile." Perhaps that view could be dismissed as snobbery (certainly Loewy attacked car design as "vulgar"), and perhaps Detroit had accurately targeted a mass desire for excess.[8] In any case, excess was the hallmark of 1950s American cars. For all the obvious utility of the automobile, any attempt to explain Detroit's products as practical or functional quickly rang hollow. The great symbol of the automotive flight of fancy was the tail fin, first introduced on the 1948 Cadillac and, a decade later, reaching the literal heights of extravagance on many Detroit models. Fins were the epitome of pseudo-rational design. World War II aircraft, in particular the dual tail of the Lockheed P-38 fighter, inspired the celebrated head of General Motors Styling, Harley Earl, to design tail fins that evoked the plane. Marketers promoted the tail fin as an aid to automotive efficiency, but a shape that made aerodynamic sense on a flying machine served no practical purpose on an earthbound automobile. (Or as the enthralled French philosopher Jean Baudrillard put it a few years later, "Tail fins were a sign not of *real* speed but of a sublime, measureless speed.")[9] When the car companies stopped pretending that aerodynamics justified tail fins, they claimed the dubious benefit of mounting taillights up high. Obviously they thought some buyers needed a sober rationale for their purchase, but the explanations for tail fins in particular and car designs in general were rationalizations, not rationality.

The auto industry's immense advertising budgets (long the biggest of any industry worldwide) have filled magazines, television screens, and billboards with seductive images. (And since cigarette ads were banned from television—in 1965 in the U.K., in 1971 in the U.S.—the occasional car hater has argued for a ban on automobile advertising as well.) The notorious high-pressure sales tactics of car dealers also helped to make automobiles the most controversial products in the world of consumer marketing. A fear of manipulation was a nagging undercurrent of the burgeoning consumer society of the fifties, most famously expressed in Vance Packard's best-selling 1957 book, *The Hidden Persuaders*, which claimed to expose advertisers' deliberate manipulation of the unconscious minds of vulnerable consumers. Packard attacked big business, notably Detroit, for infantilizing Americans by robbing them of their ability make rational choices. The linguist S. I. Hayakawa agreed that things had been taken to an absurd extreme. Automobiles served many needs, he observed, but "the 1957 cars are nevertheless unique in sacrificing *all* else—common sense, efficiency, economy, safety, dignity, and especially beauty—to psychosexual wish fulfillment." In a later article, he concluded that the carmakers' flight from reason had finally gone too far for their own good, arguing that they apparently assume "that the majority of the population is mentally ill."[10]

The fall of 1957 saw the extravagant rollout of Ford's new Edsel line, which quickly became a spectacular failure, both in critical opinion and in sales: it was discontinued after just two years. In a market already saturated with interchangeable chrome-encrusted, fin-bedecked monsters, the Edsel offered nothing sufficiently new or different to attract buyers. Hayakawa trumpeted the Edsel's failure as evidence that Detroit had entirely lost touch. And in fact the industry did change a bit in the following years. John Keats, who compared the Edsel and other 1950s behemoths unfavorably with that model of practical automobility, the Model T, also reserved praise for little American Motors' new and relatively small Rambler models. In recognition of the demand for smaller cars (also apparent in the rapidly growing sales of the Volkswagen Beetle, the first imported car to make a dent in the American market) Ford introduced its compact Falcon, Chrysler its Valiant, and Chevrolet its innovative if ill-fated Corvair in 1959.

POSTWAR EUROPE

During the first bleak years after World War II, new, often tiny cars were the most visible signs of a welcome new prosperity in western Europe, but they did spark some rancor among the carless majority. Urban pedestrians had to endure the noise and smoke, and they could scarcely help feeling threatened in the streets. Some of the same indignation that fueled J. S. Dean's 1947 rant against British motorists was apparent in another treatise written shortly after the war by a Dutch engineer by the name of Valderpoort. *The Selfish Car* denounced the small minority of arrogant "autocrats" whose vehicles, whether speeding or parked, claimed the cities for themselves at the expense of the inconvenienced and endangered majority.[11]

If this indignation had been confined to a few pamphleteers, it probably would not have caught the attention of West German chancellor Konrad Adenauer, the canniest of politicians. As mayor of Cologne in 1930 he had already voiced suspicion of the powerful auto lobby and warned that the city's old streets "are not there primarily for autos."[12] In a conversation in 1954, he is reported to have mused, "if I weren't chairman of the strongest party in the Federal Republic, I would found an anti-automobile party, which would be even stronger."[13] But Adenauer kept his sentiments private, and the moment passed, as the majority of West Germans and western Europeans became aspiring motorists, if not yet actual drivers. Pedestrians' resentments faded in the face of the liberating possibilities of auto travel. And no one loved cars more than the West Germans, who were being encouraged by their leaders as well as their foreign allies to embrace individual freedom and initiative in order to distinguish themselves both from their own Nazi past and from the Communism prevailing in the eastern part of their homeland. Driving an automobile became synonymous with individual opportunity, and the Nazi heritage of Volkswagens and autobahns proved easy to repress.

Soon the postwar embrace of the automobile was remarkably close to unanimous, even though motorists were a small minority in every European country in 1950. Prewar resentments against the motoring class faded quickly, perhaps because auto ownership became less identified with the idle rich, perhaps because people adjusted to having cars around them. Munich's longtime mayor Hans-Jochen Vogel later recalled, possibly with an excess of drama, that "it was nearly suicidal for a politician in the Fifties to take a position against the automobile."[14] Things were little different in France during that decade, when, according to the prominent economist Alfred Sauvy, the nation developed a flourishing culture of free speech, in which nothing was taboo except the automobile. Much the same has been said of Britain; and Italian car advocates zealously denounced a mostly imaginary hostility to cars. By 1960 the Zurich newspaper editor Ernst Bieri could haughtily dismiss the "not quite extinct dinosaurs of the age of autophobia."[15]

By then, much of Europe was making the same transition as the U.S. in the 1920s, with the once exclusive luxury of car ownership now normal or even necessary. In 1960, many northern European lands were down to about ten inhabitants per automobile; by 1970, approximately four— that is, close to one per family, although a substantial carless minority remained in every country. During the 1960s West Germany and its smaller neighbors caught up to Britain and France. A few years later, so did Italy (and Japan as well). The auto boom came later to Spain, Portugal, and Greece as they emerged from dictatorship and poverty.

As in the U.S., pro-auto attitudes as well as policies could generally be found across the political spectrum. British, German, and Italian conservatives might occasionally try to score political points by accusing their labor-party rivals of collectivist anti-auto tendencies, but they had scant grounds to do so before the 1970s. Politicians seeking the working-class vote knew that a car (or at least a motorcycle) was the European worker's proudest possession, whether already acquired or merely aspired to. Typical was the sentiment of the German Social Democratic politician (and later chancellor) Helmut Schmidt in 1965: "Every German should have the opportunity to buy his own car. Therefore we want to build him the roads he needs."[16] Concern about the finances of Europe's state-owned railways sometimes countered the desire to finance roads that aided the rapidly growing motor-freight business, but the auto lobby usually prevailed.

Europe's new consumer culture found no more visible outlet than the purchase and display of automobiles. This material frenzy repelled some cultural conservatives and technoskeptics, whose views bore a curious resemblance to an emerging French Marxist critique of the automobile as the most egregious example of an industrially produced object with a remarkable power to hold workers and consumers in its thrall. Cars interested these theorists mainly as material evidence of the ravages of capitalism. Guy Debord, for example, denied that the private automobile was "essentially a means of transportation"; it was, rather, "the most notable material symbol of the notion of happiness that developed capitalism tends to spread throughout the society. The automobile is at the center of this general propaganda, both as supreme good of an alienated life and as essential product of the capitalist market."[17] This "unimposing technical object," in the words of Henri Lefebvre, somehow serves "as a substitute for eroticism, for adventure, for living conditions and for human contact in large towns."[18] In acknowledging the extraordinary allure of the automobile, these critics agreed with the car's intellectual fans, most prominent among them Roland Barthes, whose admiration for the new Citroen DS moved him to declare, "I think that cars today are almost the exact equivalent of the great Gothic cathedrals: I mean the supreme creation of an era, conceived with passion by unknown artists, and consumed in image if not in usage by a whole population which appropriates them as a purely magical object."[19]

Before the Edsel era, the extravagant size, power, and inefficiency of American cars came in for little criticism, although the automotive writer Christy Borth conceded the absurdity of using "two tons of automobile to transport a 105-pound blond."[20] A "blond" was a woman, of course (and half a century later trim women in hulking SUVs would provoke virtually identical comments). It was scarcely less absurd to use the car to transport a slightly larger and darker man, but a woman's driving was understood to be more frivolous than a man's. As people moved to the suburbs, as streetcars and buses became unattractive or simply unavailable, few questioned that men needed cars to go to work. But did they need such big ones? Perhaps they did, in order to attract women. Millions of men have certainly thought so, and many a fortune has been made selling "chick magnets." Nor did the central role of automobiles in American life erase their long-established aura of forbidden sexuality. Whereas the bustle of city life, epitomized by downtown hotels, retained a veneer of sophistication, the suburban motor hotel (or "motel") had not shed its aura of debauchery, iniquity, and tawdry trysts. Vladimir Nabokov gently mocked this image in his notorious 1955 novel of forbidden desire on the American highway, *Lolita*: "All along our route countless motor courts proclaimed their vacancy in neon lights, ready to accommodate salesmen, escaped convicts, impotents, family groups, as well as the most corrupt and vigorous couples. Ah, gentle drivers gliding through summer's black nights, what frolics, what twists of lust, you might see from your impeccable highways if Kumfy Kabins were suddenly drained of their pigments and became as transparent as boxes of glass!"[21] Another work that provoked a scandal, a decade later, was Ed Kienholz's sculptural piece *Back Seat Dodge '38*, with its explicit and untender depiction of backseat sex.

Americans' oft-proclaimed "love affair" with their automobiles (and the same thing was soon being said about the Germans, the Italians, and everyone else buying cars) was sometimes thought of as a couple's or a family's delight in use of their car, sometimes as a man's extension of his masculinity, and sometimes as the man's treatment of his car as a sex object. The German auto writer Alexander Spoerl wrote, as was typical, for a male audience: "Perhaps a car is like a woman after all. It is all a matter of compromise and, as there's no such thing—when you come to know her better—as a really ugly woman, there is no such thing, when you really get to know it, as a thoroughly bad car."[22] John Keats opened his sprightly 1958 attack on the car culture, *The Insolent Chariots*, with an overtly gendered (and sexual) metaphor that managed both to embrace and to mock hoary clichés of the decade: "Once upon a time, the American met the automobile and fell in love. Unfortunately, this led him into matrimony, and so he did not live happily ever after." The beginning of the affair, like the mythic origins of America, was rustic: "He joyfully leaped upon her, and she responded to his caresses by bolting about the landscape in what can only be called a succession of bumps and grinds." But marriage spoiled everything: "Quickly the automobile became the nagging wife, demanding rubbings and shinings and gifts. She put eyebrows over her windshield in the 1920s, plucked them out in the late 1930s, put them on again in the middle 1940s, and took them off once more in the 1950s. She nagged him for bits of chrome and cursed him for his extravagance when he brought them home. She lifted her face—expensively—from year to year; incessantly demanded new gauds and different colors, developed ever more costly eating habits, threatened to break the family budget and often succeeded, and the American,—poor dolt, not only catered to her whims but decked her out in door-edge guards and silvery Kleenex dispensers." In short, it could only end badly, and soon. Keats believed he was chronicling the end of an era: "the American's marriage to the American automobile is now at an end, and it is only a matter of minutes to the final pistol shot, although who pulls the trigger has yet to be determined."[23]

Keats was inspired by the sterner outrage of Lewis Mumford, whose prewar optimism about the automobile as a tool to empty the slums had turned into a passionate hatred by the 1950s. Mumford, too (writing the same year as Keats), saw the car as a woman, one who brought not amusement but tragedy: "the American has sacrificed his life as a whole to the motorcar, like someone who, demented with passion, wrecks his home in order to lavish his income on a capricious mistress who promises delights he can only occasionally enjoy."[24] Usually, however, Mumford described the car not as a woman but as something like a goddess, referring to the American "religion of the motorcar" and the "sacred cow of the American religion of technology."[25]

The 1950s were probably the golden age of "woman driver" jokes, which bolstered a male conviction that females were inattentive and incompetent behind the wheel, a belief consistently belied by accident statistics. The humor may have masked deeper anxieties about the unleashing of male aggression. Auto racing had been used to drum up car sales since the 1890s, and drivers who used public roads as racetracks had been a menace for just as long. Critics of 1950s auto advertising argued that carmakers were encouraging antisocial and dangerous behavior in the form of aggressive driving and excessive speed. The extraordinary increase in the horsepower of American automobiles during the 1950s, making ordinary cars capable of going a hundred miles per hour and more, inflamed old worries about the carnage attributable to drivers' aggressive habits. Overpowered cars with poor handling guaranteed deadly crashes, and traffic deaths were becoming a leading cause of mortality, especially among the young and healthy. Car crashes were the typical cause of headline-grabbing celebrity deaths, such as those of the speeding James Dean in 1955 and the drunken Jackson Pollock in 1956. Yet they were not a major public issue in the U.S. or any other country during the 1950s. In 1951, a brief flurry of press coverage called attention to the fact that the American death toll from automobiles was about to reach one million. Then the millionth death was duly recorded, and, in renewed obscurity, the numbers continued to climb.

As the preeminent symbol of the heady combination of freedom and prosperity that sprang up so rapidly in the two decades after war had ravaged Europe, the car was bound to be a target of critics troubled by the libido and aggression so openly on display. By the 1960s, a few articulate voices in western Europe lamented the substitution of automobility for sociability in a world where people wrapped their bodies in robust metal skins and pretended they were invulnerable. The Italian futurists had once hailed the driver as a modern centaur, but intellectuals now pondered a world in which these centaurs threatened to overwhelm ordinary two-legged wanderers. Whereas Georges Portal recycled the glorious image of the superhuman centaur to conclude a 1967 French paean to the automobile, a Paris city councilor had already, a few years before, employed the same metaphor to lament the plague of new roads that were "transforming Parisians into automotive centaurs" who "can cross the city only in their cars."[26] Similar thinking informed Robert Poulet's anti-auto essay, published as a counterpart to Portal's, in which he denounced the car for making human beings forget the greatness of their own hearts and bodies.[27] In the age of mass automobility, the image of the heroic centaur ceased to be persuasive; soon it yielded to that of the more ominous cyborg, half human and half machine.

Pessimism about the effects of modern technology has probably always been stronger in Europe than in America, and that old-fashioned

technoskepticism suffused the French environmentalist Bernard Charbonneau's 1967 fulminations against "l'hommauto" (the auto man) and
Hans F. Erb's treatise on the new "Automensch" (auto person). Cars, in
Erb's view, promoted social isolation, antisocial behavior, and disre-
spect for the law. They also made life easy for Germany's rulers, he suggested: people feel free and equal as soon as they have their speed limit
abolished, and "horsepower replaces democratic convictions."[28] (Poulet
added that horsepower also drove out self-possession, responsibility, and
intelligence.)[29] Erb's gentle satire hinted at a harder edge in the provocative title of his 1966 book, *Auto, Auto über alles*, an obvious play on the
banned opening words of the German national anthem, "Deutschland,
Deutschland über alles." At the time it was distinctly unfashionable in
Germany to recall the Third Reich heritage of cars or autobahns, but Erb
credited Hitler with the idea that auto ownership could overcome social
divisions, creating a unified "society of Volkswagen drivers." Instead of
bread and circuses, Erb suggested, the Nazis had offered bread and automobiles. Of course the Nazis had offered war as well, whereas postwar
Germans "have surrendered their dreams of national greatness in favor
of the dream of one's own family car. . . . The Germans have become the
nation of auto-supermen. Today they fulfill the maxim of their philosopher Nietzsche—live dangerously!—only on their roads. Here they give
vent to whatever will to power still lurks in their subconscious."[30]

This was not the prevailing view of life on the highway. A technological optimist like the German sociologist Janpeter Kob, writing at the
same time as Erb, argued that the more striking fact about the new society of drivers was the civilized restraint with which the great majority
exercised the power of their machines.[31] Even those who acknowledged
the dark side of motoring might still interpret it as a good thing: make
tracks, not war. Erb, however, did not see things that way. His point was
that Germans' penchant for violence had not been sublimated: "Just as
before, on the battlefields, here too they are ready to tender their offering in blood. Death comes easily on Germany's roads."[32]

Erb was not the only critic who thought that automobiles awakened
the dark spirits of his own national culture. Across the Atlantic, in an
essay on demolition derbies (an American invention that followed automobiles around the world), Tom Wolfe observed, "As hand-to-hand
combat has gradually disappeared from our civilization, even in wartime, and competition has become more and more sophisticated and abstract, Americans have turned to the automobile to satisfy their love of

direct aggression."[33] The government policy adviser and later U.S. senator Daniel Patrick Moynihan argued along similar lines to explain the widespread resistance to the imposition of safety standards: "It is surely clear that the largest reason we have not done anything to tame the automobile is that we have not much wanted to. That the automobile has a powerful symbolic, emotional role in American life is a proposition few would doubt. It is a central symbol of potency and power: the equivalent of the sword, or the horse, or the spear of earlier ages. It is both a symbol of aggression, and vehicle thereof. It is a sanctioned form of violence. In American Society one can injure and kill another person with an automobile at virtually no risk of *physical* reprisal. It is also a prime agent of risk-taking in a society that still values risk-taking, but does not provide many outlets."[34] A few years later, at the height of the Vietnam War as well as a wave of public hysteria about crime, Ronald Buel put it this way: "We are a violent people.... The auto falls solidly within this tradition. It keeps people from treating other people as human beings. One thinks of passing the car in front of you, or beating the other car to a parking place, instead of passing the *person* in front of you or fighting the *person* for a parking place. The auto prevents casual contact with others unlike oneself. And because we don't understand the humanity of others, there are fewer limits to our aggressive tendencies."[35]

In France, Alfred Sauvy invoked anthropological clichés to make a sardonic comment on the pleasures of automobility: just as many cultures have practiced human sacrifice to please the gods, "modern society consents to a regular sacrifice to conserve its way of life." In other words, although the carnage on the roads could easily be reduced, we choose not to be inconvenienced. Sauvy raised his irony to a high pitch: "Looked at in retrospect, perhaps from the year 2000 or 2500, this attitude will appear to be gilded with a certain grandeur: for its noble refusal to put any brakes on progress, or what appeared to be progress, our distant descendants will say that twentieth-century society sacrificed itself for our benefit."[36] Writing at about the same time, the iconoclastic British economist E. J. Mishan argued that "primitive" peoples came out well by comparison: "The sacrifice of a life or two by primitive communities in the belief that it ensured a good harvest seems humane in comparison with the implicit decision to kill some tens of thousands yearly that the pleasures of private motoring be upheld."[37] Charbonneau offered up ironic praise of the futurist intoxication with speed. After all, "what does death matter to those in ecstasy!" The automobile was an eminently practical device, indeed a vital one, he explained: it enabled people to squander enough blood and treasure on the weekend so that their orderly weekday lives might continue without disruption.[38]

Automotive eroticism and violence has long troubled social critics as much as it has fascinated writers and artists. An obvious example is F. Scott Fitzgerald's *The Great Gatsby* (1925), in which automobiles embody both glamor and death. In it, as in many other stories and films, a car crash serves as a convenient plot device because it had become the most common kind of violent death suddenly intruding into ordinary lives. Poems such as Karl Shapiro's "Auto Wreck" and Allen Ginsberg's "Car Crash" contemplate the violence done to human bodies. Harry Crews's novel *Car*, in which a character sets out to eat an automobile, offers a comic but still bloody take on car culture. It was only a small step from familiar obsessions to stories of demonically possessed cars, such as Stephen King's *Christine* (1983).

European writers first contemplated the specter of mass automobility by observing its development in America. The prolific Belgian writer Georges Simenon, for example, conjured an ominous atmosphere of brewing violence in his 1953 novel *Feux rouges* (*Red Lights*) by setting it on the crowded highways of New England during a holiday weekend. Françoise Sagan's *Bonjour Tristesse* (1954) is an entirely French story, but its plot turns on the fatal crash of a powerful American car. French cinematic fascination with cars, violence, and the fragile veneer of civilization reached a kind of culmination just after Charbonneau's book, in Jean-Luc Godard's 1967 film *Weekend*, in which the petty nastiness of bourgeois life degenerates into Hobbesian violence amid the endless carnage of car crashes during a sojourn in the country.[39]

The deadly side of the celebrated youthful car culture surfaced in popular 1960s American songs like "Dead Man's Curve" by Jan and Dean and "Leader of the Pack" by the Shangri-Las. Even before that, Andy Warhol, with his talent for enshrining icons of popular culture, exploited the vicarious thrill of automotive violence in the lurid "car crash" paintings of his "Death and Disaster" series of the early 1960s. Anticipation of crashes has of course never been the only reason people watch auto racing, but it is part of the excitement—as is apparent in the international appeal of demolition derbies (and their progeny, monster-truck rallies) where people pay to watch cars and trucks destroyed. (The Italian writer Primo Levi melded this tradition with an older one from his homeland in his whimsical 1978 story "Gladiator," in which spectators watch humans battle cars.) Meanwhile, car-chase scenes—the more crashes, the better—had become a staple of movies as soon as directors figured out how to film them. Before the recent spate of violent automotive-themed video games, children were socialized to car culture in carnival games of bumper cars, another American invention that spread around the globe. It is also impossible to overlook the hungry gazes from cars passing fresh auto wrecks on the highway, evidence of a fascination that may not be as unabashedly sexual as that of the characters in J. G. Ballard's lurid 1973 novel, *Crash*.

FROM HELPLESSNESS TO BLAME

The fact that people were behaving foolishly in their cars was much lamented. The fact that carmakers indulged their foolishness ultimately proved to be more controversial. Government and industry consistently blamed accidents on poor driving habits. They paid some attention to safer road design, but little to improved car design. Although some of the smaller American auto manufacturers (notably Kaiser-Frazer) incorporated safety features in their designs, they failed to survive in competition with the Big Three. At the instigation of one of its top executives, Robert S. McNamara, Ford introduced improved door locks, a collapsible steering wheel, and optional seat belts on its 1956 models, and the company briefly emphasized safety in its advertising. However, other executives remained skeptical of the safety pitch and chose to deemphasize it. Sales figures that failed to match Ford's rival, Chevrolet, led them (as well as their competitors) to conclude that "safety doesn't sell." Although some Ford employees believed that the safety campaign had in fact attracted customers as well as saved lives, most auto executives feared that any emphasis on safety features might scare off potential buyers by turning their minds to the dangers of driving, whereas annual styling changes kept everyone happy.[40] When they were later condemned for selling dangerous products, the manufacturers could argue in all honesty that they were giving Americans the killer machines they wanted.

However justified the assault on Detroit—which did have a great deal to answer for—it proved far more effective than any carping about the poor habits of ordinary motorists. The public was willing to believe in its own helplessness, but not in the innocence of the carmakers. When the journalist David Cort, writing in the *Nation* in 1956, lamented that the automobile had "converted the descendants of American pioneers, the toughest, most energetic and open-minded people in the civilized world, into lazy and fat seated invalids in forty years," his target was the industry that had created these invalids.[41] In the following years, other critics built a damning case against the carmakers' indifference to safety. Keats's 1958 book was in fact largely a caustic attack on Detroit, lambasting the industry for products that were shoddy and unsafe as well as ridiculous. In a 1959 article about the "epidemic on the highways," Daniel Patrick Moynihan urged government regulation of car design.[42] Some critics began to unearth evidence that the auto industry was hiding the dangers of its products. Although General Motors, for example, rejected rounded dashboards in the early 1960s in favor of a stylish and angular design deemed more marketable, the latter became known within the corporation as the "meat cleaver" because of what it did to human bodies in crashes.[43]

It was a few years later that the safety issue finally caught the nation's attention, notably in 1965 with the publication of Ralph Nader's book *Unsafe at Any Speed* (a phrase borrowed from Keats) and in U.S. Senate hearings organized with Nader's participation.[44] His book and testimony described design flaws that made collisions deadly. Nader's graphic account of the "second collision" between human bodies and steering wheels or dashboards highlighted Detroit's failure to design cars that would enable drivers and passengers to survive crashes. Even more sensational was his exposé of design defects that made cars, especially the Chevrolet Corvair, likely to go out of control. His gripping compilation of the deadly consequences of Detroit's refusal to pay attention to safety in car design might well have created a stir even if General Motors' overreaction hadn't made Nader famous. GM executives, facing lawsuits prompted by Nader's lurid descriptions of the fate of drivers who had lost control of their Corvairs, hired private detectives to dig up dirt that would discredit the man. The story might have turned out differently if their target had been more vulnerable than the austere Nader. As it happened, the result was a fiasco for GM. Not only did they get nothing on Nader, their skulking was uncovered and GM's president had to apologize in front of the Senate committee. The Corvair's worst defect had actually been quietly corrected in the 1964 and 1965 models (as the book made clear) but its sales never recovered from the bad publicity.

Nader's research showed that Detroit had taken its belief that "safety doesn't sell" too much to heart. GM's engineers recognized the problems with the Corvair (and it was the worst, but by no means the only problem model) but they were told to keep quiet. The car companies spent little on safety research and resisted design changes known to make cars safer. Among the problems that endangered drivers and passengers were rigid steering columns, dashboard knobs, faulty door latches, unsupported roofs, poor brakes, massive front and rear overhang, poor visibility through stylishly curved windshield glass, and the absence of seat belts. Nader's moment of fame drew attention to state and federal legislative hearings publicizing the problems and led to the passage of the 1966 National Traffic and Motor Vehicle Safety Act. The result was a fundamental if gradual change in public attitudes toward automotive safety and regulation. Nader used his GM monetary damage award to make himself an institutional presence in Washington, providing a counterweight to the auto lobby's resistance to safety mandates. The 1966 law established an agency, later named the National Highway Traffic Safety Administration, which institutionalized a process of setting and evaluating safety standards for car design. Soon only the car's most fanatical defenders dared to shrug off the highway death toll as the price of progress and mobility. Over the auto industry's shrill objections, government mandates forced carmakers to redesign their vehicles. Door latches, padded dashboards, collapsible steering columns, safer glass, better brakes, seat belts, and (later) airbags became nearly universal. There is little doubt that these efforts made a difference. The annual death toll on American roads finally ceased to increase in 1972, and it fell by a quarter over the next two decades.

The automotive safety revolution was international. Although Nader's book looked exclusively at American cars (later he took on the Volkswagen Beetle), it became a worldwide sensation, inspiring critics of Japanese and European cars as well. Japan started a major auto safety push in 1970, and along with Australia and New Zealand it led the way in mandating the use (not just the installation) of seat belts by 1972. Most European countries also passed mandatory seat-belt laws during the course of the 1970s (whereas most U.S. states and Canadian provinces, as well as Britain, waited until the mid-1980s). As in the U.S., the safety regulations clearly saved lives. European and Japanese highway death tolls have fallen more sharply than those of the U.S.

As people drove more and more, the annual American death toll ceased to decline in 1992 and began a slow increase. American car boosters point out that the death rate per mile driven continues to decline, which is relevant if one is comparing cars to trains or planes (which are still far safer by the same measure), and if one assumes that all miles driven are necessary. However, the death toll itself is the relevant statistic for understanding the price Americans (and others) pay for their car-centered lives. According to the World Health Organization, traffic accidents are now the leading cause of death (worldwide) among young people aged 10 to 24. Driving is also perilous for elderly people, many of whom keep driving longer than they are really able to, because they know that nondrivers are ill equipped to maintain independent lives. It has proved difficult to change casual attitudes toward driver misbehavior, especially drinking and driving, although the American tolerance for drunk drivers decreased during the 1980s, thanks to the moralistic campaign of the organization Mothers Against Drunk Driving (MADD).

Certainly one is better off inside these cars, with their many safety features, than as a pedestrian negotiating the same roads. All the improvements in vehicle and road design have helped to increase the speed and density of traffic, lowering the death rate per million miles driven, but also making the road more forbidding than ever for those who venture onto it without a steel cocoon. Meanwhile, the rapid spread of cars to the crowded cities and villages of Asia and Africa has exacted a fearsome death toll. It is reasonable to expect that, as in the West, better roads, cars, and rules will follow, and that eventually the death rate will fall. Indeed, the sheer growth in the number of cars will almost certainly bring down the rate of death per kilometer driven, even as the absolute death toll continues to climb. That is cold comfort to today's and tomorrow's victims in the poorer countries, home to a third of the world's cars and 90 percent of its million annual traffic deaths.

CARS AND MODERNITY

For the past century, ever since Henry Ford's first astonishing success with assembly-line production, automobiles have been synonymous with industrial society. With travel by automobile (including motor freight) as one of the pillars of modernity, the automakers became mainstays of industrial production and employment. Governments hastened to do their bidding, and when they failed to do so, they could count on a scolding from the industry's lobbyists and powerful allies. Usually, however, there was no need for political arm twisting. Governments wanted to promote industry and mobility, and that meant cars, trucks, and roads. Highway construction became a basic task of government and tool of economic development, in rich countries and also in poorer lands advised by development experts such as those at the World Bank.

Suspicion of the auto industry grew slowly during the second half of the century. When President Eisenhower nominated GM's president, Charles Wilson, to be secretary of defense in 1953, he was asked at his confirmation hearing whether he could make a decision in the interest of the nation if it were adverse to that of GM. "I cannot conceive of one, because for years I thought what was good for our country was good for General Motors and vice versa. The difference does not exist." Wilson was simply trying (if clumsily) to affirm the generally accepted role of the major industrial firms in the economic growth and rising standard of living that cemented an American political consensus. However, dissenters have pilloried Wilson ever since. They have decried every attempt by the largest American corporation to influence public policy, accusing it of the arrogance they saw revealed in Wilson's words, which were consistently misremembered as a resounding declaration that "what's good for General Motors is good for the country!"

Something like that has, in fact, been widely believed. Most major centers of automobile production that arose to compete with the earliest ones—the U.S., Britain, and France—have been promoted by governments eager to bring home the benefits of automobile production and use. The most famous case may be Hitler's Germany (along with Mussolini's Italy) in the 1930s, but other, mostly authoritarian governments have developed domestic car and truck production even more systematically. Japan in the 1950s is the greatest of these success stories. Francisco Franco's Spain in the 1960s is another, as are Korea at the same time and China since the 1990s.

Other notable examples are the Communist states of eastern Europe. Recent defenders of the automobile are fond of citing Communist hostility to cars as further evidence that automobiles are vital tools of individual freedom. Communist dictators, they argue, wanted to confine their people to the limited and controlled mobility of mass transit, and contemporary Western car haters want to do the same thing. This is, however, not an entirely accurate summary of the automotive history of eastern Europe. The leaders of the new Soviet Union in the 1920s were, like Hitler, great admirers of Henry Ford. Nearly all Communist leaders were enthusiastic proponents of mechanization and technological progress, in transportation as in other areas. Their visions of the modern socialist society, as revealed in the cities they built, resembled those of

Figure 6. Wide streets in the car-friendly Communist city: East Berlin, 1987. Author's photo.

early twentieth-century modernist architects, with their gleaming towers, broad avenues, and free-flowing traffic. Although their collectivist ideals left some of them less enthusiastic about private cars than either their fascist or democratic rivals, by the 1960s most envisioned a socialist future that included widespread car ownership, as part of their desire to match Western living standards.

They contemplated alternatives, but rarely for long. Traffic jams in Western cities made some Communist leaders wonder whether cars might be a luxury their people were better off without, but they typically concluded that superior central planning would enable them to handle motorization more efficiently than their rivals had.[45] (Similarly, Chinese officials in the late 1970s boasted of the absence of Western-style pollution and traffic jams, but soon fell silent as China began to mass-produce cars.)[46] In a 1960 speech, the Soviet leader Nikita Khrushchev proposed that socialist motorization take the form of collectively owned vehicles, a kind of rental fleet that would fulfill practical needs without becoming a measure of living standards or an object of conspicuous consumption. (The fact that "car-sharing" has recently been promoted as an alternative to car ownership in European and American cities confirms fanatical autophiles in their belief that enemies of the car are communists at heart.) Khrushchev's suggestion was poorly received, however, and private ownership of cars soon became entirely acceptable.[47] Eastern European auto ownership grew at rapid rates in the following years, although it lagged behind the capitalist west.

Attempts to satisfy consumer demand foundered not on hostility to cars but on internal contradictions of the centrally planned economies. Communist leaders were generally eager to give people the material goods that made them happy, but economic planners imposed limits on the production of consumer goods in order to promote industrial investment.[48] It was these planners who drew the line between necessities and luxuries (apparent in their pricing systems: cheap bread and expensive chocolate, subsidized mass transit and overpriced cars). Behind the structural contradictions of Communist car policy undoubtedly lay a certain ambivalence about automobiles. Although cars had practical uses, just as, say, refrigerators did, people persisted in wanting their cars to make them stand out from the crowd—behavior that good socialist leaders were loath to encourage. Nor, of course, was individual mobility an unquestioned good in the land of the Berlin Wall. Even as some Communist moralists fretted about cars becoming status symbols or tokens of social inequality, official policies continued to endorse auto ownership.[49] By the 1960s, Communist dictators saw cars as a way of both keeping up with Western technology and keeping the masses happy and distracted. They did not see automobility as a threat to their control of their people.

The threat came, rather, from the lack of automobiles. Anyone without special connections had to expect a long wait for a car—in these societies, money alone did not open every door. By the 1980s in East Germany, eighteen-year-olds routinely put themselves on the central waiting list for the humble national car, the Trabant, anticipating that in ten years (the usual waiting period) they would want and be able to afford one, or have no problem passing it on to an eager buyer on the black market. Among the many consumer shortages stoking popular discontent, cars loomed the largest. In a 1989 internal report, the East German secret police concluded that the supply of automobiles had become, for many citizens, the measure of their economy's success.[50] The opening of the Berlin Wall five months later dramatically revealed their poor opinion of the economy as well as their pent-up desire for mobility.

Cars bring liberation. Yet authoritarian regimes of many kinds—Nazi Germany, Communist Germany, Spain, China—have eagerly promoted automobiles. And car critics of a Marxist or structuralist bent make a persuasive case that the automobile is ideally suited to imprisoning people in a technocratic cage, leaving them helplessly addicted to highways and suburbs, to the governments and corporations that build them, and to the merchants of petroleum. The carmakers advertise their wares as freedom machines, and millions of us—European women, Chinese men, American teenagers—eagerly make ourselves slaves to our cars and to the entire automotive infrastructure. Perhaps that makes us fools or dupes—on a bad traffic day, some of us feel that way. Still, all but the most hardened car haters recognize that cars bring not only a potentially illusory sense of liberation but also the very real advantages of mobility.

The car is an instrument of both oppression and freedom, not only when a motorist terrorizes a pedestrian, but also when the pedestrian yearns to sit behind the wheel, and when the motorist feels trapped there and wonders whether automobility is worth the price in money, time, pollution, and nerves. In the early days, cars (and car-oriented public policies) were vulnerable to attack as oppressive tools of the rich and powerful—as they still are in some countries. In the age of mass automobility, they can be criticized as unfair to the unmotorized poor, but they can also be defended as tools of equality and opportunity. The democratization of driving gives millions of people the real power of a machine along with the illusory sovereignty of the road. (Meanwhile, the car bomb democratizes violent terror.)

Certainly the gender politics of automobility cuts both ways. Throughout the automobile era in nearly every land, men have far outnumbered women in the possession of driver's licenses as well as the ownership of motor vehicles. That was the case across Europe until nearly the end of the twentieth century. Only where car ownership and use became nearly universal did the gender gap vanish. One result—but sometimes also a cause—of this imbalance is that women have been less mobile. When they do travel, women have often been disproportionately represented among the pedestrians, bicyclists, and transit users forced to cope with auto-oriented roads, cities, and societies. Feminists have drawn conflicting conclusions from this state of affairs. Some argue that male- and automobile-centered mentalities and policies have disadvantaged women by failing to acknowledge and plan for their use of non-automotive modes of transportation, or by making women bear the burden of auto dependence.[51] That view is more commonly heard from European feminists, whereas some Americans argue that women's travel itineraries make them more likely to benefit from automobiles than men do, and that policies to restrict auto use are therefore the greatest enemies of female mobility and freedom. Not only do women typically need to go more places in their daily "trip chains" of work, shopping, and family duties, they also (according to this line of argument) need to feel secure in an enclosed automobile, rather than having to brave the unprotected public spaces of streets, stations, trains, or buses.[52] Thus we have two contradictory interpretations of the affinity of suburban mothers (Americans and those who have followed the American model) for spacious minivans and SUVs. Either they know and value the benefits of automobility, recognizing that they would be in dire straits if they had to manage all the same trips without their own vehicles, or they resent their roles as the chauffeur slaves of suburbia and wonder if there is an alternative to a family life assembled from far-flung destinations connected only by mom's van.

It is also no surprise that the automobile has played its part in America's troubled race relations. In 1910, for example, the flamboyant African American boxing champion Jack Johnson, much hated because he openly flouted white Americans' expectations of black men's submissive behavior, crossed yet another line when he challenged the racing driver Barney Oldfield to an automobile race. (Oldfield accepted the challenge, to the chagrin of some white racists, but, to their relief, he easily defeated his amateur opponent.) In the early decades of the twentieth century, many middle-class African Americans acquired cars, in part because they provided a welcome alternative to the humiliations of travel on the segregated trains and buses of the American South. Many of them testified to the liberating experience of automotive travel. It was, however, a temporary liberation: autocamps and other places of accommodation (even national park campgrounds) often did not welcome them. The writer Chester Himes bitterly recalled a "frightening" 1946 cross-country drive with his wife—through the North, not the South: "literally none of the white people en route who operated hotels, motels, restaurants, or even local YWCAs or YMCAs would serve a clean, respectably dressed couple in a new Mercury car."[53]

Nor is there much evidence that African Americans found the automobile to be a means to the racial integration or political rights they sought. Pro-auto propagandists of our day sometimes cite the 1955 Montgomery bus boycott as evidence of the irreplaceable liberating power of the automobile. During that trying time, which brought fame to Rosa Parks and Martin Luther King, Jr., and helped break the hold of legal segregation in the U.S., those who boycotted the segregated public buses of Alabama's capital had to arrange alternative transportation to reach jobs and other destinations, and the cars of supporters proved invaluable in keeping the boycott going. Cars meant freedom, in other words, while public transit was oppressive. But there is little evidence that the boycotters considered their makeshift travel arrangements, or their abandonment of public transit, adequate compensation for the equal treatment on public buses that they were fighting for.[54] This may be a case in which the dynamics of gender and race point in different directions: whereas for many women, mobility itself has been the very liberation they sought, for African Americans it was no substitute for civil rights.

Yet there is no denying that many African Americans since Jack Johnson have proudly displayed their cars as tokens of real or imaginary wealth, status, and potency. Further evidence of the liberating power of cars, but especially of its limits, is the experience of many African American drivers, mostly men, who have been stopped by the police. The frequency of these checks aroused the suspicion that many white police officers resented or mistrusted black men driving their own cars and stopped them on the flimsiest of pretexts, to harass them and let them know they were being watched. The well-documented experience of "racial profiling" spawned bitter jokes that African Americans were likely to be stopped on suspicion of "driving while black." This is just more one example of the recurring fear that cars may be permitting the wrong sort of people to go where they shouldn't go, do what they shouldn't do, and escape proper control. Such attitudes nourished some of the earliest hostility to cars, reappeared in the anti-auto arguments of the American wilderness movement, fed the fears that draw people into gated communities, and remain apparent in the prohibition enforced against would-be women drivers of the luxuriously motorized Saudi Arabian upper class.

One country after another has crossed the threshold of mass automobility, attended by many of the same tensions. The most recent case, and perhaps the most dramatic of all, is China, partly because of that country's sheer size, partly because of its rapid economic growth and the sudden transformation of its society. China may be compressing a century of Western automotive history into a few years, as the car is rapidly transformed from rare luxury, to symbol of success, to routine tool of prosperity, to scourge of the cities. Until the 1980s, Chinese cities not only had few cars, there was little mobility at all. The Communist system assigned nearly everyone to a work unit (*danwei*) that provided employment, housing, and access to a limited range of consumer goods, all within a single corner of the city. Most people were expected not to want or need to travel far, even within the city, and the means to do so were not readily available. Not only were cars a rarity, public transportation was in limited supply, and even access to bicycles was restricted to a privileged minority with a certified need for them. After that rule was changed in 1978, as part of the reforms promoted by the Chinese leader Deng Xiaoping, bicycle ownership grew rapidly, as the bicycle became both the symbol and the tool of individual mobility. But the bicycle's reign was brief. Within a few years, automobiles, too, were becoming available. A tiny but growing minority owned them, while other urban Chinese came to rely on taxis, jitneys, and buses. As the *danwei* system was dissolved, people suddenly felt both the need and the opportunity to seek work, shopping, and leisure far from home (or to move far away from work and leisure, which had the same effect). Cars were more prestigious possessions than bicycles, but they were also more practical for transporting families and goods across the vast expanses of Beijing or Shanghai, especially since the government has responded with a crash program of urban road construction. Whether cars can long remain an efficient form of urban transport is far from certain amid the growing smog and traffic jams.[55]

In China as in other lands, a desire for freedom continues to sell cars, yet the automobile sometimes looms as the biggest obstacle to that very freedom. From the beginning, the need to regulate automobiles threatened to spoil all the fun. Even if a ban on cars like Graubünden's, or rules amounting to a virtual ban, like Britain's Red Flag law, were doomed by the early twentieth century, they were replaced by an ever denser labyrinth of restrictions. Around the world and across the past century, the tyrannical reign of motorists has been at war with the tyrannical impositions placed on motorists. Because speed was the first attraction of cars as well as the first threat to bystanders, speed limits and speed traps have always been a bone of contention. The same goes for all the other rules regulating stops and turns and rights of way, as intersections became contested spaces in more ways than one. Police forces found themselves diverted more and more to traffic duty ("Mother, what *did* policemen do when there weren't any motors?" asks the little girl in the 1927 *Punch* cartoon) while prominent citizens protested the indignity of being hauled into court for their motoring offenses.

Surprisingly little has changed in a century. In wealthy lands, average people encounter law enforcement primarily through traffic infractions. Most see themselves as law-abiding citizens, except when it comes to traffic laws. Many eagerly seek arcane information about getting speeding tickets "fixed," or even trade tips on how to get away with having a few drinks before the drive home. (In other places, the topic of discussion is the appropriate etiquette for bribing a traffic cop.) Early motorists were offended at the idea that they should have to display an official identification plate on their vehicles, as if they could not be trusted to control their vehicles. That, too, quickly became a general rule, if not a universally popular one. The recent proliferation of cameras installed to record traffic infractions, notably in Britain, has not only alarmed some civil libertarians who see it as yet another automobile-related threat to freedom, but it also seems to have created a market for fake mud splashed across the fenders (and license plates) of 4x4s that never actually encounter the muddy roads for which they were supposedly built.

The testing and licensing of drivers also became universal, despite early misgivings. In the United States, occasional qualms are raised (by nondrivers, noncitizens, civil libertarians, and, more recently, "homeland security" officials) about the long-established fact that the driver's licenses issued by the individual states function as ersatz national identification cards. For better or worse, the driver's license is the badge of citizenship, and the computers of the fifty state departments of motor vehicles have become major repositories of private secrets. Meanwhile, in the northern borderlands of Germany, "Flensburg" merely designates a modest town that happens to house the national registry of traffic infractions, but among motorists elsewhere in the nation, the name summons a cold chill. New worries have arisen in many lands with the growth of electronic tolling via windshield-mounted transponders that can be used to trace drivers' paths. And a further step looms in the form of long-promised new technologies to increase freeway capacities and decrease the danger of accidents by transferring control of a car from the driver to a central computer that packs the cars into freeway lanes, or onto fixed guideways. This traffic engineer's dream could become a dystopian nightmare for motorists in search of mastery and escape on a road that calls itself a *freeway*.

CHAPTER THREE

Cities in Motion:
The Car in the City

Remarkably soon after cars appeared, critics had registered the full range of visceral objections to them. What subsequently changed, more than people's attitudes, was the world in which the cars circulated. They quickly transformed the countryside, shattering its tranquility or its backward isolation, depending on one's point of view. Although most automobiles were found in cities, their first appearance in city streets was less disruptive. An occasional car was enough to make country people feel dispossessed of their roads, but in town it took a few more. On streets choked with clanking wagons and shouting teamsters, residents were less likely to complain that cars disturbed the peace. The first motorcars merely joined the maelstrom of slow-moving wagons, fast carriages, darting bicycles, and electric streetcars. Soon, however, the confrontation between car and city would transform urban life, as cars changed the character of human interaction in city streets. Their speed, plus the layer of glass and steel encasing the motorist, made encounters in the streets far more impersonal and anonymous than those of pedestrians, cyclists, wagon drivers, and even the few privileged riders in closed carriages.

THE BATTLE FOR THE STREETS

Even before automobiles, no one thought of city air as healthful, with coal smoke, sewage, and horse dung assaulting the nose. The dust churned up by cars was a problem, but less noticeably than in the country, since major city streets were typically paved before the automobile era, or, if not, were regularly sprinkled with water. A worse nuisance was the concentration of exhaust fumes. Decades before smoggy skies made auto exhaust a major scandal, some scientific evidence pointed to its dangers to human health, and medical experts joined lay people in decrying the foul fumes.[1] Car exhaust was also blamed for contaminating the pristine countryside. A German doctor wrote in 1911 that "even a trip to the nearby surroundings of the cities often no longer offers the desired rehabilitation for the lungs," since the air around busy country roads was now so contaminated.[2]

Although aesthetes as well as peasants decried the loss of pastoral quiet, city dwellers were the ones who had to bear the relentless din of traffic. The urban noise problem was not new, yet even in bustling city streets the roar of automobiles was a shock. In 1908, the German scholar and social reformer Theodor Lessing published a tirade against the plague of urban noise and founded an "Anti-Noise Society" in Hanover, which quickly established branches in other cities as well.[3] Lessing reserved particular ire for "that depopulation machine," the automobile. His movement's major victory was the mandatory use of mufflers, which abated the noise, at least until the volume of traffic became the ceaseless if dull rumble that modern urban dwellers must endure. Punctuating the roar of engines was the piercing blare of car horns, which many city dwellers found not only vexatious but also indicative of motorists' boorishness. Anti-noise crusaders like Lessing denounced the selfishness of motorists who robbed city-dwellers of the chance for quiet contemplation and civil interaction. By 1926, even the ardent motorist Rudyard Kipling, on a visit to Monte Carlo, lamented that "the motor car has made the Riviera a hell—and a noisy, smelly one."[4] The racket of Rome's thirty thousand cars (it seemed like a lot at the time) also disturbed the motor enthusiast Benito Mussolini. His misplaced optimism assured him, however, that their ever-increasing number would solve the problem by itself: when there are many cars, "all must channel themselves one after the other, and then there will no longer be any motive for annoying the public with useless honking."[5] But not even Mussolini could orchestrate this fascist fantasy of regimented motoring.

At first the electric car showed promise as a vehicle compatible with city life. Electrics were less smelly and noisy, and not so ostentatiously fast and powerful. They were sometimes exempted from rules banning cars from urban parks (such as New York's Central Park), restrictions intended to preserve those oases of urban tranquility. In hindsight we might call the electric a Trojan horse that helped make cars acceptable.[6] It gained a reputation as a good car for women (even Henry Ford bought one for his wife), meaning that it was not so dirty or powerful or frightening—or thrilling. Those very qualities, of course, partly explain the electric's ultimate failure to compete with the gasoline engine.

The sound of a car quickly became a sign of danger, since its speed was deadly. Booth Tarkington's 1918 novel *The Magnificent Ambersons*, in which automobiles are the key instruments of change in a fictional midwestern city, describes the disruption of the quiet evening from the point of view of the disgruntled old guard: "Then, like a cowboy shooting up a peaceful camp, a frantic devil would hurtle out of the distance, bellowing, exhaust racketing like a machine gun gone amuck—and at these horrid sounds the surreys and buggies would hug the curbstone, and the bicycles scatter to cover, cursing; while children rushed from the sidewalks to drag pet dogs from the street. The thing would roar by; leaving a long wake of turbulence; then the indignant street would quiet down for a few minutes—till another came."[7] Here we have the street as an urban public space, under threat from the new machine. The "machine gun" was the opening shot of a battle for control of the streets, one soon won decisively by the automobile.

The tyranny of the road predated the horseless carriage: for more than a century before motorcars appeared, the fast carriages of the rich had menaced poor people in city streets.[8] A vivid pre-automotive example is the shocking scene in Charles Dickens's *Tale of Two Cities*, written in the 1850s and set in 1780, in which an aristocrat musters only cold contempt after his speeding coach kills a child in a Paris street. Still, early motorists often felt besieged, blamed for taking city streets away from pedestrians and bicyclists, and, most dramatically, from children, whose deaths under the wheels became all-too-routine news. Grieving parents denounced reckless and arrogant drivers, while motorists (and courts) often blamed the careless children and their parents. During the first years of the twentieth century, accidents or heedless motorists in poor neighborhoods of American cities sometimes incited stone-throwing mobs. Some motorists responded with anger, some with indifference, others with a missionary impulse. The Chicago Automobile Club, among others, sponsored automotive outings for potentially delinquent youths, so that they might share rather than resent the joy of motoring.[9]

Indignant Driver. "Hi! 'Ow much more o' the blinkin' road d'yer want?"

Figure 7. Motorists claiming the street all for themselves. *Punch* cartoon by J. C. B. Knight, 1922.

It soon became clear that cars had fundamentally changed the dynamic of city streets. Paris, the first city where cars appeared in large numbers, was also the foremost city of urban strollers, a place where both motorists and flaneurs could count on articulate, upper-class support. Paris was better suited to the automobile than most old cities, thanks to the wide boulevards Georges-Eugène Haussmann had torn through the city during the nineteenth century. Nevertheless, strollers soon realized that the new form of fashionable urban display posed a mortal threat to the older one. Although this new German technology was still chiefly a French fashion in 1902, one Parisian critic denounced its rush through the boulevards as a pernicious Anglo-Saxon invasion, "a thoroughly English impertinence: Time is money! What else matters?"[10] Short-lived French attempts to mobilize against the new danger dated to the first decade of the century, and a Parisian "league for the defense of pedestrians" emerged in the 1920s, but decades would pass, and many rows of beloved street trees would be sacrificed for traffic lanes, before serious restrictions were put on the car in Paris or most other cities.[11]

In 1906–7, over 90 percent of the two thousand cars registered in Berlin were involved in an accident.[12] Too often the victims were pedestrians. Most were poor and anonymous, but not all: in 1914 two members of the German parliament were run down on a Berlin street.[13] Already in 1905, a member of the Prussian parliament had complained that "there is hardly a person in Berlin who has not been on the verge of being run over." He lamented that "here the pedestrian is now no better than a second-class person."[14] Baron Michael von Pidoll made the same point about Vienna in 1912: from the motorists' point of view, pedestrians were nothing but "an annoying accessory of the street."[15] The problem, in other words, was not merely the motorists' arrogance, bad as that was. Pidoll, an Austrian government official, was one of the few early observers to attack the car as a fundamental threat to city streets. His book denounced "the view that the purpose and function of public ways and streets begins and ends with traffic." City streets and squares "are more than mere thoroughfares," he explained. "Rather, they belong to the whole layout of the city; they are the population's site of settlement; they form the surroundings of the buildings, the milieu in which the personal, social, and economic life of the city in no small part takes place; and they satisfy city dwellers' indispensable need to go for a stroll."[16]

Not only did automotive traffic threaten to supplant all these other needs; motorists had the audacity to claim a right to drive mere pedestrians off the streets. "Perhaps the public streets should be kept free of people?"[17] Pidoll meant his question rhetorically, but in many places the answer would soon be yes. With the arrival of automobiles came a flurry of traffic regulations, the upshot of which was to make the street a place exclusively for cars. This was a revolutionary change in the use of urban public space. Pedestrians, horses, and the vehicles they pulled had long ranged freely across streets and squares, while menacing street railways were at least confined to their tracks. Either cars had to adapt to the slow pace of the street—a solution adopted only decades later, and only in a few places—or other users had to be forced aside.

FROM CONGESTION TO SPRAWL

An emerging profession of traffic experts pondered how to attain what motorists sought: the smooth and rapid flow of automobiles. The problem was congestion, and other users of the street simply blocked traffic. Pidoll's street, a place of leisure, beauty, and commerce, had little in common with this new understanding of the street as a traffic artery. The imperative of traffic flow became the argument that trumped all other uses.

This way of thinking first became established law and practice during the 1920s in southern California. Motoring organizations, supported by the automobile industry, countered popular images of the spoiled "joy-rider" with a campaign against the heedless pedestrian, even using the power of their advertising dollars to demand that the press cease its attacks on innocent motorists and direct its attention to the real trouble-makers. They popularized the word "jaywalker" to denigrate those rubes whose obliviousness to the new realities of the street endangered their own lives and snarled traffic as well. After 1925, Los Angeles became notorious for its strictly enforced jaywalking laws, which restricted pedestrians to authorized crossings and punished them for venturing onto the roadway anywhere else.[18] During the following decades, this way of thinking remained dogma among traffic engineers, one of whom still proclaimed in 1969 that "the only impediment to free and efficient traffic circulation in downtown Los Angeles is the pedestrian."[19] Only the rare skeptic recalled that a "jaywalker" was someone who treated the street as the public place it once had been. Motorists generally agreed that city streets should approach the ideal of the limited-access freeway, where nothing was permitted to impede the flow of traffic. This way of thinking about streets later attracted more critics, as we shall see, but it still lingers—apparent in motorists' daily grumbling around the world as well as in an Australian newspaper columnist's recent suggestion that the solution to Sydney's traffic congestion was to ban bicycles from the roads, and in Chinese policies to do the same thing on major thoroughfares.

The building of cities, or at least of roads, proceeded without regard to people who were not in cars. Pidoll's fears about the death of the traditional street came to pass. Viewed through the windshield, pedestrians were simply fools, daydreaming relics of an archaic pace of life, as in a poem published in an Australian motoring magazine in 1947:

Shy and timid, never caring,
If the lights be red or green
He will saunter, stop—eyes staring,
At a far-off distant scene.

Tooting horns will not affect him,
Swear words brush by either ear;
Would the gods-that-be inject him,
With some sense of sight or fear.

But my plea to you, dear reader,
Is to spare this simple lout;
He's a dill without a leader,
Soon the species will die out.[20]

No one doubted that automobiles posed a grave threat to pedestrians and bicyclists. Nor, however, did the authorities place the onus on motorists or their vehicles. Motorists should be more attentive, everyone agreed, but generally the blame lay with the victim. A writer in 1916 had no doubt: "With an automobile properly driven there is no menace to life, except that precipitated by those on foot who make improper uses of the streets and thoroughfares."[21] Later generations of safety experts generally agreed. In 1950, an American traffic safety consultant lamented that pedestrians, unlike motorists, could not be licensed. Most pedestrians who died were breaking the law—that is, jaywalking—or "engaged in some obviously unsafe act." The same was true of cyclists: "Like the pedestrian, the bicyclist is his own worst enemy."[22] This way of thinking carried over to the Nader-inspired reforms of the 1960s, which made car passengers safer but did little for anyone outside a motor vehicle.

Making the cities safe for cars was supposed to usher in the utopia of free-flowing traffic. Snarled city traffic predated the automobile age, whether in imperial Rome or in the Paris of 1610, when a traffic jam enabled the Catholic fanatic François Ravaillac to leap onto King Henry IV's stalled carriage and stab him to death. In the most thriving nineteenth-century cities, swarms of pedestrians fought for street space with trams as well as horse-drawn buses, carriages, and wagons. The first cars were merely caught in the chaos. Early in the century, Daniel Burnham and other bold urban planners of the City Beautiful movement in the United

Figure 8. Policeman directing traffic: Michigan Avenue, Chicago, c. 1917. National Archives.

States drew on European precedents such as Haussmann's Paris to propose the construction of broad streets through city centers, opening them up to light and air as well as horses and fast carriages. The new automobiles seemed ideally suited to these wide streets. Thomas Edison, contemplating New York's horse-drawn chaos in 1908, envisioned a future free of traffic congestion as soon as fast-moving motor vehicles supplanted all the horses.[23] Early American traffic engineers agreed that the automobile offered the solution to urban traffic problems, once the streets were cleared of slower vehicles and redesigned for the smooth flow of motorized traffic.[24] Yet already before World War I, cars brought their own traffic jams to American downtowns, and all subsequent victories over congestion proved short lived, while a smoother flow of traffic only exacerbated the problem of finding space to park all the cars.

The combined problems of parking and congestion added up to a fundamental conflict between the new automobiles and the old cities: there simply wasn't enough room. By the 1920s, visionaries were declaring that the automotive age had made the old cities obsolete. Only a fundamental reconstruction could make room for wide roads and parking spaces—whether at ground level, above, or below. American civic-improvement schemes led the way, but the crowded cities of Europe demanded more radical surgery, as was proposed by the Swiss architect who called himself Le Corbusier, and who emerged as the most forceful advocate of rebuilding old European cities to suit the needs of the fast-moving modern age—an age of high-speed trains and air travel, but above all an age of automobiles. His Radiant City of 1922 was the most stunning model of a completely new metropolis of generously spaced apartment towers, set in spacious parks, and knitted together by high-speed roads. Nothing came of his notorious 1925 proposal (sponsored by the Voisin car company) to raze most of Paris to make way for such a city, but where no cherished old town stood in the way—as in North America, Australia, Asian Russia, and colonial settings, not to mention the Paris suburbs—many elements of the Corbusian model became reality. In eastern Europe, Communist governments, unrestrained by private-property rights, rebuilt many cities in Corbusian forms that left ample room for the few cars there.

Proposals to build roads exclusively for cars dated to the early days of automobility. Because cars traveled so much faster than other vehicles and because they quickly destroyed traditional pavements, both their enemies and their friends wanted to segregate them. At first, motor interests were wary of the idea, fearing it as a first step toward a complete ban on cars. Soon, however, it became clear that auto-only roads promoted more and faster motoring. Le Corbusier went a step further, proposing to organize the new city around the movement of automobiles. He declared that the problem was not merely congestion in the street; it was the street itself, especially the crowded, tenement-lined street of the European city, with its promiscuous mixture of vehicles and bodies. Like Pidoll, he recognized that streets had long served many functions: commerce, pedestrian circulation, vehicle movement, communication and socializing, open space and recreation. Le Corbusier proposed to separate these uses. His visionary city of towers housed as many people in the same area as the old tenement city, while leaving generous open space separating homes from high-speed transit corridors, elevated or at ground level, and reserved for trains and automobiles. This tabula rasa appealed to the emerging profession of traffic engineers, who hoped to narrow the yawning gap between the automobile's potential for rapid movement and the painful reality of its tortuous journey through city streets.

Fast roads for cars proved the most attractive element of Le Corbusier's scheme. They became the key to the future American city envisioned in the most popular exhibit at the 1939 New York World's Fair, the Futurama, sponsored by General Motors. Five million people stood in line to be transported on moving benches through a diorama organized around "magic motorways." Its designer, Norman Bel Geddes, offered a vision similar to Le Corbusier's, and it was his genius to let people experience it as if seated in a car, where they could enjoy a panorama of the open countryside as well as a smooth and rapid ride through the congestion-free "City of 1960." Bel Geddes offered Futurama, however fantastic it appeared, as a genuine model for future traffic planning. And he wanted to assure Americans that their love for cars was not misplaced: "Automobiles are in no way responsible for our traffic problems. The entire responsibility lies in the faulty roads."[25]

The planners' ideal of separating cars from pedestrians, and from other uses of streets and public space, reigned supreme from the 1920s to the 1960s, and in most places its influence lasted much longer. In the American suburban context, the foremost model was designed in the 1920s by Clarence Stein and Henry Wright for the New Jersey suburb of Radburn. Stein declared that the standard American street grid was unsuited to the age of the automobile, because cars drove all other uses from every street. In its place Radburn offered a hierarchy of streets—from wide and fast to narrow and slow—and in particular a network of residential "cul-de-sacs," dead-end streets that serviced only a few houses each. Radburn's street plan became the model for the postwar suburb in the U.S. and beyond, and the cul-de-sac, combining easy car access with protection from through traffic of any kind, became the residential location of choice for the rest of the century.

The point of all these plans was to accommodate the automobile, whether out of love or fear. Burnham and Le Corbusier eagerly promoted their visions of new cities opened up to rapid movement by car. Stein, by contrast, concluded that "the automobile was a disrupting menace to city life" and that "quiet and peaceful repose disappeared along with safety. Porches faced bedlams of motor throughways with blocked traffic, honking horns, noxious gases. Parked cars, hard grey roads and garages replaced gardens."[26] His solution was to embrace the suburb as the only alternative—an alternative made feasible by the widespread ownership of those very automobiles. Thus he might have subscribed, bitterly, to Le Corbusier's proud boast that "the automobile has killed the great city; the automobile must save the great city."[27]

Although both kinds of plans encouraged driving, they also tried to preserve other uses of public space by giving them their own, car-free paths and zones. Le Corbusier's Radiant City envisioned people living in the middle of urban parks. Radburn, inspired by the horse-and-carriage model of New York's Central Park, incorporated picturesque pedestrian and bicycle paths equipped with underpasses to avert all conflict with motor traffic. What subsequently happened, however, was that thousands of plans for other new places borrowed the idea of separating cars from other uses, but left out the other corridors. As traffic planning became a science, the emerging profession of traffic engineers understood "traffic" to mean the flow of motor vehicles only. After World War II, when urban leaders agreed that their cities were "blighted" by the noise, vibration, fumes, and congestion of auto traffic, their solution was to propose bigger and faster roads. Pedestrian and bicycle paths became an optional feature—indeed, walking and bicycling were soon classified as recreation rather than transportation. (As recently as 2007, U.S. secretary of transportation Mary Peters lamented the diversion of a small portion of her department's budget to bicycle and pedestrian paths, which were "not transportation.") Planners and politicians looked at existing paths and saw them little used. It was not clear, and soon didn't matter, whether they were little used because they were poorly designed and maintained, or neglected because they were little used. Driving and parking had become so convenient that most residents didn't seem to care. Whatever the reasons, plans for pedestrian access withered away, and the eventual result in the typical American suburb (and often in other countries as well), even in large quasi-urban commercial developments, was that the roads and ramps designed exclusively for speeding automobiles were the only ones built. Access to the increasingly popular cul-de-sacs was barely possible without a car, and by the late twentieth century many houses communicated with the world outside only through a prominent garage door. In these places, pedestrians, bicyclists, and bus riders were left even worse off than they had been in the teeming streets that both Stein and Le Corbusier detested. Meanwhile, the very presence of sidewalks in older areas often came to signify a less than desirable neighborhood.

Burnham's and Le Corbusier's idealized sketches of the future city typically show wide roads with little traffic. This utopia was not to be.

Figure 9. Traffic jam, 14th St. and the Mall: Washington, D.C., 1937. National Archives.

Even after World War II, however, and even in the United States, civic leaders were slow to recognize the implications of growing car ownership. As the journalist Francis Bello wrote in 1958: "A great many city officials and city planners continued to believe—until very recently—that the urban transportation patterns of the last half of the century would differ relatively little from those of the first. Automobile use in the city could be expected to rise, of course, but presumably most sensible people with business in town would continue to patronize public transit. But they didn't."[28] More and more of them said goodbye to streetcars and buses, reluctantly or eagerly, and drove into town, and many moved to auto-dependent suburbs.

The continued growth of these suburbs was a certainty. The battlegrounds would be the districts that predated the automobile. In 1920, and still to a great extent in 1950, office employment and retail trade in major American cities was concentrated "downtown," in a dense agglomeration of tall buildings. Most downtown businessmen and their allies in local government were eager to open downtown to motor traffic, unaware that cars would prove to be its undoing. Government and business leaders had been grappling with downtown traffic jams since the 1920s; by 1950 the problems were worse than ever. There was talk of revitalized mass transit, preferably in the form of underground railways, which could take pedestrians and trams off the streets, leaving more room for cars. But the automobile generally won the battle for funding, which went to widen streets and to construct major inner-city highways such as the Brooklyn-Queens Expressway and Boston's Central Artery.

American traffic planners were confident that they could build their way out of congestion. Downtown leaders agreed that the key to stopping the decline of city centers was to make them more auto-friendly, using such tools as on-street parking bans, one-way streets, and timed stoplights, providing plentiful and convenient parking, and ultimately by building express highways into the city center. What they failed to foresee was that the highways could also channel traffic out of the center, to peripheral areas where driving and parking were less arduous.

The real solution to their problem thus emerged outside the vision and jurisdiction of downtown leaders. Shoppers found their way to new stores built outside the old downtowns, in more spacious areas with good road access, room for parking, and, often, poor connections to bus and streetcar lines. When the mighty catalog retailer Sears, Roebuck decided in 1925 to build its own stores in major cities, it chose locations on busy streets far enough from downtown to avoid its traffic jams and parking crunch. The first city in which this approach became the typical pattern of development was Los Angeles, where the original "Miracle Mile" of Wilshire Boulevard emerged as a major retail center by 1930.[29] Civic leaders elsewhere in the U.S. (and, ultimately, around the world) failed to recognize the extent to which their old cities would follow the L.A. model. Visible signs of change came soon after World War II, when large new shopping centers were constructed on the fringe of many cities, entirely separate from the existing urban fabric but uniting multiple department stores, numerous smaller shops, and often supermarkets as well, all surrounded by vast parking lots. These "malls" attracted hordes of shoppers. In 1956, Edina, Minnesota, a suburb of cold Minneapolis, became the site of the first shopping mall to be fully enclosed, setting an example soon imitated in all American cities and climates.

Office jobs followed stores to the strips and suburbs, although at a slower pace. (Industry had actually led the decentralization in earlier decades, driven outward by the need for large assembly plants, and soon freed from dependence on rail lines and waterways by the growth of the trucking industry.) The combined result was a fundamental reshaping of U.S. urban geography, and also a partial solution to the traffic problem—immediately, by distributing traffic over a wider area, and in the longer term, by the massive construction of new roads on the urban fringe. Critics soon denounced the cure as worse than the disease, as once-bustling downtowns in many cities emptied out, leaving mostly low-income residents (and often not many of those), stores targeting that market, and few jobs of any kind.

That first Minnesota mall, like many others that followed, was designed by the very successful firm of Victor Gruen Associates. Gruen, a refugee from Hitler's Europe, hated cars and loved old cities like his native Vienna. He envisioned the mall as a new American downtown, a car-free, pedestrian-centered space that would replace the ever-lengthening highway strips. For many Americans, perhaps most, malls became a more than adequate substitute for downtown. Not for Gruen, however. He wanted to make his malls diverse places by attracting churches, government and professional offices, and educational institutions, but he was working for real-estate developers who preferred the rents paid by retailers, so, to Gruen's chagrin, malls in the U.S. and around the world became main streets defined entirely by shopping.[30]

Meanwhile Gruen turned his skills to downtown revitalization. Here, too, he saw the main problem as the car, and he was enough of a salesman to capture the attention of downtown leaders who feared that traffic jams were driving customers and businesses to the suburbs. Gruen's 1956 plan for Fort Worth, Texas, became the talk of downtown planners across the country and beyond. Its centerpiece was a car-free city center, a place for pedestrian strolling that could be landscaped like an outdoor suburban mall.[31] Several other elements were required to make the pedestrian zone work, in Gruen's view. A wide ring road would move cars smoothly around it; an archipelago of parking garages would let commuters park within a short walk of the center; an underground freight-delivery network would provide truck access; and an efficient bus system would take enough pressure off the roads and parking ramps to keep traffic flowing. This last component in particular was one that downtown leaders in Fort Worth and elsewhere did not want to hear about. The city built the ring road, but the rest of the plan remained on paper.

Lower levels of car ownership were one reason that land-use patterns changed more slowly in Europe. The cars were also much smaller, better adapted to the old cities. Higher land prices, too, helped preserve denser patterns of urban development, with less room for cars. (The land values, in turn, had their own causes, but it is difficult to know how much was attributable to the heavy hand of government regulation, a cultural attachment to place and proximity, or simply the inevitable lot of crowded countries.) Although most European city centers never had the concentration of buildings and jobs typical of American downtowns, they held onto their economic importance more tenaciously. And that is why the car in the city first became a crisis in Europe, although there were far fewer automobiles there during the first two decades after World War II.

European cities were less car-friendly to begin with. Even pre-automobile American cities like New York and Chicago boasted much wider streets than their European counterparts. Traffic jams in the largest European cities grew so quickly that the pessimistic German philosopher Oswald Spengler, famous for his treatise on *The Decline of the West*, could hope in 1931 that the new machines would soon dig their own graves: "In the great cities the motor-car has by its numbers destroyed its own value, and one gets on quicker on foot."[32] When the Dutch engineer Valderpoort, observing the trickle of automobiles in the early 1950s, declared that "the car makes itself impossible in the cities," he meant that "if we do not drive the car out of the city soon, it will drive us out."[33] The ravages of World War II, especially in Germany, offered a chance for a new beginning. Reconstruction made many concessions to cars, notably wide streets torn through war-damaged districts, as prescribed by modernist planners like Hans Bernhard Reichow, whose 1959 book *The Auto-Friendly City* summarized the principles of reconstruction in "progressive" German cities.[34] Foreign visitors sometimes envied the blank slate that had been the Anglo-American bombers' gift to German towns.

Still, even rebuilt German cities bore little resemblance to Le Corbusier's visions, and they remained far less auto-friendly than American ones. Nor did any European city approach universal car ownership. There were over twenty Britons per automobile in 1950, and everywhere on the Continent the number was much higher, at a time when the U.S. had an

Figure 10. Automobile and street-car competing for street space: Luxembourg, 1950s. Courtesy of Tramways and Bus Museum of the City of Luxembourg.

Figure 11. Old town square as parking lot: Salisbury, England, 2006. Author's photo.

automobile for every three people. Whereas American postwar sprawl was taking the form of low-density suburban tracts that could function effectively only with near-universal car ownership, that was an impossible dream for European and Japanese planners in 1950. While generally welcoming cars for the additional mobility they offered, they continued to organize cities (and suburbs) for the convenience of transit riders as well as motorists. Reichow's postwar German cities, like Le Corbusier's imagined ones, were auto-friendly but not auto-dependent. Reichow and other planners did not envision them being overwhelmed by too many cars, nor did it seem likely that most commuters would abandon mass transit. The goal was a smooth flow of traffic in cars, buses, streetcars, and (in the largest cities) underground or elevated railways.

Although many people still relied on their feet, bicycles, or motor scooters to get around European cities—far more than in the U.S.— planners and politicians paid them little heed, and then only to wish them away, much as had happened in U.S. cities during the 1920s. The influential German traffic planner Kurt Leibbrand, observing that the essence of the city was its seething cauldron of motorized traffic, argued in 1957 that "to demand a pedestrian city is to destroy the city."[35] Even more provocative was a Berlin planning document from the same year, which serenely predicted the disappearance of the traditional street—following the ideas of Le Corbusier—in favor of new tunnels and raceways for cars. "And the pedestrian? The new street has no place for unreconstructed Neanderthals. Anyone who has a destination should be sitting in a car. Anyone who doesn't is on a stroll and should proceed immediately to the nearest park."[36]

By 1960, although the postwar reconstruction of Europe's impoverished and devastated cities was by no means complete, the die was cast: driving was encouraged above all else, yet there was not enough room for everyone to drive. No one could fail to notice the growing traffic jams and the parked cars blocking streets and sidewalks. Among the most common responses during the 1950s were the removal of streetcar lines and the creation of more parking spaces, often by turning old town squares into parking lots. Advocates of the auto-friendly city proposed more and larger roads, and theirs was the prevailing view through the 1960s, but they had to face growing doubts about the feasibility of their solution. Although the dramatic growth in car ownership caught leaders by surprise, the fact that European and Japanese cities were less able to accommodate the cars left them, paradoxically, better able to resist their onslaught.

Britain, which had more cars than any other place outside the U.S. in the 1950s, was the first European country to undertake a systematic study of urban traffic problems. The planner Colin Buchanan, who directed the study, insisted that he was not hostile to cars. To be anti-car was presumably to be hopelessly anti-progress, and thus not serious about practical solutions to the problem at hand, which was the flood of automobiles overwhelming the old towns. Buchanan aimed to reconcile city life to the automobile. The car in the city was a "mixed blessing," as he entitled his 1958 book, but it was "pulling the whole fabric of cities about the ears."[37] He assumed car use would continue to grow, and he did not wish to reverse that trend. However, the crush of traffic in England's old town centers was not merely dangerous and inefficient, he thought, it was incompatible with everything that made them pleasant and functional places. His efforts to limit the penetration of the car into cities made him known as one of the most prominent European car critics. The British minister of transport chose Buchanan to chair a commission charged with examining the problem of "traffic in towns," the title of its much-cited 1963 report. Buchanan and his colleagues concluded that careful planning would be necessary to keep the growing volume of cars flowing through and around towns, and that any attempt to build roads as quickly as people acquired cars, as the United States seemed to be doing, would be futile as well as destructive to town and country. Instead, limits needed to be placed on the movement and parking of cars in town centers, with car-free areas carved out to separate pedestrians from motor traffic. The panel also recommended subsidies for mass transit.[38]

At first, few local governments followed the Buchanan report's recommendations to any great extent. It proved difficult to reverse the practice of leaving streets open to all vehicles, especially when restrictions were aimed at private automobiles. Cars being associated with freedom—freedom of movement—the firmly established British discourse of rights had long since embraced a "right" to drive an automobile. As far back as 1927, when urban traffic jams had already incited talk of restricting car use in towns, the transportation expert Lord Montagu was aghast: "But shall we ever stand such a denial of individual liberty? If I am right in my opinion that the right to use the road, that wonderful emblem of liberty, is deeply engrained in our history and character, such action will meet with the most stubborn opposition. More street space and more road space will have to be provided whatever be the plan for it or the cost of it."[39] His attitude remained firmly entrenched (and not only

Figure 12. Traffic-choked British high street: Caerphilly, Wales, 2006. Author's photo.

in Britain) into the 1950s and beyond, but ever more observers concluded that street space in cities could not be expanded indefinitely, and that "the cost of it" was becoming unbearable, as measured both in money and in the disruption of town life.

Before the Buchanan report, nearly everyone assumed that cities simply had to make room for the rapidly growing fleet of cars. The report proposed to combine the tools of land use and transportation planning in order to limit the impact of cars. At first, in lieu of any serious proposals to restrict driving, the effect of Buchanan's recommendations was to reinforce support for the construction of high-speed urban "motorways," sacrificing selected slices of a city in the hope of sparing others. Motorways held out the promise of faster city driving as well as reduced traffic flow in residential streets. But they would prove even more controversial than any previous attempts to reconcile cars and cities (as the next chapter shows).

The Buchanan report attracted a great deal of attention on the Continent (German and French translations had appeared by 1965). The plight of West Germany was particularly striking: just as gleaming new cities were rising out of wartime rubble, automotive traffic began to choke them. As one journalist lamented in 1961, the rebuilt cities, for all their splendor, "are threatened by chaos. Just as swarms of grasshoppers descend upon fields, the automobiles are taking control of streets and squares, settling into parks and woods and, in their insatiable greed, demanding ever more space."[40] Suddenly cars were a problem, even a threat. Far more than in the U.S., there emerged an awareness of an urbanity incompatible with cars. It had long since become normal to describe urban transportation using organic metaphors, with roads as "arteries," cars understood to be vital blood, and the movement of traffic equated with commerce and with life itself. But now the logic of traffic flow was coming under challenge. In 1960 a Cologne city official felt it necessary to warn that roads are "only arteries to the heart of the city," not ends in themselves.[41] Sociologists and municipal officials began to argue that the need to keep city centers accessible by car had to be balanced against the need to keep them pleasant enough places to be worth visiting in the first place.[42] Planners, politicians, and journalists debated whether the German cities that had most aggressively modernized their street networks after the war (such as Hanover) offered models for their more conservative and traffic-choked rivals, or whether they had surrendered their charms and perhaps even their sustenance to the automobile.

The Buchanan report's appeal for limits on cars in cities joined a few Continental voices such as the Italian art critic Leonardo Borgese, who denounced the "horrible and foolish sacrifices" demanded by "the cult of the automobile," and the Dutch engineer Valderpoort, who called cars and motorists "selfish" because they took city streets away from everyone else.[43] Progressive planners, put on the defensive, insisted on the necessity of allowing cars access to the city center. Few dared contradict them, but the movement of automobiles gradually became one competing priority among others, no longer the measure of urbanity. One of the first youth movements of the era, the Amsterdam "Provos," agitated in 1965 to ban all cars from the city center, and introduced a fleet of communal bicycles, painted an unmistakable white and offered for the free use of all (but promptly confiscated by the police). An anti-car organization in Helsinki advised supporters to carry hammers to bang on the hoods of cars blocking crosswalks.[44] By 1971, as Spain began it own belated automotive revolution in the late Franco years, one critic chided his countrymen for their childish pride in the nation's first traffic jams.[45]

Bernard Charbonneau decried the growing damage to Paris wrought by efforts to make the city accessible to the automotive horde: bulldozing trees, pushing pedestrians off the boulevards, transforming open spaces from parks to parking, and making the streets too noisy and fetid for strolling. Like the German critics who blamed zealous postwar planners for completing the work of the Anglo-American bombers, Charbonneau proclaimed that he was about to see a world in which "Paris is no more. Renault, not Hitler, has destroyed it."[46] He was not the only French intellectual who feared that Paris would become no better than an American city—which was to say, not a proper city at all. In a 1965 book on Paris, the art historian Michel Ragon bemoaned the failure to learn from the American example. In Americans' desire to open up cities for cars, "they have destroyed so much for freeways and parking that they will soon realize that there are no longer any cities!"[47] A more dispassionate glance across the Atlantic had convinced the Buchanan commission that growing prosperity would soon saddle densely settled British cities with far more cars than they could accommodate. But Buchanan declined to look to America for solutions. Critics of the Buchanan report argued that it overstated the threat of congestion by assuming that the growth in car use would not promote the decentralization of jobs and shopping.[48] (They were right.) This urban sprawl was, however, precisely what Buchanan wanted to avoid. He liked the cozy English towns with their medieval street patterns, and he argued that it would be neither practical nor sensible to make old England look like New Jersey.[49]

THE AUTOMOTIVE METROPOLIS

By the 1960s, European urban critics shuddered at their cities' slight but growing resemblance to the quintessential new American metropolis, Los Angeles, where people spent their lives behind the wheel and never arrived at their destinations, indeed, where there were no destinations left, only parking lots. A Spanish sociologist described L.A. as "the anti-city by definition" because it was "the first place in the history of humanity conceived solely and exclusively for the automobile: networks of freeways, boulevards, and loops that obligate its citizens to travel countless kilometers and hours daily from one place to another, that have consumed vast amounts of land" and caused dreadful pollution as well.[50] An Argentine critic invoked the cliché of L.A. as "seventeen freeways in search of a city."[51] Munich's mayor, Hans-Jochen Vogel, writing for a popular magazine in 1971 about the automotive threat to German cities, concluded that the worst possible solution would be "to rebuild our cities so that anyone can drive to any place at any time and also find a parking space there. In Los Angeles you can see the result of such an effort. That city is closer to a catastrophe than any other I have seen."[52]

A generation later, even L.A. haters admitted that these overwrought descriptions failed to do justice to the city's peculiar vitality. If you let the car shape the city, what you got was Los Angeles, in all its chaotic and disturbing splendor. By the 1950s, L.A. was the third most populous U.S. city, with by far the largest land area. Its residents owned more cars and drove them more than their counterparts in other American cities (to say nothing of the rest of the world): already in the 1930s there was a car for every third Angelino. They took it for granted that nearly everyone drove to nearly every destination. They left behind the old, circumscribed patterns of urban mobility and sociability, and the rest of the U.S. followed. The case for Los Angeles was most famously put by the English architectural critic Reyner Banham, whose 1971 book about L.A. architecture portrayed the automotive mobility offered by the freeway network as an essential element of the city's stunning beauty. Los Angeles was a new kind of city, Banham argued, not an urban void.[53]

It was difficult to surrender the idea that a community ought to have a center, or at least be a recognizable place. A South African visitor struggled to make sense of the California highway strip in 1957: "Nowhere along its length does the road contract, confine itself, center itself for a community around it. There are no parks, no statues, no plaques commemorating notable events; there are no vistas, no views, no streets that radiate from this point or that; no steps leading to public buildings." The automobile, he recognized, had created this placeless place, where "everything is built on the supposition that everyone has a car."[54] It could be an alienating place for those who tried to negotiate it without a car. L.A. pedestrians traded tales of being treated as freaks if not criminals. The young science fiction writer Ray Bradbury set his 1951 story "The Pedestrian" in the year 2053, when aimless walking was unheard of and apparently illegal. Bradbury was inspired to write the story after being stopped by the L.A. police on Wilshire Boulevard one night in 1947, just for being a pedestrian.[55]

Most Angelinos, and most Americans, adjusted to the new reality. Perhaps they had their moments of disorientation; sometimes they lamented the distances they had to drive; and certainly many of them eventually realized that their cherished mobility was a mixed blessing. L.A. became the poster child for automotive liberation and for urban sprawl— a term that came to connote all the disadvantages of the dispersed city.

L.A.-bashing is a paradoxical affair. The automotive metropolis offered liberation from old constraints, yet the car's defenders were increasingly those who called themselves conservatives. Its critics were the ones demanding both the conservation of natural resources and the defense of the traditional city, views that offended the free-market sensibility that gloried in the "creative destruction" wrought by capitalism. (This memorable phrase, popularized by the Austrian economist Joseph Schumpeter and beloved of American free-market fundamentalists, is, ironically, derived from Continental philosophies of cyclical history and particularly from the work of Friedrich Nietzsche, although it also carries echoes of Christian apocalypticism.) This endorsement of dynamic change helps explain the spirited defense of urban sprawl by those who see the bulldozer in the countryside as productive activity rather than wanton destruction. Sprawl, the car-borne escape from the old city, can be defended as a philosophical stance as well as a practical solution to the problem of cars in cities. Many libertarians, for example, wholeheartedly embraced sprawl as a solution that people freely chose but no one really planned.

Certainly we can point to apostles of sprawl, although they praised it by some other name. Suburban life has had its fervent advocates in the Anglo-American world for two centuries, often because they despised urban life and wished to see the crowded and dirty cities deconcentrated if not dispensed with entirely. Among the utopians who envisioned the complete abolition of cities were nineteenth-century socialist critics of the industrial revolution, including Karl Marx, who envisioned a communist future in which city and country would melt together, as well as individualists such as Henry Ford, who hated both socialists and urban crowds. Another anti-socialist version of the anti-city came from the great American architect Frank Lloyd Wright. His 1935 manifesto of "Broadacre City" (contemporary with, but more radical than the plans of Le Corbusier and Clarence Stein) envisioned every family living in an individual house at the equivalent of the lowest suburban densities, linked by universal car ownership and fast roads. Hardly anyone took his plan seriously, but many elements of it resembled the exurban sprawl that by the end of the century had engulfed Wright's own desert retreat, Taliesin West, outside Phoenix.

Cars were certainly not the sole cause of the dispersed urban form in L.A. or the other emerging suburban metropolises. Even without cars, populations had become more mobile, with weaker ties to local neighborhoods—first in the U.S., then elsewhere as well. Greater prosperity among broad segments of the population—here too, the U.S. led the way—gave people more leisure as well as greater residential luxury and privacy. For a few decades, streetcars and suburban railways were the transport technologies that reshaped cities, including Los Angeles. Automobiles proved to be not only more popular but also more disruptive to the pedestrian scale of existing towns. Motorists, traffic engineers, and assorted visionaries dreamt of a new kind of city.

Or would it be a city at all? After the middle of the twentieth century, the combination of freeway (and airliner) speed and advances in telecommunications kindled new speculation about the disappearance or at least the superfluousness of cities. Whereas architects and urban planners had envisioned new, low-density cities, apostles of the electronic age proclaimed that the restraints of physical space were simply irrelevant. The planner Melvin Webber, writing in California at the height of the freeway boom, foresaw the future "community without propinquity," in which people would, for the first time, be freed from having to consort with their neighbors or any others who happened to live, work, or travel in their immediate vicinity.[56] The idea, much trumpeted ever since, is that we can choose to spend our time with people we might journey far in order to see (presumably by automobile or airplane) or (in a vision predating the Internet age, but recently given more emphasis) we can each assemble our own community from the people we work or play with via electronic media, people who may be next door or halfway around the world.

In a placeless world, there is no virtue in proximity. Instead, the goal is free communication and rapid mobility. This ideal of placeless community is very American, since Americans have long been notably willing to uproot themselves in search of new opportunities. (And for decades their favorite destination was California.) By some accounts, the rest of the world is merely catching up to the American level of liberation from place, while skeptics argue that Americans now long to restore some of the rootedness that lingers elsewhere.[57]

Whatever their reasons, most people have been opting for both mobility and urban life. Contrary to predictions of the "annihilation of space" and the irrelevance of place, recent decades have seen a continuing influx into large metropolitan areas in the U.S. and most other nations.[58] Cities' expanding landscapes of office parks, shopping strips, and residential subdivisions (and, in poor lands, shantytowns) make them more important, if more sprawling, than ever. Liberation from place has not meant the disappearance of cities; rather, it has meant the sprawling metropolis, held together by freeways.

Even within these metropolises, the prophecies that distance would cease to matter have not yet come true. The new cities depend entirely on movement by automobile, and that has not proved as convenient as predicted. Rapid, painless travel is what the freeway promised, but the reality is quite different. Although greater Los Angeles continues to grow and thrive, it is a notoriously difficult place to get around. Its vast distances (vast, that is, for a city) are suited to high-speed automobile travel—and, at least for now, to no other means of transportation—but high speeds are seldom attainable during the many busy hours of the typical day. L.A. is the perennial leader in surveys of the average American commuter's congestion delays (seventy-two hours per year, as of 2005). The traffic jam has long since become a quintessential L.A. experience (the same goes for many other cities of the world by now), time to be spent enclosed in one's vehicle, usually alone, in air-conditioned, well-amplified musical comfort, in nonstop telephone conversation (in more recent years), in "zen" isolation, or in tense frustration. The average American now spends over an hour a day in the car. Many Americans, and not a few people elsewhere, spend more time in their cars than with their families. Some drivers value this involuntary extension of the cherished freedom their car provides. Others, wishing there were some alternative to the hours trapped behind the wheel, think the promise of automotive freedom has turned into automotive slavery. For better or worse, the automobile has certainly not reduced to insignificance the experience of crossing urban space.

The tedium of the freeway becomes a half-buried secret of people's lives, bemoaned in casual conversation and occasionally highlighted in literature and film. Freeway life can be alienating, dangerous, thrilling, even relaxing, but, it seems, seldom joyous or enriched by social interaction. Even in the early days, the fabled experience of driving the L.A. freeways might serve at best as an escape into the freedom of emptiness. In Joan Didion's 1970 novel *Play It As It Lays*, Maria Wyeth takes long freeway drives to dull the pain of her loss of connection to everyone and everything, with her sense of control behind the wheel compensating for a lack of control over her life.[59] Although many motorists long for some diversion to punctuate the freeway routine, what they get are the drama of the traffic jam and the collision, whether offering the erotic thrill of broken bodies described in graphic detail in J. G. Ballard's 1973 novel *Crash*, or as in Paul Haggis's Oscar-winning film *Crash* (2004, not to be confused with David Cronenberg's 1996 film of Ballard's novel), in which the collision of their cars is the experience that brings motorized Angelinos together in uneasy if not always catastrophic encounters.

Ballard's *Crash* is far from the only novel or film that imagines the highway as an accursed place where social niceties fall away. The Australian *Mad Max* films, dystopian twists on earlier road movies, offer an apocalyptic vision of lawless highways, fast driving, and ceaseless violence, with the car itself as the favored weapon. The stress of the rush-hour traffic jam is at the opposite extreme from the high-speed chase (or crash), but the aura of menace is common to both. In Joel Schumacher's 1993 film *Falling Down*, a hopeless freeway backup on a hot day is the last straw that sends the straitlaced William Foster (played by Michael Douglas) on a violent rampage through a Los Angeles nearly devoid of civility. Ballard's 1973 novel *Concrete Island* tells the story of a man whose Jaguar skids off London's new Westway, stranding him without hope of rescue on a forsaken "island" sealed off by impassable highway ramps from all the pressures, constraints, and proprieties of the living city. (An unwelcome confirmation of this scenario appeared to contractors preparing to widen a busy ring road through Wolverhampton, England, in 2000: in an inaccessible median strip they discovered the decomposed body of a woman who had wandered away from a nursing home three years earlier.)[60] In Matthew Bright's 1996 film *Freeway*, a modernized retelling of Little Red Riding Hood, the drive up the entrance ramp is the step into the woods, the place of anarchy and terror. The image works because the freeway (if not the entire freeway-centered city) does seem to be a place beyond civility and order, where few of us would want to be caught without the protection of our steel cages. The freeway, the domain of the automobile, is no place for human beings. In the film, in fact, the modern Little Red Riding Hood's terrors begin when her car breaks down on Interstate 5.

RUMBLES OF DISCONTENT

It was easy enough to concur that the city on wheels was the modern city, the city of freedom—and that there was no turning back. Some dissenters argued that cities were, in their essence, rooted in place, and that ceaseless automobility came at too high a price. Their interpretation of urban history was open to question: much of the history of cities has been about uprooting old certainties. But there was no denying the growing resistance to the destruction of buildings, streets, and neighborhoods that stood in the way of the automotive metropolis.

In London, for example, the Buchanan report's plea to save town centers from auto traffic coincided with the first stirrings of what became known as gentrification, as educated professionals began to cherish, claim, and renovate vast swathes of London's previously unfashionable Victorian terraces.[61] This trend, along with its distinctly English name, spread to neighborhoods of similar age around the world—whether in Melbourne, Toronto, San Francisco, or Frankfurt—where residents united against plans to sweep away their homes. Gentrifiers sometimes joined forces with long-established middle-class or working-class residents. They were galvanized by a shared conviction that these old houses and neighborhoods, with their sometimes chaotic admixture of pedestrians, slow-moving vehicles, and parked cars, were superior to the newer automobile-oriented suburbs. Jane Jacobs's 1961 book *The Death and Life of Great American Cities* became, for decades thereafter, the touchstone of efforts to protect these old neighborhoods around the world. Jacobs prized the webs of social interaction made possible by high densities, a mixture of shops, offices, and different kinds of homes, and the face-to-face meetings that took place on foot. She was less interested in the intrinsic qualities of old buildings, but at the time her book appeared, the historic preservation movement had begun to defend intact neighborhoods of pre-twentieth-century buildings, of which Jacobs's Greenwich Village was one. Although preservationists seldom singled out the car as the main threat to old buildings and neighborhoods, they increasingly attacked the modernist urban planning and architectural design that promoted mobility at the expense of stability, tradition, and urban community.

Part of what appalled gentrifiers and preservationists was the unholy alliance between Le Corbusier's modernist aesthetic and the "urban renewal" programs that promised to replace unsightly and obsolete "slums" with sleek skyscrapers suited to the automobile age. Jacobs argued that the old neighborhoods were in fact the most stable ones, and that the fetish of mobility destroyed not worthless slums but the most cherished human bonds. Preservationists, drawn to the beauty of old buildings and neighborhoods, praised an older architecture whose ornate forms bespoke stability rather than dynamic movement. From inside a moving car, impatient motorists were more likely to see old buildings and neighborhoods as mere obstructions. Richard Sennett highlighted this incompatibility of car and city in his influential book *The Fall of Public Man*: "Today, we experience an ease of motion unknown to any prior urban civilization, and yet motion has become the most anxiety-laden of daily activities. The anxiety comes from the fact that we take unrestricted motion of the individual to be an absolute right. The private motorcar is the logical instrument for exercising that right, and the effect on public space, especially the space of the urban street, is that the space becomes meaningless or even maddening unless it can be subordinated to free movement."[62] A few years earlier, the German sociologist Hans Paul Bahrdt had already tried to describe the ineffable urban character sacrificed to the automobile: "As imposing as the flood of motor traffic may be, participation in a city's public sphere, or movement in public, requires a composure that is available only to a pedestrian."[63]

In other words, something vital—if hard to describe—was being lost in the new vision of urban life that prized mobility above all else. This was what Lewis Mumford and Jane Jacobs concluded. These two influential urban critics cherished divergent visions of an ideal city—Mumford's sheltered hothouse of cultural achievement and Jacobs's bustling street life— but they found common ground in opposing the conventional postwar wisdom. While Mumford was America's most prominent car hater, Jacobs did not stand in the front ranks of car critics. She described cars as more a symptom than a cause of the damage inflicted on the city life she loved so passionately. Yet she came close to sharing Mumford's bitter conclusion that "instead of planning motor cars and motorways to fit our life, we are rapidly planning our life to fit the motor car," revealing "that we have no life that is worth living."[64] In her 1961 book, Jacobs argued that if we fail to stop "the erosion of cities by automobiles," then "we Americans will hardly need to ponder a mystery that has troubled men for millennia: What is the purpose of life? For us, the answer will be clear, established and for all practical purposes indisputable: The purpose of life is to produce and consume automobiles."[65]

CHAPTER FOUR

Freeway Revolts: The Curse of Mobility

Suburbanization and urban sprawl have been driven by a desire to escape the city's woes, not the least of which has been the plague of automobiles. A growing middle class created a market for sprawl, and transport technology provided the means to move outward. The handful of early nineteenth-century English suburbanites relied on sturdy carriages to convey them beyond London's smoky confines. Later, railroads made it possible for prosperous commuters to live in villages with rail depots while continuing to work in nearby cities. After the middle of the nineteenth century, horse-drawn omnibuses and streetcars extended European and American residential quarters outward; by the end of the century, electric trams made the same commute possible for more people and over greater distances. But the automobile outdid all its predecessors. For a century it has been extending commuters' range farther and faster than ever.

In addition to being a means of urban flight, transportation technology sometimes furnished a reason for it as well. Railroads concentrated people and industry near stations, making cities more prosperous and exciting but also noisier and dirtier. The "decongestion" of these crowded cities was a central goal of urban reformers a century ago. The automobile seemed to answer their prayers, and it deserves credit for helping to make cities more livable places—by banishing horse manure from the streets, to be sure, but also by moving people from tenement slums to verdant suburbs. The young Lewis Mumford was among the reformers who praised cars in the 1920s. Soon, however, he concluded that the automobile was the sorcerer's apprentice: even as cars offered the means to leave the city, they also created the dirt, noise, and danger that made people want to flee, leaving cities worse off than before. Whereas railroads blighted relatively small areas, automobiles destroyed urban tranquility wherever there were busy streets. As the Austro-French philosopher André Gorz reflected bitterly in 1973 (while invoking a rosy image of the urban past): "'The city,' the great city which for generations was considered a marvel, the only place worth living, is now considered to be a 'hell.' Everyone wants to escape from it, to live in the country. Why this reversal? For only one reason. The car has made the big city uninhabitable. It has made it stinking, noisy, suffocating, dusty, so congested that nobody wants to go out in the evening anymore. Thus, since cars have killed the city, we need faster cars to escape on superhighways to suburbs that are even farther away. What an impeccable circular argument: give us more cars so that we can escape the destruction caused by cars."[1]

This combination of attributes—cars make people want to get away, and able to get away—places the automobile at the center of the NIMBY phenomenon. The thousands of local government authorities of the United States, which largely control land-use planning, made suburban America the exemplar of local veto power over construction projects. By the late twentieth century, planners and real-estate developers complained that Jeffersonian smallholders' democracy had degenerated into the routine spectacle of neighbors organizing to oppose projects on the single principle of "Not in My Backyard." Thanks to their cars, people no longer felt the need to live especially close to work, shopping, or recreation. Most preferred not to live close to anything, except perhaps a handful of neighbors with similar housing budgets and tastes.

At first NIMBYism was narrowly associated with opposition to particular projects that few people would ever want to live near: either social service institutions housing addicts or ex-convicts, or industrial projects that posed actual or potential environmental hazards, such as noisy factories, nuclear power plants, or toxic waste dumps. Many suburbs went a step further and legislated the exclusion of multi-family, high-density, or low-income housing. Ultimately the power of neighborhood opposition infected the entire process of land-use planning. Its role became particularly striking in automobile-oriented suburbs, where access to shopping centers, office parks, or housing subdivisions was rarely made easy for pedestrians or transit riders. Developers, eager to avoid neighbors' opposition to any new project in their "backyards," found it easiest to acquire sites set some distance apart from any existing development. Planners leavened their frustration with sardonic humor by identifying a corollary of the law of NIMBY: the BANANA imperative ("Build Absolutely Nothing Anywhere near Anything").

There was of course nothing new about conflicts between neighbors or aversion to noisome activities: the deafening clatter of chariots had plagued imperial Rome, and medieval towns banished stinking tanneries beyond the walls. But the assumption that everyone would drive everywhere made it relatively easy for NIMBY to triumph in the form of BANANA. Most developments could be tolerated if they were a short drive away, out of sight and out of earshot. This kind of sprawl permitted suburbanites to hope they could keep a safe distance from all LULUs ("Locally Unwanted Land Uses") and their odors, noises, sights, and people. It is striking how many of those unwanted disturbances came in the form of automobiles. People did not want to endure the ceaseless roar and exhaust plumes of highways. They did not want to face the dangers of fast-moving traffic in front of their homes. They did not want too many strangers driving through their neighborhoods. They did not want to live near tacky roadside businesses, with their garish lighted signs, grease-spewing exhaust fans, ugly parking lots, and—not least—ceaseless traffic. They *did* want easy driving access to the highways and the shops, preferably via a quiet lane. So the projects they sought were roads, and the triumph of the automobile threatened to founder on the conflict between the growing need for roads and the growing damage they caused.

THE FREEWAY FROM DREAM TO NIGHTMARE

The NIMBY mentality has thrived in the suburban, automotive metropolis. But until the middle of the twentieth century, American cities (like most others) were densely populated and heterogeneous jumbles of industry, commerce, and many different kinds of housing, all in close proximity. It was not possible to build highways far away from everything. Not only did they cross backyards, they obliterated many homes and even entire neighborhoods, especially in the 1950s and 1960s. Organized opposition to freeway construction, first in a few American cities, then around the world, foiled many ambitious plans to reconcile the automobile and the city. Although the freeway revolts did not, for the most part, grow directly out of earlier animosity to cars, their effect was to drive a wedge between lovers of cities and lovers of automobiles.

The success of the automobile cannot be understood apart from the history of road construction. Although the first automobiles used existing roads, their pavements and often their width could not stand up to motor traffic, and the first great victories of the auto lobby were road-construction programs in many lands. It has been a consistent story around the world: even when motorists were a small minority, they persuaded governments to fund and build roads, often by agreeing to motor-vehicle or motor-fuel taxes. Almost without exception, road construction has remained a public responsibility, since only governments could improve existing public roads and acquire new rights-of-way across innumerable private properties. The main jurisdictional disputes have been among town, provincial, and national governments. Even in strongly federal countries such as Switzerland and the United States, the age of the automobile brought central governments into the business of building national highways, especially the new, wide, automobile-only roads that emerged as the pinnacle of highway engineering.

The great freeway-building boom began during the 1950s and peaked around 1970 in the United States and in many other countries. It was the culmination of a long-held dream of limited-access roads that separated cars and trucks from all other traffic and eliminated all stop signs and grade crossings, so that motorized traffic could speed freely across the country or the city—hence a "freeway," although many other names are synonymous: expressway, motorway (in Britain), autobahn, autoroute, autostrada. The idea of building them dates to the first years of the twentieth century in both Europe and the United States. They promised to fulfill the dream of car travel freed from all distractions of towns, farms, pedestrians, and slower vehicles. As a technical challenge, they stirred the blood of civil engineers as had few projects since the early railways. Politicians were often enthusiastic boosters as well, despite the need to finance grading, paving, bridges, tunnels, and costly new rights of way.

Limited-access highways, like the automobile craze in general, were born of automobile racing. William K. Vanderbilt II sponsored the construction of a private racing road near his Long Island estate in 1908, and he also opened it to recreational motorists who paid a toll. By 1913, construction began on a long, straight private racing road through a forest at the edge of Berlin, although World War I delayed completion of the AVUS (Automobil-Verkehrs- und Übungs-Strasse) until 1921. It was opened to the public when not used for racing, and, decades later, became the trunk of the city's urban autobahn network. In the United

States, the earliest high-speed public roads were parkways, built for leisurely recreational driving in the suburbs of New York. The first was the Bronx River Parkway, proposed in 1907 and built between 1916 and 1923. It became the model for several others built in the Westchester County, Long Island, and Connecticut suburbs during the 1920s and 1930s (most by Robert Moses) as well as a handful in other regions, such as Rock Creek Parkway in Washington. The parkways were designed to fulfill a vision of bucolic country motoring by preserving open lands along their borders while making them accessible to motorists. However, commuters and real-estate developers soon discovered them, and they spurred suburban building booms at their outer ends. They also gave traffic planners a model for the smooth flow of motor traffic and drivers a taste of the ideal conditions for which their powerful machines were designed. Another milestone came in 1940 with the opening of the Pennsylvania Turnpike, which incorporated abandoned railway tunnels to greatly speed motorists' journeys through the mountains of that state. Meanwhile, the General Motors Futurama exhibit at the 1939 New York World's Fair spread the gospel of freeways to millions of Americans.

But by then many people thought the U.S. was lagging behind the much more weakly motorized countries of Europe. Fascist Italy had led the way, opening the first autostrada in 1924 and building several other modest roads (none as long as a hundred miles) by the late 1930s. More famous and more impressive were Germany's autobahns. Private organizations there lobbied in the 1920s for a superhighway to connect the North Sea ports to the Rhine valley as far south as Switzerland. The government of the German republic moved slowly, opening its first twenty-kilometer stretch of limited-access highway from Cologne to Bonn in 1932, just months before the Nazis toppled the republic. In the first months of his Third Reich, Hitler unveiled ambitious plans for a 7,000-kilometer (4,300-mile) autobahn network. Films and photographs of the spectacular autobahns soon stirred admiration and envy around the world. Soaring bridges and gently curving ribbons of concrete testified to high standards of both engineering and landscape design. Even the outbreak of World War II in 1939 did not at first stop the project, with foreign conscripts and concentration-camp prisoners replacing German workers in some places. By the time construction finally ground to a halt in 1942, more than half of the network had been built, although work had not begun on the additional 20,000 kilometers proposed after 1939 by Nazi planners intoxicated by their cowboy fantasies of using autobahns

Figure 13. Grand Central and Interborough parkways: Queens, NY, c. 1940. National Archives.

(complete with fortified rest areas) to subdue the wild eastern steppe they thought they were conquering.

Ambitious American plans were on the drawing board by the 1930s, but were long delayed by two questions: the degree to which the federal government could usurp authority from the states, which had hitherto controlled road construction; and the question of how to pay for a massive construction program, whether by tolls, or bonds (paid off by either tolls or taxes), or pay-as-you-go taxation. In the meantime, federal money was aiding the construction and improvement of conventional highways all over the country. Even during World War II, as Detroit's tanks, trucks, and jeeps faced their German counterparts on the battlefield, and fuel and rubber rationing curtailed driving at home, the U.S. government drew up detailed plans for more and better roads. In the first postwar years, California launched an ambitious freeway program, and several other states followed the Pennsylvania model of cross-state toll roads. At the height of the cold war, the interstate highway program was sold as a contribution to effective military mobilization—more openly than the German autobahns had been, although its military use was never seriously pursued—but even more as a tool of economic development that would create jobs and open up the hinterlands. The Federal-Aid Highway Act of 1956 passed when Congress reached agreement on a funding mechanism, primarily a dedicated fuel tax, giving the states 90 percent of the construction costs for an interstate network of limited-access roads.

President Dwight D. Eisenhower could fairly claim credit for ushering the interstate act into law, but its extraordinary commitment to government spending and construction, and to automobiles, was not controversial. The law authorized an astonishing 40,000 miles of divided highways, a goal that was in fact achieved by the 1970s. These roads reshaped the American landscape along with the habits and movements of the American people. For the rural interests that dominated Congress and most state governments, the interstate program meant long-distance highways. These splendid ribbons of concrete became the bulk of the program, and their construction proceeded with little opposition, even if the engineering marvels in wide-open spaces may have been grander than necessary, with some of still them far from capacity half a century later.

The trouble began in the cities. The program was made palatable to urban interests by adding many miles of urban freeways. The expansive freeway was a fundamentally rural design, with each mile consuming some twenty acres of land, but most traffic and most traffic jams were in and around cities. Since the 1920s, American downtowns had been choked with traffic, and downtown interests had been clamoring for better highway access. The powerful economic interests in the central business districts of the major cities—department stores, real estate developers, and their tenants in the office towers—feared that the postwar traffic crunch could spell disaster. Experts assured them that highways (along with parking garages) were the solution. Grand claims were made for urban superhighways: they would not merely banish congestion and revive downtowns, they would make city driving a pleasure, beautify the city, and restore quiet to the streets and neighborhoods they bypassed.[2] Already in the 1920s Chicago's Wacker Drive and New York's West Side Highway were built as high-capacity urban roads. The parkway model, too, was made more urban and utilitarian. By the time the U.S. entered World War II in 1941, the Gowanus Parkway in Brooklyn was open, as was the first southern California freeway, the Arroyo Seco Parkway (now the Pasadena Freeway). Between 1945 and 1956, construction began on several other new roads in the largest cities, and many more were on the drawing board, awaiting funding.

The interstate highway program marked the highpoint of a kind of technocratic planning (along with its smaller but more glamorous contemporary, the space program). It placed a great deal of power in the hands of highway engineers.[3] These men (as nearly all were) took pride in their scientific skills and their professional integrity. They knew that their work promoted the interests of many large companies that manufactured automobiles, tires, petroleum products, concrete, and steel, did heavy construction, and operated road transport, but in their own eyes they were not doing those companies' bidding. Rather, they were fulfilling a broader public interest by creating roads that benefited everyone in the land. They could certainly be forgiven for believing they had unanimous support. Virtually no one doubted that the growing fleet of cars needed more road space. Discouraging car use was on almost nobody's agenda, nor were efforts to encourage the use of other modes of transit, or to compare the cost or efficiency of highways to those other modes.

The highway engineers, confident of their scientific methods, estimated the flow of traffic on the new roads, and proposed the most direct routes they could find, while also seeking the least valuable land that would have to be expropriated. Often that led them to draw relatively uncontroversial lines across old rail yards or declining industrial districts. In many cases these followed the cities' waterfronts, cutting them off from their rivers, lakes, and bays—a matter of occasional controversy at the time, and much regret in later decades, when cities wanted to reclaim these assets. Public parks offered even cheaper land for roads, and some of the earliest cases of local opposition to freeway plans arose where they sliced through parks, spoiling what remained of them with noise and exhaust fumes. Philadelphia's Schuylkill Expressway, for example, built in the 1950s on a riverbank in the center of Fairmount Park (and quickly nicknamed the "Surekill" for its frequent and deadly crashes), might be defended as a necessary traffic artery, but once it was finished and choked with traffic, no one thought it enhanced the city's main park. A brief flurry of attempts to protect the park failed to block construction.[4] The same story played out in many cities that sacrificed parts of major parks to freeway construction, including San Antonio (Brackenridge Park), Boston (the Fens), Buffalo (Delaware Park), St. Louis (Forest Park), and several parks in New York City. Citizens of Memphis, however, successfully halted Interstate 40 short of Overton Park, Milwaukee stopped a lakefront freeway, and after Baltimore saw Druid Hill Park sliced by Interstate 83, residents prevented Interstate 70 from destroying Leakin Park.

To the delight of urban reformers eager to raze the slums, many routes also sliced through the lowest-value residential neighborhoods, which were typically where African Americans lived (and often had to live, since legal or widely tolerated discrimination kept them out of most areas). Calculations of cost justified the decision to traverse the black "slums," and in any case the white politicians who ran every city were unlikely to protect black neighborhoods. Freeway construction even became a welcome tool of segregation, reinforcing other isolating effects of the automobile. The residential dispersion made possible by the automobile had already accelerated the separation of classes as well as the racial segregation that was so typical of American cities. In southern cities, roads had been a tool of segregation since the beginning of the automobile age. As early as 1917, Atlanta used the construction of a boulevard to create a barrier between black and white neighborhoods.[5] The wider and more impassable urban freeways of the 1950s and 1960s posed much more formidable obstacles, as urban politicians quickly realized—not only in Atlanta, where the freeway built along the eastern edge of the central business district wiped out poor neighborhoods and left others isolated from downtown.

Freeways were wielded with astonishing frequency to destroy African American neighborhoods. Particularly egregious cases were Nashville, where a desire to spare all white-owned businesses led to the routing of Interstate 40 through the heart of the city's black commercial district; and Miami, where city-center freeways nearly obliterated Overtown and successfully pushed most African American residents into a more remote quarter. Protests and lawsuits failed to stop either project. Southern cities that carried out similar plans included New Orleans, Montgomery, Birmingham, Columbia, Tampa, St. Petersburg, Orlando, Pensacola, and Charlotte. The practice was by no means limited to the South, however: it also occurred in Los Angeles, Pasadena, Indianapolis, Columbus, Cleveland, St. Paul, Milwaukee, and Chicago.[6] In nearly every case, little or nothing was done to help displaced residents find new homes. What worried the authorities were their ugly neighborhoods, and that problem would be solved. As one journalist wrote: "A happy by-product of all these expressway developments is that they invariably do an excellent job of slum clearance as they knife through the poorer sections of the city."[7] If the slum dwellers disappeared too, so much the better.

Amid the civil rights movement of the 1960s, newly empowered African American neighborhood organizations protested "white men's roads through black men's homes." African American community groups on the west side of Baltimore finally managed to attract attention in 1966 by threatening to block Friday afternoon rush-hour traffic.[8] In the following years, organizations from poor and middle-class black neighborhoods in different parts of the city formed a united front with white neighborhoods threatened by other freeways. Their combined influence forced a redesign of freeway plans and stopped several planned segments.[9] Washington, D.C., offered another case in which African American opponents ultimately succeeded by building alliances with wealthier white neighborhoods such as Takoma Park, Maryland, as well as Cleveland Park, home of one of the first anti-freeway organizations in 1959.[10]

Residents of most poor neighborhoods targeted by freeway planners had to resign themselves to the disruption of their lives. As in Washington, however, alliances with wealthier neighborhoods sometimes turned the tide, as did biracial coalitions uniting disparate neighborhoods in the path of a single freeway. Such a coalition managed to kill Chicago's Crosstown Expressway in the 1970s. Philadelphia's planned South Street freeway might have become a racial wall like Atlanta's, but local opponents rallied support from University of Pennsylvania faculty and students in a successful campaign against it. In Boston, a proposed Inner Belt freeway spawned an opposition coalition of neighborhoods in its path, supported by the Roman Catholic archbishop as well as a roster of Harvard and MIT faculty including Daniel Patrick Moynihan. The project paralyzed municipal politics until it was killed in 1970.[11]

Racial and class friction elevated the opposition to highways beyond the mere defense of neighborhoods by raising not only the issue of civil rights for African Americans, but also the broader question of who was benefiting from freeway construction. Freeways were promoted as beneficial to downtowns and to rural areas alike. They brought economic development that was understood to benefit everyone, not just motorists—although it was generally assumed that virtually everyone was or would soon be a motorist. In fact, though, the benefits of urban freeways seemed to flow mainly to the middle classes who were moving in great numbers to the new suburbs in the decades after World War II, while the costs of freeways, in the form of destroyed or blighted neighborhoods, were disproportionately borne by residents who remained behind in older, more central areas. A freeway torn through a city neighborhood might save time for suburban commuters, but it also disrupted the movements of residents in the neighborhoods traversed by the new highway. The commuters' estimated time savings justified the road; the disruption and loss of time of the urban residents counted for nothing.[12]

Not all middle-class or white neighborhoods were spared in the plans, and the first successful opposition movements arose to protect middle-class white neighborhoods, or showcase urban parks such as Golden Gate Park in San Francisco, or celebrated historic districts like New Orleans's French Quarter. Although the French Quarter was far from a rich area, freeway opponents could draw on a network of well-established and influential families to make their ultimately successful case for historic preservation and against the highway.[13] In other places as well, the influence of wealthier, better-connected, and better-organized opponents proved decisive. It also increased the likelihood that freeways would traverse poor towns or neighborhoods. Whereas wealthy Brooklyn Heights was able to get the route of the Brooklyn-Queens Expressway shifted away from it in the late 1940s, for example, nearby Red Hook was not. In 1965 in Philadelphia, rapidly gentrifying Society Hill near the Delaware River enlisted the aid of vice president Hubert Humphrey to get the adjoining section of a new riverside freeway depressed and covered. Poor neighborhoods and towns lacked the kind of clout brought to bear when the state of California proposed to build a freeway through the city of Beverly Hills in 1965. Opposition from residents of that famously wealthy Los Angeles suburb soon killed the project.

The first successful freeway revolt—one that stopped a road, rather than merely moving it somewhere else—took place in San Francisco,

Figure 14. The freeway in the old city: Albany, New York. Author's photo.

where, five years before the federal interstate act, city planners had unveiled plans for an extensive superhighway network through the city. By 1955, a proposed road across Golden Gate Park was the first to face organized opposition. As later happened in many cities, neighborhood groups lined up against an alliance of downtown interests and suburban commuters, raising objections about the loss of parkland, waterfront views, historic buildings, and housing stock, as well as the failure to consider improved mass transit as an alternative. Neighborhood organizations' coordinated efforts made it difficult for planners to find a path of least resistance. Opponents even persuaded the city's governing board of supervisors to join their side. California law was unusual in permitting local governments an effective veto over highway plans, so the city was able to stop nearly all freeway construction in San Francisco by voting down most of the state's proposed freeways in 1959—a break with precedent so startling that its import was not clear until the board rejected several revised plans in the following years.[14] The stump of the elevated Embarcadero Freeway along the San Francisco Bay waterfront stood as an ugly monument to the freeway wars from 1959 until damage it suffered in a 1989 earthquake finally led to its removal.

The early 1950s also saw vehement opposition to the demolition necessary for New York's Cross-Bronx Expressway. In the end the city's powerful master builder, Robert Moses, tore his highway through poor but stable neighborhoods, greatly speeding cars and trucks traveling between New Jersey and New England. Moses built several other freeways at the same time, but he was less successful a decade later with his proposed Lower Manhattan Expressway, which would have replaced Broome Street and vicinity with ten elevated lanes of traffic connecting the Holland Tunnel to the East River bridges. The opposition rooted in nearby Greenwich Village boasted some impressive intellectual and political clout, including Jane Jacobs, Eleanor Roosevelt, and the local congressman, Edward Koch (later the city's mayor). Also joining in were artists who had recently settled in the old warehouses of SoHo, much of which would have been sacrificed to the road. Lewis Mumford contributed an open letter condemning "the first serious step in turning New York into Los Angeles."[15] The project was ultimately canceled, along with Moses's two other elevated trans-Manhattan highways at 30th and 125th streets. (One plan for the former envisioned it passing through the tenth floor of the Empire State Building.) Moses's rival, governor Nelson Rockefeller, fared little better. Fierce opposition to his proposed Hudson River Expressway in 1965 led to its cancellation six years later.

The freeway revolts blotted the reputation of Robert Moses, who had used his several New York state and city offices to sponsor an astonishing array of public-works projects over four decades. New York City is scarcely imaginable without his bridges and tunnels. His early parkways were widely emulated and are still much admired, as are the city playgrounds and Long Island beach parks he created. One could scarcely say the same about the urban freeways that he saw as vital to the future of New York (and indeed of every city: he served as a consultant for several other cities' freeway plans). The construction of the Gowanus Parkway before the war, and of the Cross-Bronx and Brooklyn-Queens expressways afterward, made him many enemies in the outer boroughs before his plans came to grief at the hands of a more influential Manhattan constituency. In 1974, Robert Caro's withering biography of the retired Moses painted him as a villain responsible for "the fall of New York," in large part because he built expressways while neglecting mass transit. His ruthlessness, the key to his success, was on routine display when he declared, "When you operate in an overbuilt metropolis, you have to hack your way with a meat ax."[16] For opponents like Jane Jacobs, the city was not a hunk of meat, nor was it "overbuilt."

Moses's early parkways, modeled on the winding carriage paths that Frederick Law Olmsted had designed for Central Park, were sold as enhancements to the countryside, attractively landscaped roadways that opened up recreational opportunities in woods and valleys now easily accessible to motorized city dwellers. In the 1930s Lewis Mumford, not yet a vehement car critic, was enchanted by the ride on the scenic Taconic State Parkway (a northern extension of the Bronx River Parkway up the Hudson River valley) to his rural retreat in Amenia (his wife did the driving). Some early wilderness advocates in the western states also promoted roads and motoring as a way to broaden the appreciation of pristine landscapes.[17] At first, engineers and architectural critics praised the grandeur of the postwar freeways as well, but these new urban and suburban roads, designed to handle more and faster traffic, quickly proved to have little visual appeal from the point of view of a harried motorist and even less from that of a stationary observer. The crush of traffic guaranteed that express highways—even the old parkways—would not be pleasant places to linger. Only on the drawing table or from a great distance was anyone likely to admire the sublimity of what Mumford called "these vast spaghetti messes of roads and clover crossings and viaducts that provide excellent material for aerial photography but obliterate the towns they pass through."[18]

FREEWAYS AND FUNDING:
A COMPARATIVE PERSPECTIVE

The 1956 Interstate Highway Act put federal fuel-tax revenues into a Highway Trust Fund, meaning that the money could be used only for freeway construction, and ensuring that the pressure to build freeways in the United States would be relentless. Highway opponents later argued that its very existence created American highway addiction. The logic is just as compelling the other way around, of course: the American love of automobiles and highways made possible the political commitment to the trust fund. In fact, the federal trust fund followed the example set by the individual states, most of which imposed dedicated fuel taxes during the 1920s. The case has been made that gasoline taxes dedicated to road construction are the most popular taxes ever levied—although their popularity may have been a passing phase, judging by the fierce resistance to many recent proposals for fuel-tax increases. The Highway Trust Fund was a master stroke by wily bureaucrats, powerful economic interests, and congressional power brokers, who ensured that the love of highways would not have to prove itself in every subsequent budgetary year, and that funding would be guaranteed even after the ardor for roads had cooled.

Dedicated road taxes have existed elsewhere, but have enjoyed less support. Although the chancellor of the exchequer David Lloyd George created Britain's Road Fund in 1909, it was not legally sacrosanct, and in 1926 and 1927 his successor, Winston Churchill, raided it to fund other priorities. Churchill shared the view of finance experts that it was poor fiscal procedure to lock up tax revenues in advance of budgeting, and (in an internal memo) he insisted on the principle that a tax was a tax:

> Whoever said that motorists were to contribute nothing for all time to the general revenue of the country, or that, however great their luxury and wealth, or the inroads they make on the convenience of pedestrians, they were to be exempt for all time through their character of motorists from the smallest contribution to our revenue? Entertainments may be taxed; public houses may be taxed; racehorses may be taxed; the possession of armorial bearing and manservants may be taxed—and the yield devoted to the general revenue. But motorists are to be privileged for

all time to have the whole yield of the tax on motors devoted to roads. Obviously this is all nonsense. Whoever said that, whatever the yield of these taxes, and whatever the poverty of the country, we were to build roads, and nothing but roads, from this yield? We might have to cripple our Trade by increased taxation of income, we might even be unable to pay for the upkeep of our Fleet. But never mind, whatever happens, the whole yield of the taxes on motors must be spent on roads![19]

Churchill's opposition to the privilege enjoyed by cars and roads was a minority view in the 1920s, and rarer still by the 1950s. Switzerland also established a dedicated road fund before the U.S., in 1949, and France created a more modest version in 1951, while West Germany followed suit in 1960, although after 1966 its fuel-tax revenues were increasingly shared with mass-transit projects (a step the U.S. also took, to a much smaller degree, in 1974). In other lands, the absence of guaranteed funding has been no impediment to highway construction: many national networks on the interstate model soon followed, some financed by tolls. The growth in car use and the logic of traffic planners ensured that highway construction would be on the agenda around the world. But a substantial difference remained: by any measure—in proportion to population, number of vehicles, or national wealth—the U.S. has built far more freeway miles than other lands; and Americans also drive much more.

Even more than the rest of the world, Australia followed American models in highway building, as in much else. Sydney drew up an ambitious freeway plan already in the 1940s, but had completed only one major road by the 1960s, when other cities followed suit. Soon, however, fierce opposition killed or stalled a great many of the projects. Perhaps the success of Australian freeway opponents was partly due to the fact that Australia never managed to establish a dedicated road fund. Freeway fights in the major Australian cities followed a script quite similar to the U.S. in the late 1960s and 1970s, with the added complaint that highway planners were slavishly following American traffic models. Several familiar themes—the neglect of mass transit and of the natural environment, the reliance on the car and on American experts—found voice in a single protest poem from late-'60s Adelaide, composed in the ordinary-bloke argot of the Australian folk poet C. J. Dennis:

'Oo do they think they bloody are?
God 'isself 'cos they drives a car?

Thy're makin' such a 'spensive fuss
Wen wot we wants is a flamin' bus
An' a few more trains and a subway too.

But these poor b's ain't got a clue
'Stead o' usin' brains, they got them Yanks
'Oo when they seen the Torrens' banks
Where some kids fish an' others play
Said, "There's the track f' y' new freeway.
That useless creek an' them scrappy trees
Wavin' about in the mornin' breeze
Will be transformed into concrete piles
With curvin' roads stretchin' out f' miles.[20]

Australian freeway opponents held up Toronto as an alternative model.[21] Although Toronto built two urban freeways during the 1950s, it also created a new underground rail system, and official plans during the 1960s contemplated various combinations of highway and rail transit. In the late 1960s, the first of several proposed new freeways through the city center provoked fierce opposition (including from Jane Jacobs, who had recently moved from New York, and Marshall McLuhan) and became a major issue in the 1969 municipal elections. When the Ontario provincial government canceled this Spadina Expressway in 1971, Premier William Davis, sounding more like a European than an American politician, declared that "cities are for people, not for cars." Vancouver's transformation was even more dramatic. Fierce opposition killed a proposed freeway through its Chinatown in 1967 and beat back other freeway plans over the next five years. Plans and funding then shifted toward mass transit, and the city of Vancouver (although not its hinterland) remains nearly freeway-free. Most Canadian cities proposed extensive freeway networks during these years, but in the face of opposition (and the absence of federal funding) they built a fraction of the freeway miles of American cities, while in the following decades Canadians continued to own fewer cars, drive less, and use mass transit more than their neighbors to the south.[22]

EUROPEAN FREEWAY REVOLTS

American car critics often point to Europe as a model for what they wish they had at home: governments that restrain auto use and support healthy transit systems. Listening to their European counterparts, however, leaves a different impression. Transit advocates in all the major western European lands (and most of the small ones too) have often accused their governments of promoting auto use while neglecting transit. While American car critics stress transatlantic differences, European critics (and, sometimes, American car lovers) see a close resemblance. Europe had far fewer cars than the U.S. in the 1950s, but it also had more crowded cities. As car ownership grew, proposals for highways began to catch up to those in the U.S., while opposition caught up even more quickly. It is striking how many countries saw widespread—and often successful—opposition to highway construction in the years around 1970.

Britain was behind the U.S. but ahead of the Continent in its plans for "motorways." In addition to a handful of major intercity motorways, the early 1960s saw a slew of plans for radial and ring roads in and around the major cities. Many of these plans, like their Continental counterparts, emerged in response to growing dismay at traffic-choked city centers. The Buchanan report of 1963 promoted a widespread consensus that the growth in automotive traffic had to be planned for, preferably by finding channels for it to flow smoothly through the cities. Traffic planners concluded that the solution was urban motorways. But by late in the decade there was a dramatic shift in opinion.

The most celebrated case was London. On the very day of its establishment as a new metropolitan government in 1965, the Greater London Council (GLC) announced plans for a "motorway box" around central London to collect and distribute traffic from existing roads as well as from the new radial motorways soon to connect London to the rest of Britain. At first the plans were popular. Indeed, in 1967 a campaign in favor of speedier motorway construction helped the opposition Conservative Party oust the Labour GLC government that had launched the project. What ensued was instead an ever-more-heated controversy, peaking in the early 1970s. In addition to suspecting that any relief from traffic congestion would be too paltry to justify the enormous cost of the roads, residents of inner London (most of whom did not own cars) saw little benefit in roads designed to make it easier for suburbanites to drive in and out. Those whose homes stood in the path of the proposed roads joined forces with housing advocates convinced that the need to respond to London's housing shortage trumped a roads program that would destroy thousands of dwellings. More outrage than applause greeted the one section of the motorway box that was built, the elevated Westway that carried traffic in to Paddington. Upon its opening in 1970, pictures of speeding cars a few feet from upper-story bedroom windows proved to be very bad publicity for the rest of the project.

Because both major political parties backed the motorway project, opponents organized a "Homes Before Roads" party to run in the 1970 GLC elections, after which they took their efforts into the established parties. Soon the Labour opposition succumbed to the rising tide of anger and withdrew its support for the project. After Labour swept to victory in the 1973 GLC elections, probably aided by its anti-motorway stance, the motorways were dead. When the Conservatives regained power in 1977, they made no move to resurrect the program.[23] By then, several other British cities had abandoned their own motorway plans, and government policies were turning toward efforts to discourage car use and promote mass transit. Anti-motorway protests were also spreading across the English countryside, with environmentalists and country dwellers allied against long-distance motorways as well as ring roads through urban greenbelts.

The story was not very different in Europe's second metropolis, although opposition to highways was never as potent in France. Paris, too, had seen explosive growth in car ownership lead to dire traffic congestion. The most ambitious solution was the eight-lane Boulevard Périphérique, encircling the city along the course of its former wall. Although it took a long time to complete—its first segment was approved in 1954, its last one opened in 1973—the "Périph" quickly became indispensable to drivers entering or leaving the crowded French capital. However, motorists still had to negotiate congested old streets on the rest of their inward journey. One remedy was the modest Right Bank Expressway built into the bank of the Seine River between 1964 and 1967. Highway planners also proposed other Paris freeways, notably a north-south road across eastern Paris and a Left Bank Expressway. Whereas the right bank highway had not been controversial, opposition to its left bank counterpart became a cause célèbre among Parisian intellectuals in the turbulent years after the 1968 student uprising. Opponents rallied in defense of the tranquility and greenery of the riverbank as well as the sanctity of its historic ambience. They decried the specter of traffic roaring by Notre Dame Cathedral. Like its right bank counterpart, the proposed road was a pet project of the prime minister and later president, Georges Pompidou, so its fate became mixed up with high politics. After Pompidou's death in 1974, both candidates to succeed him came out against the road, sealing its fate. The other Paris expressways soon died a quiet death as well.[24]

Most other western European lands made similar plans. Hitler's autobahns were strictly rural, but by 1960, growing traffic problems in the newly reconstructed West German cities persuaded planners to propose American-style urban freeways in most of them. West Berlin led the way in the 1950s, planning an intra-urban ring plus an inner-city box like the one later proposed in London. The first segment of the ring, connected to the old AVUS racing road, opened in 1958. The new highways reflected a commitment to a vision of urban modernity more than a response to a pressing need: since the planned roads extended into East Berlin, their completion awaited some future German reunification. The construction of the Berlin Wall in 1961 left West Berlin quieter and more isolated than ever, yet the highway plans remained in place, with the western portions of the ring and box slated to encase West Berlin in a more modest freeway loop. During the 1960s, while construction continued in Berlin, several other German cities built high-speed urban highways as well, although, in contrast to the U.S., few built full-fledged freeways near city centers. None of these projects faced much resistance before 1970. Around then, however, passionate and sometimes militant opposition sprang up in many cities, notably Berlin. Opponents promoted mass-transit alternatives and argued broadly against the intrusion of the car into the city. They decried the air and noise pollution from automobiles and the sacrifice of parks and housing for the roads, and they argued that the highways and traffic would shatter stable neighborhoods. Some of the battles raged for years, and most inner-city freeways were ultimately stopped.[25]

Switzerland's dedicated fuel tax after 1949 gave it the funds to catch up to its German and Italian neighbors. It went them one better, becoming a European pioneer in plans for urban freeways. The national highway system mapped during the 1950s was a rare display of central government power in this strongly federal state. Swiss highway engineers quite consciously followed U.S. models, proposing to connect the major cities and to run freeways through their centers as well. At first, the architect Hans Marti waged a lonely campaign against the proposed urban freeways, arguing that highways alone would not solve urban traffic problems. By 1961, when the national architects' association endorsed his view, proposed routings provoked residents of affected neighborhoods to oppose roads through Zurich, Geneva, and Basel. A 1960 referendum in Bern even stopped a project, if only temporarily; a 1964 petition with twenty thousand signatures protested one in Basel; and a broad opposition coalition had emerged by 1960 in Geneva. Many opponents merely asked that the roads be built as bypasses around their cities, which is what ultimately happened in Geneva, Bern, and Lausanne. After more fundamental objections to roads emerged from the environmental movement around 1970, few of the original urban freeway plans survived. The citizens of Zurich, for example, canceled theirs in a 1972 referendum. The previous year, the strongly pro-auto *Neue Zürcher Zeitung* editorialized that the opposition "appears to be fundamentally an expression of a growing autophobia. Soon the unfortunate carriage will be blamed for everything: people make it a scapegoat, damning it in order to sooth their guilty consciences about the long-neglected problems accompanying civilization and technology."[26]

ENGINEERS AND OBSTRUCTIONISTS

It was true enough. The freeway revolts made highway construction the touchstone of modernity's traumas, as old ways of life rooted in the land—farms, villages, neighborhoods, parks, even suburbs—were bulldozed at the behest of faceless bureaucrats and swept away in a stream of empty progress. The freeway's emblematic character is apparent in Douglas Adams's celebrated 1978 BBC radio drama (later adapted for novels and films) *The Hitchhiker's Guide to the Galaxy*, in which the character Arthur Dent learns, first, that his English home is about to be demolished to make way for a highway bypass, and then that the construction of an intergalactic bypass entails the imminent destruction of planet Earth. Another detail of the story was all too recognizable to contemporaries: opponents were told it was too late to object, since official notice of both the English and the galactic plans had been duly posted in obscure district offices (in the latter case, at Alpha Centauri).

The freeway revolts began as quintessential NIMBY phenomena. After all, hardly anyone wants a superhighway in their own backyard. Neighborhood activists seized upon every tool available to them, whether lying down in front of bulldozers (as Arthur Dent did, with typical futility), storming public meetings, hounding bureaucrats with their own rules, or filing lawsuits over procedural issues. Some tightly knit neighborhoods were able to spring into action quickly. Elsewhere, the threat of freeway construction probably did a great deal to forge communities, especially in gentrifying neighborhoods.

Highway planners grumbled about these "cranks" whose refusal to look at the big picture threatened "to strangle desperately needed progress."[27] Engineers saw themselves as guardians of the public good against short-sighted and parochial interests. The head of the Swiss federal highway department warned his colleagues against going soft in the face of resistance: they could be sure that "the great majority of people indirectly affected as well as the users of the road certainly share our belief that there has been enough talk: now it is finally time to build."[28] Or as a 1956 American magazine article put it: "The dissident minorities who find themselves in the path of this interchange or that expressway can help if they will stop to realize that every foot of the new highways is necessary for the national well-being."[29] The frustration was understandable: crying "not here!" would do nothing to ease the traffic problems the engineers were charged with solving. It was, however, precisely the opponents' failure either to grasp or to respect the technocratic logic of the highway program that made them such a threat to it. Local objections could be brushed aside to build projects "necessary for the national well-being," but the national and international anti-freeway movements outgrew their parochial origins because many people disputed that very necessity.

Well-founded objections to particular routes or projects could be dismissed as quibbles, easily solved by proper design. When the grievances of the freeway opponents reached the pages of the American mass-circulation magazine Life in 1967, its editors did not doubt the necessity of the roads: "Do we need all those big highways we're building? Of course we do, but we also need them to be very nimbly placed in the context of our complicated cities."[30] After all, highways had long been sold as assets to a community, even as aesthetic improvements. Anti-freeway activists in many lands now argued that they were nothing of the sort. They also realized that NIMBY cries would do little more than pit one neighborhood against another. To stop the freeway juggernaut, they needed to change national transportation policies by knocking the political and bureaucratic props out from under the highway programs.

Activists in many cities argued that the transportation planning process valued the flow of automobiles above the stability of neighborhoods. Not all their arguments were new, but their influence was: the views of lonely critics in earlier years now began to affect local and national policies. Nor were all the critics hostile to cars, but the effect of their rebellion was to permanently sully the reputation of the automobile as the salvation of city and society. They argued one or more of several propositions: that powerful interests were foisting the highways on an unwilling populace; that the justifications for the projects rested on narrow thinking and faulty logic; that mobility was not an end in itself, and it was foolish to promote movement at the expense of urban stability; and that the roads both presumed and promoted an unhealthy reliance on automobiles to the exclusion of other modes of transportation.

Beyond any objections to individual projects, critics attacked the constellation of economic and bureaucratic interests profiting from highway construction. By the late 1960s, when the American freeway revolts had passed from the NIMBY stage into a national movement, attacks on the "road gang" proliferated. In 1968 a Baltimore anti-freeway organization declared that "expressways are being built in cities not for the sake of the people who live there, but for the sake of cement, tire, automobile, and other private interests."[31] These sometimes divergent interests had agreed to the Highway Trust Fund in 1956 and then made themselves a permanent presence in Washington. The auto manufacturers (usually supported by the powerful auto workers' union), manufacturers of tires and other auto parts, oil companies, trucking syndicates, concrete and asphalt manufacturers, and construction companies all supported the Washington trade associations that cultivated cozy relationships with powerful committee chairmen in Congress who could be counted on to speak out in favor of automotive mobility as well as the appropriations necessary to grease the wheels of the highway machine. Highway engineers and other civil servants in the Bureau of Public Roads may have had less of a financial stake in road construction, but their philosophical commitment to highways made them comfortable allies of both the trade groups and the elected representatives. As local freeway opponents encountered hostile responses in Washington, they became aware of the highway lobby's power and of its dubious claim to represent the broader public interest. But they also began to find allies. By 1966, cracks in the political consensus appeared when several U.S. senators spoke out against excesses of the highway program. Even the popular press began to question its value. In 1969, the widely read and staunchly conservative *Reader's Digest* published an article by its Washington reporters with the title, "Let's Put Brakes on the Highway Lobby," reflecting a widespread if recent belief that unneeded highways were being built because sinister forces were subverting the popular will.

Anti-highway activists in European lands also marshaled evidence that the "road lobby" called the shots in the road or transport ministry.[32]

Italy's multiparty parliamentary caucus "Friends of the Automobile," for example, included many ministers and other powerful figures, raising the suspicion that they did the highway lobby's bidding.[33] Because freeway construction has typically entailed opaque government decisions that meant big money for powerful interests, similar complaints have been heard around the world. Japan's notorious "road tribe" ultimately became the world's most entrenched jobs-and-highways machine.

Thus the madness of highway construction could be explained by the undue power of economic interests, compounded by bureaucratic inertia. But there still remained the fact that for each and every proposed highway, dry and rational calculations proved its benefits to traffic flow and to the local or national economy. How could these be challenged?

Obviously it would be a mistake to believe that the engineers, or even the highway lobby, simply foisted new highways on an unsuspecting public: many people were clamoring for them. Still, it was a self-perpetuating system: where funding was guaranteed, as was most clearly the case with the American Highway Trust Fund, and where respected experts were charged with building highways, not with planning cities or coordinating modes of transport, the result was bound to be more highways. When politicians' wishes (in this case, for highways) were turned into technocratic calculations, policies sometimes became far more unassailable than they should have been. Plans for new or wider roads have remained popular with the motoring public, but the freeway revolts raised widespread doubts about the authority and expertise of the traffic engineers—part of a broader questioning of authority associated with the 1960s in most industrialized lands.

No one was promising mobility at any cost, but at first there seems to have been no doubt that the going price of mobility was well worth paying. American traffic planners developed survey techniques and mathematical formulas to transform statistics on car ownership and road use into estimates of the road capacity needed to keep traffic flowing. When they said a six-lane freeway was needed between point A and point B, their word went unquestioned, especially after the 1956 Interstate Highway Act ensured that the road could be paid for. The traffic engineers' models of human behavior owed less to psychology than to hydrology: they assumed that the sum of choices by individual drivers could be measured statistically according to a "gravity model," as if it were a physical phenomenon like flowing water. Their formulas ignored the possibility that their recommended policies—more roads—might influence people's choices to drive alone, to carpool, or to take mass transit—and thus to change the traffic load on future roads. They assumed that the plummeting use of mass transit in 1950s American cities neither could nor should be stemmed. Their standard calculations completely ignored pedestrians, who did not count as "traffic." Bicycles and motor scooters, likewise, did not count, since in American cities (in sharp contrast to much of the world) they were considered appropriate only for those too young to drive. The formulas assumed that everyone would drive everywhere, if possible.

In short, they treated traffic as an independent variable, a given quantity to which policies had to respond. Critics, however, began to question that very assumption. Although the sight of traffic jams was certain to provoke demands for more and wider roads, it quickly became apparent that new roads did not always fulfill their promise, thanks to what became known as "induced traffic." As early as 1907, an American magazine observed that "the greater the facilities for transportation, the greater the congestion becomes."[34] During the 1920s and 1930s, occasional observers admitted that expanded roads seemed to attract more vehicles. Even the leading traffic planner of the era, Miller McClintock, acknowledged the problem in 1925: "Any reasonable increase in street capacity, either through a more rapid movement of traffic, or through a widening of the thoroughfare, will not reduce the density of traffic, for the places made available will be taken by those drivers who may be said to be on the margin of convenience."[35] At the time, though, the need for wider roads seemed too obvious to doubt: experts like McClintock did not let this realization stop them from recommending more road construction.[36]

In the freeway era, a later generation of skeptics had to raise the issue anew. In 1949, the planner Theodore J. Kent predicted that a proposed freeway in the San Francisco Bay area would be "hopelessly overcrowded and choked by the time it is completed."[37] The next year, another American planner, Walter H. Blucher, roundly denounced traffic engineers for their failure to take account of induced traffic—to little avail.[38] Only in the 1960s, as highway critics began to band together, did the theory of induced traffic become well known. The fact the Lewis Mumford had been preaching about it for years probably prompted Daniel Patrick Moynihan, in 1960, to detect an increasing awareness that "to do nothing more than build bigger highways only produced bigger traffic jams."[39] He could point to many cases in which new roads seemed to be full almost from the day of their opening. The promised reductions in traffic congestion and commuting times either failed to materialize, or were short lived. Highway construction and traffic seemed to advance in a vicious circle. A famous but typical example is the Long Island Expressway, the major highway built to speed commuters from that growing suburban region into New York City. Soon after its first segment opened in 1958, drivers stuck in its chronic traffic jams began to call it the "world's longest parking lot."

In 1962, the economist Anthony Downs declared rush-hour congestion to be inevitable, the product of what he later called a "triple convergence": a new highway drew commuters who had formerly avoided the peak hours; it attracted drivers from other roads; and it induced former bus, train, or carpool commuters to take the wheel. And in the long run, it actually turned out to be a quadruple convergence, since new roads also fueled decentralization and sprawl, tempting some people to drive farther than they had before, in order to reach more distant shops, say, or to live farther from their jobs.[40] If the goal of road construction was, as often proclaimed, to banish congestion and guarantee fast driving, it was bound to fail.

The vicious circle of induced traffic was no secret to the highway lobby. The asphalt industry, for example, celebrated the "magic circle," a "cyclic and beneficial process" in which new roads "ease traffic congestion and develop even more travel," creating a demand for yet more roads.[41] When defending controversial new roads, however, highway proponents felt obliged to deny the problem of induced traffic. As early as 1930, an American traffic planner acknowledged the theory, only to reject it: "It is sometimes said that it is useless to increase capacities in central areas as any additional capacity provided will be immediately taxed to the saturation point," but this assumption "has no validity whatever as applied to any major traffic artery."[42] In the 1960s, opponents of the New Orleans riverfront freeway were able to fight the experts on their own terms, citing a consultant's prediction that induced traffic would negate the road's advantages and overload rather than relieve the quiet streets of the French Quarter.[43] As the theory became conventional wisdom among highway critics and even transportation scholars, however, their opponents continued to deny it. Henry Ford II, for example, did so in a 1966 speech; and even as the Greater London Council officially admitted the problem, its politicians denied it.[44] Induced traffic posed a fundamental threat to the bureaucratic logic of road construction, as is apparent in the decades-long divergence between scholarly knowledge and the process of evaluating the costs and benefits of highway projects. In 1998 the UK government finally declared that it would no longer attempt to expand road capacity to keep up with demand; elsewhere, the goal remains, even if the funding to do so is out of reach.

By the 1970s, highway critics—and eventually many transportation planners—adopted the motto, "You can't build your way out of congestion." The sentiment was slow to reach frustrated commuters, who were (and are) still hearing politicians and the highway lobby promise that new roads will eliminate congestion. The controversy has continued into the twenty-first century, with no accepted statistical model for predicting induced traffic. Although it is clearly wrong to assert that new roads never relieve congestion, those who insist that road expenditures need not take account of induced traffic face mounting evidence to the contrary.[45] The most uncompromising highway advocates even claim that induced traffic is yet another argument for new roads. The fact that new roads induce people to drive more is, in their view, evidence of a "latent" demand for driving that ought to be satisfied: "travel that is 'induced' by added capacity is actually travel that had been repressed or shifted by capacity shortages."[46] In other words, since driving provides mobility, driving is good, and more driving is better. Specifically, they argue that spacious suburban living (what critics call sprawl) is something people want and is a measurable benefit of road construction. Expensive highways sold as congestion relief may not be as easy to justify, however, when they are instead fueling suburban sprawl or tempting people to abandon public transit. Instead of decreasing the average commuting time, decades of highway construction in the United States have increased the average commuting distance. That may be a desirable goal, depending on one's opinion about the suburban dream of house and yard, but it is not the calculation that justified the cost of roads.

In fact, traffic engineers and highway advocates were increasingly aligned against economists. The engineers treated mobility as an end in itself—as, in effect, a right—rather than a good to be purchased in the market. The perfunctory cost-benefit analyses used to justify new freeways measured their benefits largely in terms of time saved per mile of driving, thanks to faster roads or reduced congestion. Not only were these benefits often illusory or short lived because of induced traffic, they were also not subjected to market tests. That is, since motorists rarely had to pay for the privilege of using new roads, there was no measure of their willingness to do so. Proposals for variable "road pricing" emerged by the 1960s, notably in Britain, but neither politicians nor the public much liked the economists' idea that scarce road space at rush hour ought to cost motorists more, so with rare exceptions it received no serious consideration for decades. The same was true for parking: although garages and curbside meters charged for parking in some places, the idea of managing a city's or a district's parking space through price mechanisms long remained an economist's pipe dream. As an American journalist observed in 1955, "the city motorist shows a kind of tragic grandeur in his stubborn refusal to recognize parking at the curb as anything less than his inalienable right"—a right to occupy valuable street space for little or no cost.[47] The assumption that parking should be provided cheaply on demand was similar to the logic guiding freeway construction, and the result was an induced demand for parking, since free or subsidized parking offered motorists a further inducement to drive to a destination.[48]

Highway critics also pointed out that if auto traffic was not an independent variable, it was possible to argue the inverse of the theory of induced traffic. Traffic planners reflexively opposed the closing of streets, or a reduction in their capacity, by arguing that woeful traffic congestion would result. But traffic, it seemed, could also be induced to disappear, so the closing of streets did not necessarily worsen congestion. Jane Jacobs cited the example of New York's Washington Square, closed to cars in 1958 at the behest of neighbors. Defying the predictions of Robert Moses and city planners, traffic on neighboring streets did not even increase, much less become intolerable. Jacobs called this a rare example of the "attrition of automobiles by cities," the desirable alternative to the prevalent "erosion of cities by automobiles."[49] Along the same lines, a 1998 survey of planned and emergency road closures around the world confirmed that drivers were able to adapt without undue calamity.[50] The collapse of New York's West Side Highway in 1973 and of a Minneapolis bridge in 2007 failed to create chaos, and traffic-choked Seoul successfully demolished an inner-city freeway without worsening its congestion. Proposals to restrict inner-city motor traffic, first suggested in the 1960s by the Buchanan report as well as Jacobs's book, have thus gained an aura of respectability after having been heresy in the traffic engineers' heyday. An approach that relies on a market mechanism is the "congestion charge" levied on all cars entering a city center. Singapore imposed

Figure 15. The American downtown: parking lots and skyscrapers (Atlanta, 1992). Author's slide.

one in 1975, followed by Norwegian cities in the 1990s, London in 2003, Stockholm in 2006, and Milan in 2008. The daily tolls are intended to discourage driving, reduce congestion and pollution and, often, to fund mass-transit improvements. Their effect has been to reduce traffic within the designated zone without (contrary to some predictions) creating traffic jams outside the zone.

Traffic planners in the 1960s simply did not think about the limits of urban automobility. They assumed that car use would continue to grow, and that their job was to "predict and provide," to keep building the necessary roads and parking spaces. Critics less enamored of automobiles wondered when an undesirable situation became an absurd one. Some tried to calculate the proportion of American downtown land devoted to automobiles, estimating that half or more of central Los Angeles was consumed by roads and parking lots. Among the early skeptics was Atlanta mayor Ivan Allen, who asked the U.S. Senate for transit funding in 1962 by arguing that reliance on cars alone would eventually require his city to build 120 expressway lanes to downtown as well as a twenty-eight-lane beltway.[51] These numbers did not necessarily alarm champions of the new suburban metropolis where motorists could easily drive and park everywhere. But American downtown boosters like Allen, and the even more powerful urban interests in Europe, began to question the wisdom of adding ever more highways and cars.

National differences in rates of car ownership had surprisingly little bearing on either the nearly simultaneous proposals for freeways in many lands, or on the controversy most of them faced a few years later. This international phenomenon can be partly explained by the prestige of traffic engineers. The similarity of highway plans around the world was due in no small part to international standards of traffic engineering. During the 1950s, traffic planners from across Europe and Asia as well as Australia visited the United States, invited American engineers to advise them, hired the best-known American consultants, and adopted the standards set out in American traffic manuals.[52] Only slowly did critical minds conclude that these standards were not uniformly applicable but in fact reflected their roots in the American 1950s, where auto ownership was on its way from widespread to nearly universal, transit was in steep decline, suburbs were booming, and hardly anyone contemplated any alternative to full motorization. Even as highway opponents outside the U.S. drew inspiration from American protests, they argued that American consultants and American models failed to do justice to Australian or Swiss cities. By the end of the 1960s, they could cite the growing chorus of American critics who argued that the problem of induced traffic made new highways a waste of money. An unusually early example was a mayor of Hamburg who wrote a newspaper article in 1958 blasting the city's nascent freeway plans as the "grotesque" vision of experts who make a mess of things "because they consider automobiles more important than people." He cited Lewis Mumford in support of his argument that an autobahn would destroy the fabric of city life while failing to solve the traffic problem. His words caused a furor but not a change of policy, with one journalist concluding that the mayor had misjudged the public mood, since "any plan at all that offers the slightest hope of getting local traffic moving can be assured of the unanimous applause" of local citizens.[53] Adelaide's town planner returned to Australia from an American sojourn in 1964 warning that induced traffic and the decline of public transit would make freeway construction futile.[54] Few Australians heeded him, but things had changed by 1972, when the *Sydney Morning Herald* warned that "overseas" evidence suggests that "the expressways will be self-defeating. They will merely encourage more people to drive private motor cars into the city, thereby increasing congestion, pollution and parking problems, and drawing patronage away from public transport."⁵⁵

The problem of induced traffic challenged the highway engineers on their own ground by questioning the promised benefits of new roads, since it was the reductions in congestion and in travel times that justified a project's cost. A deeper disagreement also emerged, however. Traffic engineers and highway builders saw the rapid movement of motor vehicles as their ultimate goal. To the extent that any of them sought philosophical underpinnings for their work, they understood mobility as either an end in itself or a measure of freedom. From the beginning, motorists and their advocates had believed that automobiles held out the promise of individual freedom in the form of individual mobility. Although a handful of moralists and snobs had deplored this mobility, by midcentury there were few doubts about the desirability of individual car ownership and use.

It was the conflict between cars and cities that destroyed the consensus. In the 1920s, when visionaries like Le Corbusier were sketching the automotive cities of the future, and downtown leaders worried about their new traffic jams, hardly anyone doubted that bustling cities needed more rapid mobility. But the highway engineers' great successes of the 1950s and 1960s gave fodder to opponents. The freeway revolts became an international movement not merely because many people's homes were threatened, and not merely because American engineers recommended the same solutions everywhere, but because new roads were the most disruptive symptoms of a new kind of mobile and seemingly rootless life. Some freeway opponents concluded that the free movement of automobiles was simply incompatible with cities. They asked: Was mobility an end in itself? Did it matter where the motorist ended up? Were cities and neighborhoods nothing more than obstructions to the free flow of traffic? Freeways had been sold as the salvation of the city, but residents in the freeways' paths concluded that the cure was worse than the disease, or that the bureaucrats and engineers had forgotten what a city was. As early as 1956, the San Francisco newspaper editor Scott Newhall proclaimed that his city was in "rebellion against the automobile's encroachment upon the homes, the property, the peace and quiet of people." Citizens did not want to see their city "get twisted into the tortured shape of others that have surrendered totally to the monster's insatiable demands."⁵⁶ As a Washington neighborhood activist, Angela Rooney, argued in 1972, freeways erect barriers that "erode community interdependence and identification. We're encouraging the creation of a rootless, mobile society that has no sense of responsibility."[57]

It was his lifelong vision of the good city that prompted Lewis Mumford to write in 1957, "When the American people, through their Congress, voted last year for a twenty-six-billion-dollar highway program, the most charitable thing to assume about this action is that they hadn't the faintest notion of what they were doing."[58] Looking at the architects of the program, Daniel Patrick Moynihan assumed nothing of the sort: "It is not true as is sometimes alleged, that the sponsors of the interstate program ignored the consequences it would have in the cities. Nor did they simply acquiesce in them. They exulted in them." He cited a report praising the dispersal of factories, shops, and people: "Our cities have spread into suburbs, dependent on the automobile for their existence."[59] The highway program, Moynihan believed, was a deliberate attempt to wreck the cities.

Even as residents of devastated neighborhoods had to cope with the disruption caused by freeways, critics argued that the blessing conferred on suburban commuters turned out to be nothing more than the opportunity to spend more time in their cars. As André Gorz observed in 1973, "The cities and towns have been broken up into endless highway suburbs, for that was the only way to avoid traffic congestion in residential centers. But the underside of this solution is obvious: ultimately people can't get around conveniently because they are far away from everything."[60] At about the same time, German scholars coined the phrase "enforced mobility" to describe this paradox of the decentralized city, in which motorists are more mobile than ever, often not because they want to be, but merely because their homes and jobs end up far apart.[61]

In other words, mobility, the highway engineers' ideal, was self-defeating—a false god. In more recent years, some transportation scholars have argued that the proper goal is not mobility but rather accessibility, that is, the ability to reach the destinations one wants and needs. In car-centered cities with destinations farther and farther apart, increased mobility did not necessarily translate into greater accessibility or opportunities, even for motorists, and certainly not for the carless minority (or majority, in poorer lands). For them, automotive mobility decreased accessibility by forcing them to contend with motor traffic as well as automotive sprawl. Nor did reduced mobility have to mean reduced freedom, if cities could recover their compactness—or if, at the very least, average suburbanites could buy a quart of milk without getting into their cars. Congested highways, in other words, would not be such a problem if people did not need to travel as far. In recent years, transportation policies in some European cities (and a few others, such as Portland, Oregon) have given priority to compactness over mobility, accepting congested roads while seeking shorter commutes.

Unfortunately, mobility is relatively easy to identify, measure, and feel; accessibility is not. Rejecting mobility in favor of accessibility certainly meant opposing urban freeways, but otherwise it was far from obvious how to proceed. For Gorz, the only solution was to renounce mobility altogether. People "will have to be able to do without transportation altogether because they'll feel at home in their neighborhoods, their community, their human-sized cities, and they will take pleasure in walking from work to home—on foot, or if need be by bicycle. No means of fast transportation and escape will ever compensate for the vexation of living in an uninhabitable city"—that is, one rendered uninhabitable by motor traffic.[62] This was an utter rejection not only of the traffic engineers' vision but of the entire automobile age. Many 1960s-era radicals also insisted that the equation of mobility with freedom was part of capitalist economics' quantitative reduction of human happiness to material consumption, and environmentalists began to argue that it was foolish to measure prosperity by our consumption of natural resources. Predictions since the 1970s of the imminent demise of cheap energy supplies also inspired manifestos of rootedness and limited mobility. This way of thinking was very European, grounded in a visceral attachment to pre-automobile cities. It was not confined to Europe, but few Americans shared the pessimism of senator Eugene McCarthy, who wondered if the new interstate program might not merely hasten the day when "you'll be able to drive eighty miles an hour along superhighways from one polluted stream to another, from one urban slum to another, from one rundown college campus to another."[63] Perhaps the right sort of urban planning could restore a more human scale of mobility—that has remained the hope of many critics in recent decades. The prospect of renouncing mobility is less likely to appeal to, for example, Chinese, who might see it as a return to the limits of the *danwei* work unit they only recently escaped, if not to a world in which women's feet were bound in order to ensure their loyalty to the home.

Not everyone thought it necessary to choose between automobiles and immobility. Many critics of cars and freeways rejected technological despair and believed that a less car-dependent future might mean more, not less, mobility, as new or rejuvenated forms of mass transit revived cities.

An urban expressway at rush hour can serve as a kind of Rorschach test of attitudes toward transportation. Some people see squalor, chaos, and dreadful inefficiency: a filthy gash in the landscape echoing with the roar of steel behemoths, most of them carrying a single mortal who battles for position in the overcrowded lanes. As traffic repeatedly slows to a crawl or grinds to a halt, blood pressures rise and tempers flare. Surely, think many reluctant drivers, there must be a better way to get to work. What about the sleek, quiet, and fast trains that can be found in some foreign places?

But others prefer the comfort of the driver's seat. For them, the train or the bus may be squalid; the road is not. They share the view of the highway engineer: cars are fine; the only problem is the road's inadequate capacity (and perhaps a shortage of parking). These seemingly chaotic highways have, in fact, served the modern city as a remarkably efficient transit system by many measures, whereas, by the same standards, rail and bus transit are often notably inefficient, carrying too many empty vehicles to the wrong places and none at all to the right ones. A train or bus is no substitute for a car. After all, trains do not run from door to door, nor do they depart at a moment of one's choosing. Only a rare combination of fortuitous locations and schedules, disastrous traffic, and particularly efficient trains make a rail journey actually faster than a commute by car. Even if there happens to be a train gliding down the median strip of the clogged rush-hour highway, many commuters still prefer the comfort of their air-conditioned cocoons, with music and aromas of their own choosing as well as the ability to drive directly to their destination, spared the annoyance of stations, transfers, waits on platforms, and the proximity of strangers.

As the internal-combustion engine approached its hundredth birthday, the vision of the 1939 Futurama was far from dead. But where "magic motorways" had lost their luster, newer and better technologies beckoned. As traffic jams dulled the excitement of driving, more or less improbable new projects, sold as "rapid" rather than "mass" transit, promised to bypass both freeway traffic and the enforced sociability of the train. The privacy of individuals or families would be preserved in some kind of people pod that could whisk them directly to their destinations along high-speed corridors, with all the comfort of a car and all the speed of a spaceship. When a modified version was put into service in the 1970s in Morgantown, West Virginia (with cars that held twenty passengers, it was not quite the fantasized private pod), it was heralded as a harbinger of the future. Three decades later, it still connects the far-flung corners of the West Virginia University campus, but it has failed to conquer the world.

Sometimes the "bullet train" was proclaimed to be the future of urban transit. After all, the very name promised the most aggressive kind of progress. After Japan led the way to high-speed intercity rail in the 1960s, urban planners and transportation engineers, not just dreamers, tried to make the same technology work within cities. Still, its appeal was often that of science fiction, and the image that captured the public imagination was the sleek elevated train straddling a single track. The monorail came to symbolize the future of transportation, rivaled only by space capsules and jetpacks. Whenever chronic traffic problems were at issue, any local newspaper's letters column could be counted on to print the occasional plea for the construction of a monorail that would whoosh fortunate passengers over the stalled cars on some notoriously clogged highway. As the decades passed, the futuristic vision threatened to become a nostalgic one. But monorail advocates persisted. Since only a few short segments of monorail have ever been built, it does remain largely a technology of the future, although its iconic status has been challenged more recently by magnetic levitation (maglev) technology. As recently as 2006 the elderly science fiction writer Ray Bradbury wrote in the *Los Angeles Times* that the only sensible replacement for the city's battered network of clogged freeways was a monorail network.

Americans have been particularly prone to such fantasies during the past half century, perhaps because of their technological optimism, but also since ordinary passenger trains have become so remote from their lives. Whereas trains were a humdrum fact of urban life around the world after midcentury, in the U.S. they were fading into history. Intercity passenger service withered and nearly died, while suburban commuter trains barely hung on in a few cities. Although new underground railways—subways—were much discussed in major American cities during the 1920s, because they promised to replace streetcars and open up street space for cars, the lines that were built during that and the following decade were confined mainly to the handful of cities that already had rapid-transit systems.[64] After that, new transit systems were rarely proposed, and even more rarely built. The sole exception during the 1950s was a single subway line built in Cleveland. In most places, streetcars remained the embodiment of mass transit. With their fixed rails, their on-street boarding areas, and often the need to travel both ways on the same track, they were poorly adapted to sharing street space with automobiles. They gained a reputation as old fashioned, inconvenient, and downright embarrassing, and they bore no resemblance to the high-tech fantasies of future transportation. By 1960 all but a handful of lines were gone from the United States. What remained of transit in most American cities took the form of wheezing diesel buses sharing the streets (and the traffic jams) with cars.

Midcentury transportation planners around the world faced car-choked cities and motorists clamoring to be liberated not from their cars but from their clogged roads. They were not thinking about monorails or pods or jetpacks; they were busy building freeways. Yet even in the 1950s alternative views did sometimes gain a hearing. In the U.S., the pioneer was the San Francisco Bay area: during the 1950s, at the same time that San Francisco was inventing the freeway revolt, it was also developing an alternative. Promoters of the Bay Area Rapid Transit (BART) system presented their project as something entirely distinct from rattling old streetcars and commuter trains. BART was to be a space-age marvel, with fully automated cars. Unfortunately, the project's reliance on untested technology proved to be one of its biggest headaches, delaying completion and raising costs enormously. It finally began service on a limited network of lines in 1972.

It is noteworthy that San Francisco was simultaneously embracing cutting-edge transit technology and romanticizing its obsolete predecessor. Its cable cars were actually an older technology than the electric trams that had replaced them in less hilly cities. During the late 1940s and 1950s, in an initiative virtually without parallel until decades later, citizens rose up against proposals to eliminate the cable cars, once the backbone of the city's transit system. In the end San Francisco preserved three cable-car lines as well as a few electric streetcars.

Anti-freeway activists joined lovers of city life, conservationists (soon to be much more numerous and known as environmentalists), urban politicians, and a growing minority of transportation planners in promoting a revival of mass transit during the 1960s. The car, they believed, was reaching the limits of its usefulness, even in the suburbs. As one of the most prominent anti-freeway activists, Helen Leavitt, wrote confidently in 1970, "Anyone who has tried to drive to a suburban shopping center on a Saturday knows that highways and automobiles cannot continue to be the only transportation mode available for suburban communities."[65] It is doubtful that this would have been obvious to "anyone," but governor Francis Sargent of Massachusetts, when canceling Boston's long-planned Inner Belt freeway the same year, admitted, "Nearly everyone was sure highways were the only answer to transportation problems for years to come. But we were wrong."[66]

The late 1950s saw the emergence of a pro-transit coalition of city-center businesses and political leaders, transit operators, and railway unions, concentrated in the handful of cities with substantial commuter-rail operations, most of which appeared likely to shut down. A belated recognition that the exclusive emphasis on highways poorly addressed the needs of downtowns gave political ammunition to highway skeptics. As Daniel Patrick Moynihan wrote in a 1960 article entitled "New Roads and Urban Chaos," "to undertake a vast program of urban highway construction with no thought for other forms of transportation seemed lunatic," yet urban planning was in effect being placed entirely in the hands of highway engineers.[67] By the early 1960s, however, there was talk of the need to fight traffic congestion by improving transit enough to draw people out of their cars. The 1962 Federal Aid Highway Act introduced the rhetoric of "balanced" transportation and required local transportation plans to consider alternate modes, while, however, continuing to fund only highway construction. The 1964 Urban Mass Transportation Act offered federal funding for up to two-thirds of the cost of transit equipment purchases—a big change, if no match for the 90 percent funding for interstate highways. President Lyndon Johnson's devotion to civil rights and urban renewal, along with the nascent doubts about freeways, led to the creation of the U.S. Department of Transportation in 1966. Henceforth the work of the highway planners in the Bureau of Public Roads was at least nominally subject to broader transportation plans. At first the commitment to "multimodalism" was mostly rhetorical. It took several more years to crack open the Highway Trust Fund, which guaranteed funding for new roads but not for urban mass-transit projects. A modest change came in 1973, when the law was amended to permit some highway money to be traded for transit funding.[68]

This marked the end of an era of almost exclusive emphasis on road transportation, meaning trucks and passenger cars (buses used the roads, but roads were rarely planned with any attention to them). The change was nowhere more apparent than in the national capital, Washington, where determined opponents had defied Congress and the highway lobby to stop some of the proposed urban freeways at the same time that the federal government agreed to fund a new urban rail network, the Washington Metro, which opened in 1976.

The uniqueness of the American case should not be overstated. The scorn for and disappearance of street railways was an international phenomenon. After the war European cities repaired their transit systems out of necessity, but then proceeded to dismantle most of their streetcar lines. Proposals for new rail lines emerged mainly in response to growing traffic congestion in the streets: moving transit underground would free up more road space for cars. Outside the U.S., mass transit remained an indispensable part of urban traffic planning, but usually it was taken for granted. European planners generally assumed that the need for urban mass transit would remain more or less unchanged. (They consistently underestimated the growth in car use.) Their transit systems left them better able to respond to the rapidly growing traffic jams of the 1960s, as levels of car ownership rose rapidly. Although many European freeway battles were dramatic, the transformation of policy was less so, since cars never got the chance to dominate transportation to the same degree. From the beginning, European governments treated cars as luxury items, taxing them quite heavily, and most of these taxes were still in place when disillusionment set in, lending them further justification. The revival of mass transit also predated the European freeway revolts, since growing urban traffic jams around 1960 had prompted some planners and politicians to come to the defense of transit, even the unloved streetcars, warning that Europe had to learn from the collapse of American transit. West Berlin, to take one example, built not only urban autobahns in the 1950s and 1960s, but also two long new subway lines that compensated for transit connections severed by the Berlin Wall. On a much more ambitious scale, Paris built its high-speed suburban rail network, the RER, during the 1960s. By the 1970s, many smaller European cities decided to favor transit over automobiles, at least in the city center. Instead of building wide new roads, for example, they set aside dedicated lanes for buses and separate rights of way for streetcars, and timed traffic signals to give preference to buses and streetcars.

Canada offers an instructive comparison to the U.S. Although its levels of car ownership were closer to American than European averages, its transit policies and practices were quite different. During the 1950s, Toronto built two freeways but also a major new underground rail line. The city of Montreal built its own subway system in the 1960s, even as the provincial government of Quebec was weaving a web of freeways around the city. By the early 1970s Vancouver shifted nearly all its resources from freeways to rail. Calgary built a successful light-rail network in lieu of canceled freeways, while Ottawa chose to build dedicated high-speed busways. Transit use in Canadian cities remains far higher than in the U.S.

Still, neither the specter of monorails nor the construction of conventional rail systems succeeded in stopping the relentless advance of the automobile. For decades, American transit advocates have been inspired by European, Canadian, and Japanese cities' clean and bustling trains. But too seldom have they noticed that, in spite of fewer highways and higher costs, Canadian, Europeans, and Asians have been acquiring cars, driving more, and riding transit less. After losing many riders in the 1960s, transit systems in wealthy European lands have struggled (with some success) to maintain their much-reduced patronage. After 1990, post-Communist eastern Europe was flooded with cars, and people abandoned public transit in droves.

In the U.S., even where gleaming new systems were built, as in San Francisco and Washington, their effects were in many ways disappointing. Car use continued to grow faster than transit use, if the latter grew at all. Many train riders were former bus passengers, not former drivers. Motorists who supported transit because they hoped for relief on their crowded highways (as fellow drivers switched to the train) were disappointed. Induced traffic often negated the effects of transit expansion as well: where some motorists switched to transit, others quickly took their places on the road.

Nor did transit advocates always pay heed to fundamental differences in urban form between their cities and the transit metropolises they admired. Urban rapid transit worked best in cities with a single crowded employment center, such as New York or Toyko. The model of a different kind of metropolis was multipolar Los Angeles, home to the world's largest concentration of automobiles and some of its worst traffic problems. Where homes and destinations were so widely dispersed—a predicament lamented by some critics, but a reality for L.A. and most other cities—even congested roads offered the fastest and most convenient transportation for most people. Still, after years of wrangling, Los Angeles approved and in 1985 slowly began building a few very expensive rail lines. Many transit experts, not only diehard transit opponents, deplored the decision, believing that an express bus system offered the only practical alternative to cars in the vast expanses of southern California. Some of them blamed the decision on a foolish romance of the rails, fed in equal parts by nostalgia for the region's vanished rail network and by the mirage of a gleaming monorail future.[69] In car-choked twenty-first-century L.A., true believers in the promise of rail transit and of magic motorways accused each other of living in the past.

THE END OF THE FREEWAY ERA?

The freeway revolts permanently changed the patterns of road construction, and they did so quite suddenly. Although nearly all cities have freeways, or something like them, many have completed only fragments of the comprehensive networks once planned—as motorists are well aware. Since the 1970s, cities around the world have been littered with expressway stumps that end abruptly, with drivers forced to brake sharply as they are funneled into sluggish old streets. Commuters share the frustration of traffic planners resigned to maps that violate all logic of traffic flow.

Contrary to the hopes and predictions of the most ambitious highway opponents, however, the age of the automobile in the city shows little sign of coming to an end. One reason for the reduced pressure for new roads was the fact that the early-1960s predictions of imminent urban gridlock had by and large not come to pass, despite a rate of road construction far less than what experts had believed to be necessary. Less intrusive methods of traffic management—parking restrictions, one-way streets, and coordinated traffic signals—made a difference. So did the removal of streetcars and massive investments in parking lots and garages. More flexible working hours have probably helped as well: certainly heavy traffic is spread over more hours of the day than it once was. People have adapted their travel habits to the opportunities available. The most important adaptation was the exodus of jobs, shops, and residents from the dense city centers, a trend largely unforeseen by planners, but one that dispersed traffic over roads that were less congested, at least temporarily. This urban sprawl also helped ensure that mass transit would not take many drivers off the road, since their new homes and destinations were often far from existing transit corridors and in areas too sparsely developed to support new transit lines.

Nor did freeway construction really come to an end in many places. The influence of highway engineers may have diminished, but politicians have stepped into the void, promising their motorized constituents new highways to relieve congestion. Some European countries, such as France and the Netherlands, largely built their national freeway networks after 1970. And the world's enormous, rapidly growing, and rapidly motorizing poorer cities have been busily constructing freeways. Even places with successfully freeway revolts saw the pendulum swing back to road construction. During the 1980s, for example, Britain's ruling Conservatives promoted auto use and launched an ambitious roads program. By 1990, the Swiss cities Zurich and Basel had resumed work on modified versions of projects stopped in the 1970s. The 1990s also saw new, controversial, but sometimes successful attempts to build freeways in Sydney and Melbourne as well as the rapid completion of Hitler's autobahn network in the territories acquired when West Germany annexed East Germany in 1990. The newer American cities have led the way in building new highways on the sparsely developed but fast-growing urban fringe, where few residents have to be displaced and rapid development follows the roads. Many European cities have followed a similar pattern: although they built fewer inner-city freeways than American cities, many have built ring roads or suburban freeways. This shift has reduced, if by no means eliminated, neighborhood resistance to freeway construction, and has encouraged the growth of low-density suburbs and ever-longer car commutes—quite the opposite of the intimate urban communities envisioned by freeway opponents. In other words, an unintended result of successful NIMBY opposition to urban freeways has been the triumph of sprawling NIMBY developments elsewhere.

Opposition to new freeways, especially urban freeways, has ensured that their costs would be high. Already in the 1970s, rising construction prices helped make the case against new roads, with the delays caused by opponents raising costs even further. By the 1990s, urban highway proponents knew that their only chance lay in buying off opponents with amenities to offset the damage done by road construction. One example was the Century Freeway, planned as part of Los Angeles's original freeway network but stopped in 1972 by opponents in the poor neighborhoods it was to traverse. A later settlement permitted its construction after the state agreed to depress part of the road, build a transit right-of-way in its median, and finance a job-training program and affordable housing for residents of the affected area. (It opened in 1993.) Even greater expense accompanied the reconstruction of Boston's elevated Central Artery in the 1990s, the "Big Dig" that buried the road in a tunnel through the city center. A similarly extravagant proposal to replace New York's West Side Highway went down in defeat in 1986.[70] Proponents of urban highways in other cities (including Paris and Seoul) have argued that the extraordinary expense of tunnels would be justified in order to make the roads palatable. Even in China, the growing middle class of Shenzhen managed to force design changes in a new freeway.[71] The need for this kind of mitigation, on top of escalating construction costs, has helped ensure that few cities can build roads fast enough to keep up with the growth of driving. In lieu of any coherent alternative, however, they cling to the threadbare goal of building enough roads to stay ahead of congestion.

In 1989 the German philosopher Peter Sloterdijk grandiosely proclaimed that the end of the modern age was apparent to every motorist. Since the essence of modernity was movement, he explained, "the automobile is modernity's holiest of holies." Therefore "the enormous summer traffic jams on central European freeways" hold momentous significance for the history of philosophy and even religion, since they reveal to us "the end of an illusion" and amount to "obituaries for modernity." In other words, "on these afternoons stuck in traffic, even those who have never heard the word postmodernity are already acquainted with the thing."[72] As Sloterdijk suggests, the abstruse concept of postmodernity is not needed in order to recognize that disillusionment with earlier dreams of free-flowing urban traffic marked the end of an era by the 1970s. There were never enough freeways to reach the promised land. Although the fantasy of escape on the highway did not die, daily hours of freeway drudgery took their toll on the imagination. Already in the 1957 Hollywood heist movie *Plunder Road*, fleeing outlaws get caught in a traffic jam and fender bender on Los Angeles's Harbor Freeway, compelling the ringleader to abandon his car and jump to his death. It is, as the film scholar Edward Dimendberg observes, "a powerful image of the end of highway hagiography."[73]

CHAPTER FIVE

The End of the
Automotive Age—or Not

Americans' "love affair" with the automobile had not ended by 1970, insisted the chairman of General Motors: it had "just turned into a marriage."[1] But what kind of a marriage? This was, after all, just when the divorce rate was soaring. And other nations' automotive romances seemed to be on the rocks as well. By the early 1970s, books and magazines were filled with obituaries for the automobile age. Emboldened critics argued that the beastly machines had no future, because people were about to come to their senses and change their ways. A decade before, John Keats had already anticipated that the marriage would end badly, but these predictions were far more serious and substantial than Keats's comic eulogy. By 1972, John Jerome, a self-proclaimed "car nut" and former managing editor of the auto enthusiasts' magazine *Car and Driver*, solemnly concluded:

> The balance sheet could more accurately describe a war than an industrial success. Automobiles kill almost sixty thousand of us per year and injure 4 million more, pollute the environment more outrageously than any other industrial source, gobble natural resources like cocktail peanuts, destroy the cities, choke off development of more efficient or serviceable transit systems, spread squalor on the land, jam the courts with unnecessarily complex and unwieldy litigation (often as not in violation of the civil rights of the involved), exacerbate our unsolved problems of poverty and race, shift patterns of home ownership and retail trade as casually and whimsically as natural disasters, alter sexual customs, loosen family ties, elbow their way into living space despite our best efforts

to keep them out, rearrange the very social and moral structure of the nation, and dominate the economy to the point of subverting the hallowed capitalist system.[2]

The mobility they provided was surely not worth this price.

For many environmentalists around the world, the automobile came to embody the irresponsible squandering of natural resources—clean air most visibly, but also the land sacrificed to highways, parking lots, and suburban sprawl, as well as soil and water contaminated by the manufacture, storage, and disposal of gasoline, rubber tires, and the many other toxic components of the typical automobile. Some critics were confident that a revived mass transit would restore the railway age's healthier patterns of mobility. Others, more attuned to the technopessimism of the environmental movement and its prevailing emphasis on the "limits to growth," foresaw an end to the ostentatious consumerism epitomized by the automobile. Here is a typical American example from 1980, with its echoes of 1910: "Some day America will admit that the automobile is socially and economically obsolete. We will recognize that it is more important to heat our homes and run our factories than to assure each legal driver his or her personal automobile. The sleek white limousine will no longer be an enviable symbol of wealth and power, but will arouse ridicule and hatred for the greedy aristocrat who flaunts his disdain for the common good."[3] The 1970s energy crisis made it easy to foresee a future in which Americans would renounce their profligate ways, avoid commutes, withdraw into their neighborhoods, even crowd into smaller houses, and thus become friendlier, more civic minded, and less devoted to consumption. From its largely American origins, this way of thinking became even more entrenched in northern Europe by the 1980s, visible, for example, in a traveling photo exhibition, Automotive Nightmare, that made its way around Germany from 1986 on.[4] The new Green political parties embraced hostility to the automobile as part of their crusade against excessive consumption, pointless mobility, and irresponsible individualism.

The condemnation of automobiles as anti-environment, anti-urban, and anti-civility has never gone away, with many car critics increasingly certain of their inevitable triumph. In Europe during the 1990s, it became commonplace in some circles to discuss matter-of-factly the coming end of the auto age or "the city after the automobile," as the Israeli-Canadian architect Moshe Safdie entitled his 1997 book. Yet at the same time car use was increasing everywhere in Europe, and very rapidly in the post-Communist East. If attacks on the auto have become more strident since the 1990s, they may reflect a dawning realization that the many setbacks suffered by the car and its human allies since the 1960s have failed to dampen its worldwide appeal.[5] Critics thought that the environmental movement and the energy crises of the 1970s, coming on the heels of the freeway revolts, should have sealed the fate of the stinking, gas-guzzling, soul-crushing monster, but powerful and even sinister forces somehow kept the beast alive.

THE CAR AS ENVIRONMENTAL DISASTER

It was obvious from the beginning that the internal-combustion engine was anything but a model of clean or efficient technology, yet its pollution and resource consumption did not contribute noticeably to anti-auto sentiment anywhere before the late 1960s. That prosperous decade's growing concern with the degradation of the natural environment, especially in the United States, culminated in the observance of the first Earth Day in 1970. By then, worries about pollution had reinforced the antipathy to automobiles already apparent in the freeway revolts. These sentiments showed up, for example, in the defense of urban parks against the incursion of freeways as well as in fears that too many roads and cars would spoil America's rural beauty. The automobile junkyard became the symbol of Americans' propensity to turn nature into squalor.

Air pollution was the primary environmental sin blamed on cars. Already in the 1940s, people in Los Angeles fretted and joked about the "smog" that was rapidly spoiling their spectacular mountain and ocean vistas. During the 1950s, scientists established that southern California's ceaselessly moving automobiles were the main source of the contaminants transformed by sunlight into acrid "photochemical smog," a toxic brew that threatened not just picturesque views but also human respiratory health. As a growing body of evidence linked auto exhaust to illness and death, the carmakers and their vocal allies responded with familiar denial and obfuscation. In 1977, for example, Barry Bruce-Briggs still dismissed the dangers as "trivial" and insisted that "there is no record of anybody ever dying of photochemical smog."[6] Nevertheless, a 1959 California law gave the state the authority to mandate the installation of emission-control devices on new cars. Although the atmospheric conditions as well as the enormous fleet of cars in the southern California basin were peculiarly suited to producing clouds of smog, it soon engulfed other cities as well, and the U.S. federal government adopted similar regulations after 1965, over the vociferous objections of the auto manufacturers, who insisted (quite wrongly, as it turned out) that the rules would cripple their industry.

The other major motoring nations soon saw their air visibly fouled as well. Nearly everywhere, pollution became bad enough to spawn public anger and even major health problems before governments stepped in to regulate car use or car exhaust: by the 1970s in Japan and Europe, during the 1990s in Mexico and Thailand, and the 2000s in China, for example. Lead, a known poison, had been a component of motor fuel since the 1920s, and mounting evidence of widespread lead poisoning finally attracted enough concern to see it banned in the wealthy motoring nations by the 1980s—again, in the face of groundless protests from the auto and oil industries. After Europe finally established stringent emissions rules, it then led the way in attacking other sources of automotive pollution, for example with European Union rules mandating auto recycling, a response to research showing how much toxic waste was discarded with every junked car.

By the 1990s, automobile advocates could plausibly argue that the problem of air pollution was well on its way to being solved. New American, European, and Japanese cars spew a tiny fraction of the carbon monoxide, sulfur dioxide, and nitrogen oxides that 1960s cars did. However, the noticeable reduction in air pollution in developed countries removed some of the urgency driving the environmental movement's anti-auto sentiment. Certainly the emission controls helped many suburban environmentalists convince themselves that their driving was not really such a bad thing. Meanwhile, in poorer, rapidly motorizing lands, cars continued to pollute far more. Their governments also reacted sooner or later, but it remains to be seen how new emission controls offset the rapid increases in Asian and Latin American car use. Although the new, cleaner cars buttress the optimistic conclusion that pollution is just a brief phase of motorization, most experts do not think the problem has been solved, even in the most advanced countries. The continuing increase in miles driven, particularly in the U.S., partly negated the improvement brought by cleaner cars. Many U.S. and European cities still fall short of government air-pollution standards, which are stricter than before but still reflect a medical consensus on the dangers of toxic air. And even where many kinds of pollutants have been reduced, little has been done about the carbon dioxide emissions that cause global climate change. Zero-emissions electric cars would ease worries about both emissions and petroleum supplies without taking people out of their cars, but reluctant carmakers and oil companies have convinced governments not to enforce the kind of mandates that would be required to bring about such a basic change in technology.

Only during the 1970s did petroleum consumption become another count in the indictment against the car. The oil embargo following the 1973 Yom Kippur war, organized against Western supporters of Israel by Arab states through their cartel, the Organization of Petroleum Exporting Countries (OPEC), caused sudden fuel shortages and a spike in gasoline prices, dramatically illustrating Western motorists' dependence on oil-exporting states. The shock was repeated in 1979 after the Iranian revolution again disrupted trade with a major oil producer. Volatile oil prices profoundly disrupted the major industrial economies, and with most of the imported oil burned in automobiles, it was the fuel shortages and gasoline lines that left the deepest impression on Westerners. Europe and Japan were actually more dependent on imported oil than the United States, but the oil shocks revealed that U.S. domestic production was far from adequate to fuel the American cars that had long been designed with an ostentatious disregard for efficiency. There was, therefore, plenty of room for improvement, and when reluctantly forced to do so by government mandates, the American auto manufacturers greatly increased the fuel efficiency of their products in the early 1980s, largely by reducing their size and weight.

It is surprising to recall that the belief in the automobile's imminent demise largely predated the 1973 oil crisis. Before then, worries about the price or supply of petroleum, or the dependence on foreign producers, played little role in criticism of car use. The energy crisis offered a new reason to condemn automobiles, although the oil-induced economic woes of the Western industrial economies in the 1970s may have had the opposite effect as well: a strong desire to promote economic growth and industrial employment dampened the enthusiasm to protect the environment. Proposals to reduce auto use stood little chance against the enormous clout of the American automobile industry, along with the many other industries and services dependent on it, especially the giant oil companies. Since Japanese, German, and French carmakers, unlike the American Big Three, exported a large percentage of their production, the industry loomed even larger there, and proposals seen as threatening its health were all but taboo.

Decades later, fuel shortages have yet to break the car culture. Most motorized countries have come to rely on relatively efficient small cars. North America is the exception. This was the land of giant gas-guzzlers in the 1950s and 1960s, at a time when a combination of poverty, crowded cities, and taxes on horsepower and petroleum kept European and Asian cars much smaller. The sharp increases in oil prices amid the international crises of the 1970s, followed by U.S. government regulations requiring better fuel efficiency, ended the reign of the enormous sedan in America. By the end of the 1970s, Detroit's Big Three had retooled their product lines to produce smaller and more efficient cars, the better to compete with the newly popular small (mainly Japanese) imports. More significant in overcoming the fuel crisis, however, was the worldwide collapse of oil prices in the 1980s, which left gasoline plentiful and cheap. Most of the subsequent improvements in engine efficiency were devoted to making cars more powerful rather than less thirsty for fuel. Fuel consumption resumed its climb in Europe as well as America, as more and larger vehicles were driven more miles each year. Alternate fuels, revolutionary new technologies, and radical reductions in driving remained distant dreams.

Increased pollution, fuel consumption, and death tolls all accompanied the 1990s American explosion in the sales of "light trucks," a category previously comprising mainly the pickups that had long since become fashion accessories as much as work vehicles. Now they were outnumbered by new versions of the same vehicles that had been modified to carry more passengers and freight in enclosed comfort. This new genre, given the fatuous name "sport utility vehicle" (SUV), was in effect subsidized by existing regulations, intended for trucks, which exempted these vehicles from many of the emissions, fuel-economy, and safety standards applied to passenger cars. Their enormous popularity seemed to belie any claims that average Americans cared about those matters. The SUV's origins as well as its appeal evoked off-road fantasies of unregulated driving as well as the martial authority embodied by its prototype, the U.S. Army's famous jeep. Ever larger SUVs culminated in General Motors' civilian version of the jeep's military successor, the Humvee. Owners of this hulking "Hummer" could boast of driving the most menacing and most gas-guzzling behemoth on the road.

A 2002 book by the journalist Keith Bradsher made a powerful case against SUVs. Although his book bore more than a passing resemblance to Ralph Nader's *Unsafe at Any Speed*, with its shocking revelations of automakers' callous determination to exploit customers' most antisocial instincts, and of government's failure to ensure basic safety, it failed to stir the same kind of outrage at the height of the SUV boom.[7] Outside the U.S., higher fuel taxes and more limited road space ensured that SUVs would remain relatively exclusive fashion items (known in Britain as "4x4s," except among London malefactors who called them "Chelsea tractors"). As more conspicuous symbols of ostentation in narrow European streets, they have been more vilified in Europe, which has not necessarily dampened their appeal.

Despite myriad ideas for alternatives to the internal-combustion engine, at the beginning of the twenty-first century the gasoline-powered automobile seemed as entrenched as ever. Its critics, however, predicted that dwindling worldwide oil reserves would soon force people out of their cars. Their warnings of imminent "peak oil" were the latest version of the "limits-to-growth" thinking prevalent among environmentalists in the 1970s. The fashionable buzzword was now "sustainability," as scholars tried to estimate levels of resource use, pollution, and disturbance to ecosystems that would avert long-term disaster. Even more than "peak oil," the threat of global climate change—caused in no small part by carbon dioxide emissions from automobiles—lent urgency to appeals for restraint in the consumption of natural resources.

BACKLASH

Although many car critics remained confident that history was on their side, few believed that their views had much current political influence. Still, after the 1960s the international transformation of respectable opinion was striking. Activists who had styled themselves as lonely voices standing up to powerful interests—the auto industry, the "road gang," highway engineers, entrenched bureaucracies—still saw themselves as underdogs in the political arena, foiled by intrigues and conspiracies, but they could point to concrete triumphs as well as a new climate of opinion.

The highway lobbies were on the defensive, as were traffic engineers who had spent their careers predicting increased auto traffic and building highways for it. Even some experts who had warned of the dangers of unfettered auto use were unnerved by the chill wind of hostility. A notable example was Colin Buchanan, whose name had become synonymous with efforts to protect towns across Europe from the baleful influence of car traffic. The success of the freeway revolts soon led him to protest that "the people who see cars as anti-social" may, "by thwarting urgently needed schemes, actually inflict far worse damage to the environment than the roads they are afraid of. . . . Why cannot we be less hypocritical and admit that a motor car is just about the most convenient device that we ever invented, and that possession of it and usage in moderation is a perfectly legitimate ambition for all classes of people."[8]

Any intellectual vanguard risks being accused of arrogance, for presuming that the majority is wrong; or, worse, of dictatorial tendencies, for trying to impose policies that fly in the face of habit and tradition; or of being entirely wrong-headed, that is, not a vanguard at all. (Critics will call them a "self-styled" vanguard, which of course they are.) Environmentalists, for example, have struggled against such accusations since the 1970s. If conventional wisdom about the automobile had changed, then what followed was a backlash, at least in the U.S. An early shot was fired in 1968 by the landscape historian J. B. Jackson, who styled himself an academic voice for the inarticulate majority. He accused urban planners of a snobbish refusal to acknowledge other people's emotional attachment to their cars: "strolling the streets, sipping wine at a sidewalk café, playing chess in the park, sampling the art galleries or gathering for darts at a pub are all considered worthwhile pastimes for the urban dweller, while repairing or grooming cars is somehow distasteful."[9]

The most vigorous manifesto of the backlash was Barry Bruce-Briggs's venomous 1977 book *The War against the Automobile*, a furious assault on the "small band of publicists and politicians" whose hatred for America's remarkable system of highways and automobiles threatened American freedom and prosperity. Bruce-Briggs argued that a snobbish contempt for the masses offered the only possible explanation for their hostility to the automobile. By the mid-1950s, when auto ownership had spread to the urban working class, "The middle classes now had to share the road with the workers, and they did not like it very much. It is no coincidence that both the agitation against the automobile and the promotion of mass transportation began when the urban workers switched from mass transit to the car. At its most vulgar level, the anti-automobile crusade is simply the attempt to drive the other guy off the road, particularly when he is not as sensitive, educated, or prosperous as we are. That lower-class slob has some nerve jamming highways in his junky old Chevy with his wife in curlers and his squalling brats beating on the rear window. People like that belong in mass transportation, in subways and buses, not clogging our roads and slowing us down."[10]

Bruce-Briggs claimed to unmask the dissembling car haters. Although Lewis Mumford, John Keats, and Daniel Patrick Moynihan had been rather blunt in their criticisms of cars, Bruce-Briggs refused to take them at their word. Their innermost beliefs, he intimated, must sound something like this: "So what are we going to do? Well, just what we've already done: convince ourselves that our interest is not selfish, but high minded. We are not cynical people like those nasty Europeans who do not mind stepping on the faces of the working classes—we are Americans, we believe in democracy, we have noble intentions. So to drive the rabble off our highways we must divine elegant justifications—that cars are unsafe, that they are polluting, that they are chewing up the landscape, etc., ad infinitum."[11] Bruce-Briggs also denounced the malign influence of environmentalists who meddled in other people's lives in order to remedy largely imaginary problems such as air pollution. But he reserved his bitterest rancor for what he saw as the sensationalism of Ralph Nader. Nader's ultimate sin was to trumpet the fact that automobiles might cause the occasional injury without calculating the damage against the immense good wrought by cars. It was demagogic, in Bruce-Briggs's view, to make too much of the death toll—50,000 Americans per year—without acknowledging that this was a price Americans willingly paid for the wonders of the automobile.

While this argument revealed Bruce-Briggs's inability to understand why anyone would be foolish enough to listen to Nader, it also offers a way of construing the battle lines in the automobile wars, with busybody Naderites aligned against satisfied consumers. The 1950s snobbery of a John Keats did indeed continue into Bruce-Briggs's 1970s and beyond. With telling spite, car supporters have long caricatured their opponents as Upper West Side liberals who can't see why everyone else won't sell their cars and just hail a taxi at their front door. Bruce-Briggs knew that even in the pessimistic 1970s he had popular opinion on his side. His boundless contempt for the anti-auto snobs fed on their failure to appreciate either the practical advantages or the emotional appeal of cars. Of Nader, Bruce-Briggs wrote, "it sometimes seems as if he thought the only function of the automobile was to crash."[12] This was a harsh take on Nader, who was merely demanding safer cars, but it offered a suggestive insight into the attitudes of the more militant car haters who soon came along. And yet it was not a new observation: a 1916 paean to the automobile lamented that the press portrayed it as "a juggernaut, a motoring speed-monster, intent on killing and maiming all who stand in its way. The motorist, in this view of the press, is an intoxicated savage, in charge of a dangerous device."[13]

Nor was this failure of imagination unique to America. The president of the French auto manufacturers' association anticipated Bruce-Briggs in 1970 when he denounced the "caricature of the automobile" propagated by "many distinguished minds . . . who see in it nothing but a cause of noise, pollution, congestion, and accidents, forgetting everything positive and irreplaceable about it."[14] Even earlier, in 1956, the Italian publisher Gianni Mazzocchi decried the "pseudo-agonistic spirit that transformed a car trip into a series of dangers," while ignoring the serene joys of motoring.[15] Indeed, European motorists had more reason to feel put upon by the 1960s and 1970s, since their cities had never been made as auto-friendly as those in the U.S., and they also had to pay much higher taxes for the privilege of driving, because of policies established during the many decades in which driving remained an exclusive luxury. Resentment of the automobile by those too poor to own one does seem to have largely disappeared after midcentury. Car ownership may not yet have been typical among the European working classes, but aspirations to car ownership were. The trade unionist who founded the Parisian "Pedestrians' Rights Association" in 1959 confessed ruefully in 1972 that his intent to organize the humble and the carless had failed; instead, he found himself at the head of an organization of well-to-do professionals, 70 percent of whom owned cars. He had, he acknowledged, not realized how many workers loved the luxury of a car.[16] What had emerged instead was an urban subculture of enthusiastic pedestrians, bicyclists, and transit riders, one that coalesced around new Green political parties in many European lands in the 1980s. These movements, in turn, sometimes generated their own backlash, for example the avowedly anti-environmental "Auto Party" that briefly emerged as a serious vote-getter in Switzerland around 1990.[17]

This was the European equivalent of the culture clash Bruce-Briggs identified, between ordinary car-loving people on one side, and meddling intellectuals on the other. His villains composed a "'New Class' of 'intellectuals,' academics, journalists, bureaucrats, and nonprofit professionals" dedicated to foisting their prejudices and ill-considered schemes on a majority that just wanted to be left alone.[18] Bruce-Briggs later published a book about this "new class," a term that became popular for some years thereafter among conservative American intellectuals who challenged the wisdom of government intervention in many areas, including urban planning.

As car critics acquired a voice, the resentment felt by early motorists re-emerged—for example, in an unofficial Conservative Party pamphlet from 1968, *The Plight of the Motorist*, by the automotive writer P. G. M. Gregory: "Become one of Britain's fourteen million drivers and it would appear that you are immediately regarded as a second-class citizen—a person to be abused, restricted, regulated, taxed almost out of existence, and shackled by a thousand different laws, by-laws and regulations."[19] The Conservative Party leader (and later prime minister) Edward Heath had already offered a more measured version of the same position in a 1966 speech opening the Motor Show: "Some people would like to push us into a frame of mind in which it is considered anti-social to own a car; selfish to drive one; and positively sinful to take it into a built-up area."[20] Germany's influential automobile club, ADAC, became famous for its strident defense of motorists' rights and its equation of motoring with freedom, as in this declaration by its president in 1967: "Personal freedom is the highest and most sought-after human good. The motor vehicle is the great means to attain this freedom. Anyone who wants to trample on freedom must first put in chains the means to this freedom."[21] ADAC's magazine even defended Charles Wilson's notorious equation of the good of General Motors with the good of the United States.[22] For all the club's celebration of freedom and mobility, a defensive tone had already crept into its 1965 "manifesto on motorized travel": "It is feeble, if not outright hypocritical, constantly to refer to the 'slaughter' or 'murder on the streets,' when one does so from an incomprehensible lack of appreciation for the goal of making the street once again into a place of humane encounters."[23] With the vision of "humane encounters," somehow made possible by traffic engineering, ADAC attempted to retake the moral high ground.

The polarization of opinion along the left-right political spectrum had begun amid the freeway revolts, as social-democratic and working-class political parties backed away from their earlier endorsements of motorization. In Europe, this partisan divide hardened by the 1970s, with conservative parties exploiting motorists' resentment against new restrictions. The automobile became, along with home ownership, the preeminent symbol of the autonomy and prosperity threatened by creeping socialism.

A prominent conservative journalist in Germany knew how to describe the choice in 1974: "In the next election this nation must conclusively decide where it wants to drive: by car to prosperity or by bus to the welfare state."[24] Germany was one of several European nations where Green parties subsequently emerged as the voice of voters skeptical of technology, unfettered markets, and automobiles. In Britain, perhaps the clearest case of an ideological split, the Conservative governments from 1979 to 1997 were determined to cut rail and bus subsidies along with much other government spending, and they did so by privatizing transit, which led to cuts in service that encouraged more driving. In 1989, the government announced a renewed commitment to ambitious motorway construction, after a combination of protests and funding shortfalls had largely curtailed the program during the 1970s. Critics responded with a wave of new anti-motorway protests, including the occupation of construction sites. These were coordinated by new, militant environmental organizations, which formed coalitions with local opponents of particular routes but proudly insisted that they rejected parochialism: rather than Not in My Backyard, their principle was NOPE: "Not on Planet Earth."[25] Although the squatters were routed, their efforts made it easier for finance experts to cancel other road projects, and for the new Labour government in 1997 to announce a shift in priorities away from road construction.

In the face of the revived anti-auto rhetoric of the 1990s, Bruce-Briggs's banner was taken up by other publicity-savvy American defenders of the automobile. James Q. Wilson, for example, a political scientist and prominent conservative intellectual, wrote a popular article in 1997 that contemplated the bleakness of a world without automobiles. The transportation scholar James A. Dunn, Jr., concluded that the manifest superiority of the automobile as a mode of transportation has been threatened by the "elitist social engineering schemes" of what he labeled "the vanguard" of self-anointed car critics.[26] By the turn of the millennium, a network of libertarian-minded American researchers and consultants (with occasional allies abroad) had launched a vigorous campaign to defend the supposedly imperiled freedom and efficiency provided by the automobile. Perhaps the automobile's most tireless defender has been the activist Randal O'Toole, who warned of the dire threat to what he called the greatest invention of the past two hundred years and the one that "has contributed more to the quality of life in America than any other."[27]

Those who deplore the enormous squandering of petroleum by cars, especially in the United States, usually think their efforts to promote energy conservation are thwarted by the entrenched interests of the oil companies in concert with the American manufacturers of gas-guzzling vehicles. They are not entirely wrong, of course, but they are also challenging sincerely held and deeply rooted convictions about the virtue of consumption, views that have not been entirely supplanted since the 1970s by the newer belief that there are limits to the Earth's capacity to absorb human exploitation of its resources. The conviction that growing auto use is unsustainable draws much of its strength from a belief that expanding highways, increased traffic, and suburban sprawl are visible evidence of an irresponsible dissipation of the Earth's resources. It follows that, among other things, people must alter their lives to prepare for the inevitable diminution of petroleum supplies and other energy sources.

It is a minority that openly and defiantly disavows this entire way of thinking. This minority contends that modern, Western, and especially American prosperity and optimism depend on a rejection of asceticism and self-imposed limits. In this vein, Bruce-Briggs argued that, among the car's enemies, "Limits-to-growth agitators favor energy conservation to discourage economic growth: 'consumer advocates' favor it because they are fundamentally opposed to mass consumption of consumer goods."[28] In the following decades, this contempt toward energy conservation remained an article of faith in certain American conservative circles, but rarely reached the wider public. A much-noted exception was U.S. vice president Dick Cheney's dismissal of conservation in a 2001 speech, when he said that it "may be a sign of personal virtue" but was no basis for an energy policy. As Cheney explained, he was wary of any imposition of limits and of "the temptation for policy-makers, the impulse to begin telling Americans that we live too well." In a similar vein, President George W. Bush's press secretary raised some eyebrows a few days later when he defended his boss's failure to promote energy conservation by explaining that "the American way of life is a blessed one" built on the use of abundant resources. A more forthright rejection of conservation could be found in such places as the *Wall Street Journal*'s opinion page, where Stephen Moore, the former head of the anti-tax advocacy group Club for Growth, scorned the intelligentsia's "perverse logic . . . that progress can be measured by how much of the earth's fuels we save."[29] Moore was updating the standard belief of a century ago, when "heavy industry" meant coal and steel, and a smoking chimney meant progress, not pollution— the belief that prosperity is best measured by how much fuel we burn.

This was the same thinking that rejected any analysis of "induced traffic" with the argument that more driving was inherently a good thing. Indeed, a variant of the belief that energy consumption creates wealth is the claim that mobility is the best measure of prosperity. Indexes of economic growth can be correlated to the physical movement of people and goods, a statistical correlation that invites us to see mobility as a proxy for growth and to conclude that more mobility means more wealth. Since mobility takes place primarily in automobiles, it follows that more driving means more prosperity, and that the "congestion coalition" that fights road construction is the greatest enemy of prosperity.[30]

Moore was confident, though, that the intelligentsia's perverse hatred of the car would never take root in the United States: even if "Green indoctrination" taught children that cars were evil, "once these youngsters got their drivers' licenses, their attitudes would change" and healthy common sense would prevail. "The good news is that environmental groups and politicians aren't likely to break Americans from their love affair with cars—big, convenient, safe cars—no matter how guilty they try to make us feel for driving them." Like Bruce-Briggs three decades before, Moore attributed hatred of the car to an influential but utterly unrepresentative minority, while the collective wisdom of the consuming public would continue to defeat the schemes of the busybodies Bruce-Briggs had labeled the "new class." In other words, the well-known emotional appeal of the automobile faithfully reflected its practical value.

Many people on both sides were confident that technology would come to the rescue. Car boosters dismissed problems of pollution, safety, and fuel supplies as overly hyped temporary glitches well on their way to solution. Proponents of electric cars, new high-tech transit systems, and other sustainable "green" technologies argued that they were the forward-looking thinkers, not mired in century-old habits and technologies. Unlike most car boosters, however, they sought government rules to make automobiles pay the full cost of their wasteful and polluting ways. New and fairer regulations, they believed, would enable the cleaner technologies to prevail. While support for energy conservation and mass transit typically reflected a belief in limits and a strain of asceticism, the world of cars remained the world of individual opportunity and free-market optimism—despite the fact that governments had devoted the twentieth century to building roads through town and country. Even as automotive technology entered its second century, the ideology of motoring remained optimistic, even heedless, while it was easy to depict car critics as pessimists and scolds. The can-do American in the tradition of Henry Ford—or perhaps of *Mad* magazine's Alfred E. Neuman ("What, me worry?")—faced off against Chicken Little, latter-day roadkill.

Bruce-Briggs's views, an echo of the auto industry's defense of its own virtue, not only ignored the powerful interests that promote cars, but also simply turned a blind eye, Nelson-like, to the disadvantages of automobility and the well-founded doubts people hold about it. Still, Bruce-Briggs's attack on the "new class," for all its conspiratorial bombast, does help explain why prophets of the car's imminent demise often failed to appreciate the depth of the automobile's hold on ordinary people—a failure most dramatically apparent in the resort to conspiracy theories to explain its triumph.

WHO FRAMED JUDGE DOOM?

One obvious reason for the persistence of American car culture in the face of all criticism was the lack of alternative means of transportation. Apart from a few cities that clung to their rail systems, by the 1960s transit had been reduced largely to poor service on decrepit buses. Why had American mass transit, especially the streetcars that were once the envy of the world, been so thoroughly dismantled? How could Americans have been so shortsighted? The answer was neither simple nor especially illuminating. Transit had been expected to pay for itself, but after ridership ceased to grow in the 1920s, the private franchises that operated most transit systems were unable to make money under the regulations imposed on them by local governments. As they cut service, former passengers bought cars, ridership and fare revenue declined further, and a death spiral ensued, leaving cities to pick up the bankrupt pieces, sooner or later, and to offer grudging subsidies to keep a barebones system running.

But there was another explanation that made more sense, one that gave the story a compelling logic, a redemptive meaning, and a villain. General Motors, the world's largest company, had knowingly sold unsafe cars; had tried to smear Ralph Nader; had invented the annual model change that made motorists slaves to fashion; had spent millions to persuade Americans that they should go into debt to have a car a little bigger and flashier than they (or their neighbors) already had. Many people not enamored of cars, of GM, or of large corporations in general had little trouble believing that GM had conspired to destroy mass transit, leaving Americans with no alternative to cars. Although the events in question occurred long before, only since the 1970s have people been ready to see the demise of streetcars in this new and sinister light.

The story's prominence can be credited above all to the zealous work of the antitrust attorney Bradford Snell, presented in a report to a U.S. Senate subcommittee in 1974. Numerous articles and books soon pointed to the GM conspiracy to explain the mysterious and catastrophic collapse of American mass transit. It became, and has remained, something close to conventional wisdom on the political left in the U.S. and beyond. Snell stated his case in an undiluted form in a 1996 documentary film, *Taken for a Ride*, which was broadcast nationally on PBS.[31] By then, however, the story had reached its widest audience thanks to the mythmakers of Hollywood. Robert Zemeckis's clever, partly animated 1988 film *Who Framed Roger Rabbit?* is set in the myth-shrouded golden age of Los Angeles. By the 1980s, frustration with that city's famously clogged and famously indispensable freeways prompted a wistful look back at the rail network of electric "Big Red Cars" that had knit together the expanses of southern California before its freeways did. The last of the Red Cars stopped running in 1961 and, for most moviegoers, had become bathed in the same nostalgia as colorful bootleggers and private detectives, fedoras, silk stockings, and Packard sedans. The film ultimately reveals the forces of evil to be manipulated by a character known as Judge Doom, who is conspiring to destroy mass transit. In the end, he shows his hand to the clueless hero:

JUDGE DOOM: Several months ago, I had the good providence to stumble upon this plan of the city council's. A construction plan of epic proportions. They're calling it a freeway!

VALIANT: Freeway? What the hell's a freeway?

DOOM: Eight lanes of shimmering cement running from here to Pasadena. Smooth, safe, fast. Traffic jams will be a thing of the past.

VALIANT: So that's why you killed Acme and Maroon—for this freeway? I don't get it.

DOOM: Of course not. You lack vision. I see a place where people get on and off the freeway. On and off. Off and on. All day, all night. Soon where Toontown once stood will be a string of gas stations, inexpensive motels, restaurants that serve rapidly prepared food, tire salons, automobile dealerships, and wonderful, wonderful billboards reaching as far as the eye can see. My God, it'll be beautiful.

VALIANT: Come on. Nobody's gonna drive this lousy freeway when they can take the Red Car for a nickel.

DOOM: Oh, they'll drive. They'll have to. You see, I bought the Red Car so I could dismantle it.

The beleaguered Valiant gives voice to the cherished belief of late-twentieth-century car haters: no one with any sense would drive if there were a pleasant alternative, as there once had been. Only in the movie is Judge Doom defeated: the real, car-choked, late-twentieth-century Los Angeles was all too recognizable as his dastardly creation.

The story that inspired this plot twist centered on National City Lines (NCL), a company founded in 1936 with support from the GM-controlled bus manufacturer Yellow Truck and Coach. NCL began to acquire transit companies in many cities (including the Los Angeles Railway, but not its regional competitor, the Pacific Electric with its Red Cars), and in most cases it promptly replaced street railways with motor buses. In 1947 the U.S. Justice Department filed antitrust and conspiracy charges against NCL, GM, and GM's partners in the venture—Standard Oil of California, Phillips Petroleum, Firestone Tire, and Mack Truck. Two years later, a jury convicted the defendants (except Mack) of a "conspiracy to monopolize" the bus business because, in return for loans from its suppliers, NCL had agreed to buy only their products, above all Yellow Coach buses. On the charge of conspiring to control the nation's transit systems, however, the defendants were acquitted. Thus the widely circulated claim that GM was convicted of conspiring to destroy streetcar systems is doubly untrue, since it was never even charged with such an act, and it was acquitted of the related charge of seeking to control the transit business.

In the puzzling illogic of the conspiracy theory, GM, through NCL, set out to destroy mass transit by acquiring streetcar lines in order to dismantle them and replace them with buses. Many streetcars were in fact replaced with buses in the 1930s and after—but buses are mass transit, too. Buses (so the theory goes) were just a means to drive riders away from transit and into cars, buses being so unpleasant, so clearly inferior to streetcars, that they could only have been intended as a ruse. Certainly streetcars offered advantages that some riders later recalled fondly, especially in comparison with the early gasoline-powered buses of the 1930s: they could be spacious (if they weren't too crowded), they could be fast (if they weren't caught in traffic), and they emitted no exhaust fumes. Even the new diesel buses that came into use during the 1930s spewed stinking smoke, and their engines were far from silent. But the nostalgia for smooth, quiet, comfortable streetcar rides departs from the reality of the 1920s and 1930s, when streetcars were in fact widely unpopular. It forgets the squealing of metal wheels and the queasy sway of crowded cars lurching around corners. And that was not the worst of it. Lingering Victorian morality, which feared wafting miasmas carrying moral as well as physical decrepitude, was apparent in a 1913 Los Angeles newspaper account of a streetcar ride: "Inside the air was a pestilence; it was heavy with disease and the emanations from many bodies. Anyone leaving this working mass, anyone coming into it . . . force[s] the people into still closer, still more indecent, still more immoral contact. A bishop embraced a stout grandmother, a tender girl touched limbs with a city sport, refined women's faces burned with shame and indignation—but there was no relief."[32] One can scarcely imagine a more urgent plea to flee the streetcar for an automobile, as millions did in the following years.

Electric streetcars predated automobiles, if only by a few years. Although they provided remarkably efficient transportation, they were also, like automobiles, a frightening menace on the streets, a fact that was soon forgotten amid the flood of motorcars. More fatefully, it soon became clear that streetcars and automobiles coexisted awkwardly at best in busy city streets. Collisions between them were common, as were even deadlier accidents in which embarking or disembarking streetcar passengers were struck by cars, just as motorists getting in and out of their cars were vulnerable to passing trams. For better or worse, hardly anyone before the 1970s thought of banning automobiles from the streetcars' paths, whereas traffic planners and civic leaders clamored for the removal of streetcars. They could, after all, be replaced by more maneuverable buses, if not by underground railways that would entirely remove mass transit from the street.

The technological limitations of streetcars were probably less of a problem than the economic circumstances in which the streetcar operators were working. Riders mistrusted companies they saw (with good reason) as greedy monopolists. Unpleasant rides in crowded cars reinforced their wish to escape from the monopolists' clutches as soon as possible. Already in the 1920s most American streetcar systems were losing passengers. Cities typically required the private franchises to operate on certain routes. In the face of declining ridership, the companies, which often were forbidden to raise the sacrosanct nickel fare, not only reduced service, but also failed to maintain their equipment. They deferred maintenance, and their trolley cars aged beyond a reasonable lifespan. (When they did raise fares, of course that made riders unhappy as well.) The cost of buying and operating buses on a given route was far less than that of laying and maintaining tracks for the more expensive rail cars, so transit companies across the country, whoever controlled them, were seeking to switch many lines to the promising new technology of motor buses. They argued that riders would prefer new buses to battered old streetcars—as, it appears, many did. Into this crisis stepped National City Lines. GM and its other backers, unlike the streetcar companies, were strong and growing businesses able to tap both deep pockets and goodwill.

The decline of the streetcar predated, outlasted, and far exceeded the alleged conspiracy. Streetcars were the old technology, compared to motor buses. Americans were buying cars in large numbers in the 1920s; they were moving to new low-density suburbs not served by trolleys; they were shopping at new auto-accessible plazas. The fixed tracks in the streets impeded the flow of cars, whereas buses could share the road space more efficiently. Even without the private franchises typical of the U.S., streetcars nearly disappeared from many other countries as well, including most of Latin America, Australia, New Zealand, India, Japan, Korea, China, Britain, France, Spain, and Italy. If there was a conspiracy, it was far bigger than General Motors and Standard Oil. The fact that highway interests had demanded the abolition of tramways since the 1920s certainly influenced the climate of opinion in many places, but so did the daily tussle of streetcar and automobile.[33]

In Europe, unlike the U.S., near-universal car ownership was conceivable only in the 1960s, and by then the disillusionment with the car was beginning to set in. Although many European cities dismantled their street railways (as early as the 1930s in Paris, among other cities), by the 1960s they were investing in other transit improvements, such as subways. If Europeans had less reason to be nostalgic about mass transit, there was still talk of the French trams having been the victim of an "automobile lobby."[34] The less elaborate French version of the conspiracy theory, widely shared among Parisian intellectuals in the 1970s, was that the recently deceased President Georges Pompidou had headed a cabal of economic and bureaucratic interests that forced freeways on a reluctant Parisian populace. As in the U.S., critics had forgotten how willing the populace had been, just a few years before. They pointed an accusing finger at the late Pompidou by citing his demand that "Paris must be adapted to the automobile." But as the historian Mathieu Flonneau points out, they have wrenched the quotation out of context. However ardent Pompidou's support for freeways, his notorious 1971 speech merely expressed a realistic acceptance of the automobile and warned against "a kind of aestheticism" that demanded a ban on cars in Paris in order to beautify the city: "The automobile exists. It is necessary to accommodate ourselves to it and to adapt Paris to both the lives of Parisians and the needs of the automobile, on the condition that motorists are willing to discipline themselves."[35]

Conspiracy theorists are right to reject the technological determinism according to which the inherent superiority of motor vehicles (buses, perhaps, and cars for certain) ensured their triumph. Streetcar technology was not inevitably doomed, as is apparent in the survival of streetcars across car-saturated Germany. But the conspiracy theorists fall for a particularly crude form of economic determinism when they argue that powerful profit-seeking interests hijacked markets and deprived consumers of choice. Political clout and cabals are not sufficient to explain the victory of road interests over rail interests in so many places. Nor can the car companies' secret influence (or their seductive advertising) explain the failure to defeat the automobile since the 1970s.

Nor is it sufficient, however, to argue that rubber-tired vehicles won out simply because people preferred them. The same partisans of the automobile who offer this explanation for the streetcar's demise often insist just as vehemently that the restoration of tram service in many cities around the world since the 1980s is the work of special interests flouting the popular will. While the automobile's defenders remind us that there are many reasons people like to drive their cars, their accounts tend to dismiss the role of the powerful interests supporting car use, as well as the path dependence—habits and entrenched structures in our economies and societies—that make the automobile an easy, convenient, even necessary, but not always wise choice. The claim that Americans (or Europeans or anyone else) drive cars simply because they want to goes only a little further in explaining our transportation system than the belief that people drive because they are forced to. Choices are always constrained by the available circumstances, and people are often complicit in creating those circumstances. Even if most commuters did, at crucial moments, prefer cars or buses to streetcars, they were choosing among the limited and imperfect alternatives available to them. Streetcars suffered not only from the limitations of their technology, but also from a political deadlock that left the transit companies, lacking the resources of a General Motors, unable to improve that technology. Healthier relationships between cities and transit companies would probably have preserved streetcar service in some places. Heavy public investments in street improvements gave a further advantage to cars as well as buses. That funding reflected partly a popular demand for roads and partly the economic and political clout of the carmakers and the highway lobby.

Among the forces influencing people's choices are taste and fashion. In the competition for street space between cars and trams, cars were newer, flashier, and more desirable. Neither efficiency nor popularity can entirely explain the fact that municipal leaders worldwide, from the 1920s to the 1980s, damned streetcars as old-fashioned and embarrassing relics. (Nor can the millions spent on car advertising, although the carmakers probably have good reason to believe they made a difference.) Long before anyone claimed to unearth a secret conspiracy to destroy mass transit, Lewis Mumford, for one, thought the "conspiracy" was there for all to see: "Our highway engineers and our municipal authorities, hypnotized by the popularity of the private motor car, feeling an obligation to help General Motors to flourish, even if General Chaos results, have been in an open conspiracy to dismantle all the varied forms of transportation necessary to a good system and have reduced our facilities to the private motor car (for pleasure, convenience, or trucking) and the airplane."[36] Mumford, while certainly ascribing more order to the process than was warranted, knew all too well that the traffic engineers and the highway lobby boasted not only political clout but also enlightened opinion and popular support in favor of their autocentric vision of transportation planning.

AUTOMOBILE DEPENDENCE

The decentralized metropolis depends entirely on convenient access by automobile. In it, driving has become a humdrum routine (if perhaps punctuated by moments of terror), even if car ads still try to seduce us with improbable images of the open road. Anyone who chooses to live without a car becomes an oddball or a recluse. Full participation in the new automotive metropolis means getting a car, driving it, and finding space on the road as well as a parking spot at every destination. The search for space perpetuates sprawl and thus requires ever more driving, which magnifies every drawback of the automobile. From the early days of automobility it has been apparent that cars not only enabled people to flee but also impelled them to do so, since too many cars create an environment that drives people away—whether with noise, vibrations, and fumes, or by putting up impassable barriers in the form of rivers of traffic or seas of parking. Driving becomes a habit and a necessity, as is all too apparent in the outbreaks of panic and hysteria that follow attempts (by governments in rich and poor countries) to raise fuel prices or otherwise reduce subsidies to motorists.

This problem is sometimes identified as "automobile dependence," a concept much discussed since the 1990s by the car's opponents as well as by scholars in various disciplines. Dependence has been interpreted both psychologically—people unable to imagine life or mobility without their cars—and structurally: if it is impossible, or extremely impractical, for people to work, shop, or socialize without driving, then they can be said to be dependent on their cars. Some critics opt for the stronger name "automobile addiction," which can also be understood psychologically, when applied to individuals, and structurally, if an entire society is addicted to its cars.

Libertarian auto boosters scoff at the notion that anyone is forcing people to embrace the mobility and freedom they get with their cars. They dismiss the concept of automobile dependence, like the General Motors conspiracy theory, as the fevered vision of people too clueless to understand why anyone would actually want to drive a car. Boosters argue that people make free choices, and that the failure to respect those choices is just a short step from a tyranny that prohibits choice, starting with draconian restrictions on driving. By their logic (drawing on conventional economics), the fact that people drive more and more is simple evidence of their growing freedom and prosperity.

Not everyone thinks this is the proper way to interpret long commutes on congested freeways and endless "trip-chaining" by the "chauffeur slaves" of suburbia. Although auto dependence is never absolute, it is real, even if it is the product of individual choices. We might consider auto dependence as being something like refrigerator dependence. Over the past century, people in many places eagerly acquired refrigerators, ever larger ones, as they became available and affordable. Owning them, they could buy more perishable food at once and not need to shop for it as frequently. A secondary result was that neighborhood food shops (and also some delivery services, notably of milk) gradually disappeared, making it difficult to shop as frequently or conveniently as before. The demise of these shops is sometimes lamented, but people who had refrigerators—that is, nearly everyone, in the typical North American or European neighborhood—scarcely noticed. As a result, though, people became dependent on their refrigerators.

The same logic applies to automobiles: because people wanted the mobility provided by cars, they paid the price. Yet surely the price has been higher. For one thing, use of a car can never be quite as universal as use of a refrigerator. Cars are much more expensive, both in what users pay to buy and maintain them, and in external costs for roads and pollution. Nor can everyone drive: some of the young, the disabled, and the infirm will always be dependent on other drivers or other forms of transportation. (Even in the United States, only two-thirds of the population has driver's licenses.) And the effect of planning for automobility has been to reduce other forms of mobility. This outcome became apparent decades ago, as many public-transit systems went into a death spiral when the loss of riders forced service cuts that encouraged even more people to drive. In addition, cities built for convenient driving and parking require ample space between homes and businesses: space for parking lots, for roads, and for buffers to placate people who do not want to work or shop, and certainly do not want to live, too close to the noise, fumes, and danger of traffic.

This sprawl causes the "enforced mobility" identified in the 1970s, and it is also the key to the structural notion of automobile dependence discussed more recently in publications by the Australian planners Peter Newman and Jeffrey Kenworthy. They are interested not in the psychology of drivers, but rather in resource use and in "sustainable" urban development, a goal they believe to be incompatible with land-use patterns organized around driving. For them, cities, not individuals, are car dependent, because of their sprawled layout. They define automobile dependence as "a situation in which a city develops on the assumption that automobile use will predominate so that it is given priority in infrastructure and in the form of urban development."[37] They equate low urban density with automobile dependence and blame it for the squandering of resources such as energy and productive land.

Their data show the cities of the United States to be uniquely auto dependent, combining very low urban population densities (even compared to Canada, although not to Australia) with long commutes and far more driving than anywhere else. In most of the United States during the past half century, and in pockets of other countries, the desire to shield homes from automobile traffic has encouraged the design of residential subdivisions with a minimum of access points to arterial roads. (The next logical step was the "gated community," where the single entrance to a subdivision is closed to unauthorized vehicles.) In other words, cities and especially suburbs have been laid out on the assumption that everyone will get around by automobile. Since that assumption is never correct, nondrivers often feel stranded, and hapless pedestrians and bicyclists are forced to negotiate the desolate fringes of roaring highways around suburban pods and commercial strips. Even in poor countries, auto-oriented development is surprisingly common, although car ownership is limited to a minority. As in 1920s America and 1950s Europe, it just happens to be the prosperous minority whose patronage is sought by business and, often, government. In such places, pedestrians and bicyclists sometimes reclaim their own transit corridors by sheer force of numbers, compelling drivers to make way for them—not that the lot of the pedestrian on the highway is less than dangerous. In most of the United States, by contrast, pedestrians are the forlorn few. Among those who are most often killed or injured in collisions with cars are immigrants from poor countries who negotiate the fast roads as best they can, perhaps as they did at home, but too often unseen by speeding drivers.

Europe lies somewhere in the middle. At the end of the twentieth century, car dependence was more of a topic of investigation in Europe than in the U.S., because there was reason to believe that much of the continent was poised on the brink, not yet having developed urban forms or individual routines as car centered as those in North America. In Europe, Australia, Canada, and in parts of the United States as well, many people live in places where it is fairly easy to keep a car, but also to use public transit or to walk or bicycle to many destinations. In most such areas, car ownership and use has grown rapidly in recent decades. It has ceased to be a luxury and become a habit, as is apparent, for example, in the growing use of cars for very short trips. Car dependence in these places is less a result of the utter necessity of driving and more a matter of choice and habit. Of course, even in the most auto-dependent parts of the United States, many car trips can reasonably be counted as optional, which suggests that this dependence is also at least partly voluntary. Although Newman and Kenworthy convincingly demonstrated that low urban densities and heavy auto use go together, they cannot prove their assumption that low density causes car dependence or, crucially, that greater densities would reduce it. In fact, efforts to reduce auto dependence, by increasing urban densities or by expanding access to mass transit and facilities for biking and walking, have often met with disappointing results.

Neither Newman and Kenworthy's models of urban geography nor simple economic formulas can effectively explain people's psychological dependence on their cars. It is helpful, however, to draw on the notion of path dependence. The French transportation scholar Gabriel Dupuy has sketched a model of structural dependence that lends itself to a psychological understanding as well. The steps of obtaining a driver's license (a "club effect"), acquiring a car (a "fleet effect"), and driving on the roads (a "network effect") draw an individual into a convenient, familiar, and popular system. "It is the fact that many others are in the system that motivates us to enter it (or to remain in it), to use a car, and thus to become dependent on it."[38] These "effects" are economic as well: once you have a license, a car, and good roads, the marginal cost of driving is much reduced. Structural dependence also begets psychological dependence where the difficulty of getting around without a car encourages car-centered habits. The Canadian transportation planner Lawrence Frank has argued that the tendency to build schools where children cannot walk to them has just this effect at an early age: "We are training the next generation to be auto-dependent."[39] Psychological dependence may also reinforce structural barriers, as growing car use leads to the deterioration of transit service, the neglect of sidewalks and bikeways, and a general failure to build communities that can effectively be negotiated except by car. Nor should we forget the intoxicating (and perhaps addicting) sensation known to early motorists and recent ones alike.

The choice to drive can be condemned as irresponsibly selfish, or as evidence of a lamentable addiction. Or it can be better understood through a careful examination of individuals' thinking, choices, and decisions, as has been attempted in a few recent studies. A British study of attitudes toward driving, entitled *Car Dependence*, was sponsored during the early 1990s by the RAC Foundation for Motoring and the Environment, an institution created (surprisingly) by the Royal Automobile Club to investigate how to "reconcile the need and desire for personal powered mobility with the protection of the environment."[40] Later in the decade, sociologists from the University of Göttingen carried out another rare survey of people's transportation choices in and around Hanover, Germany. Both studies treated car use as a matter of habit rather than structural constraint, a product of people's choices about their mobility. Indeed, an awareness of choices—driving versus walking to the store, taking transit to work, bicycling for errands—set these survey groups apart from most of their American contemporaries. The German authors could observe, for example, that getting around by bicycle was a nearly universal phase of adolescent life in the Hanover area. In Britain as well as Germany, access to transit was an accepted fact. Most American suburban youths in the 1990s, by contrast, had little experience with either transit or bicycles as practical means of transportation.

Investigators for both projects interviewed their subjects in some depth to understand their choices, going beyond the usual transportation statistics that merely count people's use of different transport modes. What they found was that the general and increasing availability of cars created growing expectations of mobility. Car owners could rarely imagine giving up their vehicles; to do so would be to exclude themselves from a good and normal life.[41] (Just as more roads can "induce" more driving, so, too, can the mere availability of cars.) The German sociologists interviewed many men and women who had recently acquired their first car, or their second car, or had moved from city to suburb in the knowledge that they would be driving much more—self-inflicted cases of the "enforced mobility" decried by car critics. These were people who had been thinking about the choice of whether or not to drive—to work, to shop, to socialize—and were aware of the tradeoffs involved. The trend toward more driving was nonetheless clear. Driving nearly always saved time (this might be less universally true in a bigger city); it made family trips easier; it offered independence and autonomy as well as mobility; and it permitted both individuality and sociability, since it opened up access to a wider choice of club life or organized leisure.[42] In other words, the equation of cars with freedom was alive and well, but so, too, was a degree of dependence. In the British survey, over a quarter of respondents said they would like to use their cars less.[43] That proportion may perhaps be offset by others who would drive more, if they could, but it does give evidence of a sense of dependence, even helplessness, or else of cognitive dissonance and a lingering sense of guilt.

Interviews can make decisions about car use seem more rational and calculated than they are. An Italian study, also from the 1990s, asked motorists to specify the maximum tolerable cost of driving, in time and money, and then calculated that most of them were far exceeding their limit.[44] Similarly, a more recent German study repeatedly observed people trying to minimize the costs of their own cars. Typically they counted fuel and parking costs as well as insurance, but not purchase price, repairs, taxes, or registration fees, ending up on average with an estimate equaling about half of their actual costs.[45] These results remind us of the extent to which the desire to have a car, or the inability to get along without one, has often trumped rational calculations.

The Germans interviewed for the Hanover project also showed an impressive awareness of the environmental cost of their driving, although they typically rationalized it by claiming that more and worse pollution came from other sources, or that technological fixes were solving the problem. Some also recognized that their behavior was counterproductive in a broader sense: for example, people who moved out of the city in part because of the plague of traffic knew that they were now, as suburban commuters, contributing to the same problem. Clearly, even a well-developed ecological consciousness prodded only a few to change their driving habits. Dutch surveys have come to similar conclusions: habit trumps ecological consciousness.[46]

These studies can certainly serve as ammunition for those who argue that the automobile is the ideal means of transportation for most people, and that policies should be directed toward making it easier to drive— by building more roads, for example. Meanwhile, even members of the anti-auto subcultures that developed in recent decades (notably in northern European cities) have acknowledged that their initial attitude—why can't everyone just kick the habit?—became hard to maintain in the face of increasing auto use everywhere, evidence of structural dependence or of an irresistible attraction. Many of these anti-auto Greens have become affluent professionals, members of a class that takes automotive mobility for granted. Out of their circles have emerged various car-sharing schemes that permit people to have ready access to a car, without owning one themselves. One of the goals of these programs is to offer a halfway step between car ownership and a completely car-free existence. Participants could be expected to drive much less than car owners, because the car would not be a habit, but rather a choice that required thought, planning, and a careful decision. Unfortunately for car opponents, these initiatives have often failed to break the car habit. German social scientists, observing participants in a car-sharing program in Berlin and Hamburg from 1998 to 2003, found that even among the ecologically minded urban milieu that gave birth to the program, there was little willingness to accept the tradeoffs inherent in car-sharing. Most people preferred to forego the choices and decisions: by owning a car, they did not have to ponder what mode of transportation to take for which trip.[47]

Auto dependence can also arise where cars are few. That may have been the case in rural and small-town America early in the twentieth century, or in Australia or Europe somewhat later. It is typical of poorer lands today, and offers evidence of the manifest advantages of the automobile: access to better residential quarters and to more job possibilities, as well as a source of employment and income, particularly in places where cars are still scarce.[48] Both the structural and the psychological notions of automobile dependence can help explain the attractions of the automobile to the poor as well. A car is not only the most visible artifact of a middle-class or first-world life, it also becomes a basic tool of such a life when cities are rebuilt with freeways, parking garages, and gated communities. In other words, this is a case of path dependence, where cultural habits and technological developments foreclose later choices.

China's rapid economic growth and urbanization makes it the most dramatic example of a newly flourishing car culture. Only since the 1980s have automobiles become available to more than a select few people in China. Those who could afford cars embraced them as both convenient tools and tokens of success. Government leaders, caught up in the enthusiasm, have worked hard to open up China's crowded cities to more cars. Their response to traffic jams has been to build new highways and to reorganize streets to improve the flow of cars. Some of their measures favor car traffic at the expense of the swarms of bicycles on which urban Chinese have long relied. Thus is added a further incentive to switch from bicycles to cars.

Traffic jams were not, of course, the only visible problem created by all the new cars. Their unfiltered exhaust (along with coal-burning factories) gave Chinese cities dreadfully filthy air and alarming rates of respiratory disease. Recent responses have included tailpipe exhaust controls as well as proposals to improve mass transit, discourage car use, and once again encourage bicycling. But these relatively feeble efforts pale in comparison to the eager promotion of automobile manufacturing and driving by many Chinese cities and regions since the 1990s. In another great triumph of the car culture, China may be on its way to adding hundreds of millions of cars to the world's fleet. (And the 2008 release of the inexpensive Tata Nano may give India a chance to do the same.) It remains to be seen whether China's culture and cities, or the world's air and petroleum reserves, can accommodate this burden.

Nor is it clear whether any policies can dampen the growing Chinese desire for cars—although models of relative restraint are available in other Asian cities such as Singapore, Tokyo, Seoul, and even Hong Kong. If there are successful examples of a lesser degree of car dependence, they may in fact come from east Asia, where most cities have very high population densities, guaranteeing that even moderate levels of car ownership will create massive traffic jams. Densities in the wealthiest Asian cities are lower than in the poor ones, but still higher than in North America or Europe. Governments have not responded with crash programs of urban sprawl, but rather with restraints on car ownership and use (along with expansion of rail transit), most drastically in Singapore since the 1970s. Although Japan ranks among the world's leaders in per capita auto ownership, its average private car is driven far less than even in Europe.

PLACES OF REFUGE: CAR-FREE ZONES

Although efforts to ban cars from entire towns have rarely been taken seriously, many cities have designated particular streets or zones from which cars are fully or partly banned. The origins of this practice can be traced partly to the most car-friendly policies. Plans to organize cities around auto-only roads, such as Le Corbusier's Radiant City, envisioned spacious pedestrian precincts between the highways. The pedestrians in Le Corbusier's drawings, mere dots dwarfed by the broad highways and soaring towers, do not appear to have interested him much, and Corbusian plans have generally left pedestrians wanting to rush from their homes or offices to their waiting cars. A different kind of pedestrian precinct, by contrast, seeks to tame the automobile, or at least to protect some places from it. The heyday for the creation of these zones was the decade after the publication of the Buchanan report in 1963 (although Britain was actually a laggard in the movement). They represented a notable retreat from postwar traffic-planning orthodoxy. The internationally active German consultant Kurt Leibbrand, for example, believed that since "the traffic problem is due to the shortage of road space," the creation of pedestrian precincts was a step in the wrong direction. "Doubtless this would be the cheapest solution at the moment. That is why the policy of traffic restraint is gaining more and more adherents. Moreover this approach takes account of feelings nourished by fear of too rapid technological progress."[49] He was wrong to blame parsimony for the

"This city is going to hell! That used to be a parking lot."

Figure 16. Pedestrianization from the motorist's point of view. © The New Yorker Collection 1975 Barney Tobey from cartoonbank.com. All rights reserved.

trend, but right to believe that it was driven by a fear that cars would overwhelm the cities.

Already in the 1920s, Bremen and Essen in Germany had experimented with pedestrian streets. Just after World War II, the most influential model was the Lijnbaan in Rotterdam, a centerpiece of the postwar reconstruction of that bombed Dutch city. Similar cases were Treppenstrasse in Kassel, Germany, and the center of Coventry, England, two other cities nearly leveled in the war and given entirely new shopping streets designed exclusively for pedestrian traffic. More typical, but harder to agree on, was the closure of an established shopping street to auto traffic. Early examples from the 1950s were especially narrow old streets such as Hohe Strasse in Cologne and Limbecker Strasse in Essen as well as several streets in Zurich. The Buchanan report's recommendation that auto traffic be channeled into major roads amounted to an endorsement of these pedestrian precincts. In the 1960s and 1970s, hundreds of European towns closed central shopping streets to cars, especially in West Germany and in neighboring lands, including East Germany. Initial controversy often yielded to widespread acceptance, as, for example, in Copenhagen, where a temporary closure of the Strøget in 1962, against the advice of traffic planners and merchants, proved to be popular and successful.

Many Mediterranean towns have de facto pedestrian zones where streets are too narrow or steep for cars. Otherwise, restrictions on cars in cities were slower to catch on in southern Europe, including France. Rome's attempt to establish an unusually wide pedestrian zone in 1965 proved to be a fiasco, so thoroughly sabotaged by uncooperative motorists that it was abolished after barely a week. Soon, however, the idea caught on across Italy, with Siena leading the way, followed by Bologna, which banned cars from a large central zone in 1972.[50]

Pedestrian streets did reach the United States, beginning with Kalamazoo, Michigan, which adopted a plan by Victor Gruen to pedestrianize its main shopping street in 1958. More typical, though, was a determination to keep traffic flowing, as in Fort Worth's rejection of Gruen's 1956 plan for a car-free downtown. Although many desperate American downtowns (especially smaller ones) created pedestrian streets, few of them thrived, and most were eventually reopened to cars. Leibbrand had predicted that a businessman on a pedestrian street "will seek a more favorable situation with regard to traffic. And so the economic decline of the old town begins."[51] He was generally wrong about Europe, at least for several decades, nor does his prediction entirely apply to the U.S., since American pedestrian zones were typically a response to a decline already well advanced. In Europe, by contrast, where most pedestrian streets were much more successful than their desolate American counterparts (few of the former have been reopened to cars), they may have benefited from having been established before the peak of the auto boom. The European stores generally held their own against suburban competitors, which was rarely the case in the U.S., where both car ownership and suburban shopping remained far ahead of Europe. Other American cities, led by Rochester, New York, in

Figure 17. A typical narrow Paris street (rue St.-Louis-en-l'Ile), dominated by cars, 2003. Author's photo.

Figure 18. A rare Paris pedestrian street (rue Mouffe-tard), 2003. Author's photo.

1961, tried to take on the suburban competition with a more radical pedestrian-oriented makeover in the form of a enclosed downtown mall. But downtown malls could not match their suburban competitors in providing either vast parking areas or convenient access for an increasingly suburban middle-class population. Instead, the true American equivalents of European pedestrian zones—later copied in Europe and beyond—were the suburban malls, which were also car-free shopping zones, albeit ones placed in the middle of parking lots. By the twenty-first century, even some European pedestrian zones were suffering in competition with these suburban shopping centers.

Wider pedestrian zones like Bologna's have typically been carved out of the venerable centers of old tourist towns. Elsewhere, there were usually too many objections to the hardship of doing without cars. What emerged as an alternative, especially for residential districts, was the practice of "traffic calming," pioneered in the Netherlands during the

1970s. Narrow or residential streets were not closed to cars, but the streets were designed to "tame" them. Low speed limits reinforced by narrow traffic lanes, cobbled pavements, and raised surfaces encouraged drivers to proceed very slowly, or to take another route if their destination was elsewhere—or even to recognize that proceeding on foot, by bicycle, or by bus or tram might be more practical. Dutch examples were widely copied in Germany, Scandinavia, and elsewhere in the following decades. Germans called them "play streets" because, for the first time since the appearance of automobiles, these streets were safe for children to play in. Elsewhere, wider bans on cars were limited to special occasions. Since 1998, occasional car-free days have been declared in over a thousand European cities at the instigation of activists who want to demonstrate that at least from time to time, city life without a car is bearable and even pleasant. In Japan, the regular Sunday street closures known as "pedestrian paradises" have been well established since the 1970s.

Traffic calming revealed a new attitude toward the automobile in the city. Because they acknowledged that cars were here to stay, the existence of these "home zones" (as they are called in Britain) might seem to be a less radical and more realistic but also more effective form of resistance to the incursion of the automobile. If earlier efforts to separate pedestrians from vehicles merely diverted the cars away from some places, to the detriment of others, traffic calming demanded that motorists yield to other uses of public space. The effort to slow down cars ran directly counter to the prevailing logic of the automotive age, since it forced cars to adapt to the pace and scale of the pedestrian city, rather than the other way around. (And indeed militant pro-automobilists denounce the practice because "the real purpose of traffic calming is to make it harder for people to drive.")[52] This European idea made inroads in the U.S. by the end of the century, offering an alternative to failed pedestrian shopping streets. "New urbanist" designers made it a centerpiece of new mixed-use developments. Major developers also embraced it, in an attenuated form, in the rapid spread of the new upscale shopping developments labeled "lifestyle centers," generic malls built as a pastiche of traditional main streets, with slow-moving cars permitted through them.

A related experiment in a few twenty-first-century European cities has been the removal of most traffic signs and signals, a radical and counterintuitive method of traffic calming based on the assumption that drivers will slow down and be more civil when they have to negotiate each interaction with pedestrians and other motorists. The experiment so dramatically reduced accidents and delays in the Dutch town of Drachten that the European Union has sponsored its emulation in several other cities across Europe. Throughout the twentieth century, traffic engineers worked to make driving more predictable and automatic as well as faster, with the goal of turning the human-automobile centaur into a driving machine. The deregulation of the street challenges the assumption that the human beings behind the windshield cannot be expected to engage in civil interaction with fellow members of a community. It also defies the general trend of the automotive age in turning its back on the ever-growing regulation and surveillance of the Western street in favor of a model more typical of India (or of the nineteenth century). It sacrifices one freedom—automotive speed—in favor of a bevy of other freedoms for motorists and nonmotorists alike.

Some crusaders hope to tame the car everywhere, while others merely try to carve out a few islands of peace and civility, whether roadless wilderness in remote mountains, pedestrian zones in city centers, or calmed traffic across residential districts. In a few North American and Australian cities and many European towns, certain urban neighborhoods have become strongholds of anti-auto sentiment, even if many of the movement's supporters still own cars. (Rarer and riskier have been newly built car-free developments, for example in Freiburg, Germany, and in Hong Kong.) These neighborhoods boast organizations working for car bans, traffic calming, and better provisions for pedestrians, bicyclists, and transit. Activists in Switzerland in 1979, followed by Germany and Austria a few years later, even founded national "transport clubs" to counter the influence of the national automobile clubs. A more confrontational approach has arisen with the monthly "Critical Mass" bike rides (begun in San Francisco in 1992 and now a fixture in many cities), when cyclists assemble in the streets to remind everyone that they exist and deserve respect—sometimes confounding and angering motorists (and police officers) unaccustomed to having to share their space. To counter motorists' blithe assumption that anyone not in a car is an obstruction to traffic, they chant, "We *are* traffic!" The sort of people who join these activities and organizations pride themselves on having arranged their lives to avoid auto dependence, relying instead on their feet and bicycles to get around their mixed-use neighborhoods, and on transit for other destinations. They are bearing out an ironic prediction made by David Riesman and Eric Larrabee in 1956, at a time when freeways and cars were widely hailed as the salvation of downtown: "The automobile may eventually be the savior of the American city, since it has restored to the decadent downtown centers their lost potentialities for uniqueness—in this case, the potentiality of the auto's absence."[53] The same year, the Swiss architect Hans Marti prophesied the movement's broader ambitions: "It could come to pass that the next generation will have to reconstruct a city destroyed by reconstructed transportation."[54]

Road Rage

"Only connect" is E. M. Forster's famous motto from his 1910 novel *How-ards End*. In it, the obstacles to Margaret Schlegel's ardent desire to main-tain her life as a coherent whole often come calling in the motorcars that move restlessly in the background of the story. Not only do automobile trips disrupt Margaret's struggle to make sense of the time and space of her life, they also seem to rupture whatever harmony still governs social relations, provoking rich motorists to brutal inhumanity as they treat other people as nothing but hindrances.

It is easy to dismiss Forster's portrait of motorists' coarse behavior as the grousing of another articulate reactionary distressed by the democ-ratization of mobility. Cars, we might conclude, simply appealed to the sort of people Forster didn't like—the very sort who ended up shaping the twentieth century. Yet the roadkill of history—technophobes mourn-ing a lost world and snobs blustering about good manners—were never alone in their qualms. Even enthusiastic motorists like Louis Baudry de Saunier and Adolf Schmal were honest enough to admit that automo-biles often brought out the worst in people.

The opening scene of Robert Musil's monumental novel *The Man without Qualities*, published two decades after *Howard's End*, plays out on a Vienna street in 1913. A strolling couple stumbles upon the com-motion following an automobile accident that has left a man lying mo-tionless after being run over by a truck. "Somewhere between her heart and her stomach the woman had an unpleasant feeling which she was justified in believing to be sympathy. After a pause, the man said to her,

'These heavy trucks that they use here have too long a braking distance.' With this the woman felt relieved and she thanked him with an attentive glance. She had probably already heard this term from time to time, but she didn't know what a braking distance was, and didn't want to know. She was satisfied to bring this gruesome event into some kind of order and transform it into a technical problem that did not affect her directly." Her salvation lies not in connecting, but in dissociating. To focus not on the anonymous victim, nor even on his broken body, but on the technological conditions of his demise, enables her to evade the pain that confronts her. The arrival of efficient ambulance attendants completes the process of turning an automobile accident into an orderly and rational event, and the escape from emotional reality is sealed with the addition of some fantastic (and utterly spurious) numbers: "'According to American statistics,' remarked the man, '190,000 people are killed there annually by autos, and 450,000 are injured.'"[1]

The novel experience of speed and dissociation was at least as thrilling as it was frightening. Just as Musil's modern woman does not want to "connect," the birth of the automobile coincided with an artistic modernism that often exalted (or at least was awed by) the disconnectedness of modern life, and automotive journeys stimulated the modernist imagination. In a 1904 story, the Belgian writer Maurice Maeterlinck praised the automobile as a magical creature that enabled speed to conquer space.[2] This reordering of time and space helped shape modern literature through its effect on Marcel Proust, who expressed his fascination with automotive travel in a 1907 article for Le Figaro and later worked the same impressions into his fiction. The speedy automobile, this "giant with the seven-league boots," yanked the veil from some of the mysteries of the countryside even as it compressed his impressions of places once observed only at greater leisure. The ever-changing view from a moving car showed him a new way of composing a picture of his world by juxtaposing multiple perspectives of once-familiar sights. (Virginia Woolf offered a similar observation in her 1928 novel Orlando, written just after she acquired her first car: "the process of motoring fast out of London so much resembles the chopping up small of body and mind, which precedes unconsciousness and perhaps death itself that it is an open question in what sense Orlando can be said to have existed at the present moment.") Soon after Proust discovered the automobile, the Italian futurists credited automotive speed with inspiring the dazzling blur of their paintings, and at about the same time this process of fragmenting and reassembling perspectives also gave birth to cubism. An explicit painterly nod to the automobile was the 1916 Matisse painting of a landscape framed by a car windshield.[3] Nor can the birth of the motion picture be separated from the view through the windshield: the automobile turned the landscape into a movie at the very time that film cameras began to capture automotive speed.[4]

Neither the flickering of memory nor lamentation for a lost world accounts for the way most people greeted the automobile. Hundreds of millions have chosen to obsess over, sacrifice for, and spend a great deal of their time in their cars. A good portion of common sense and decency advises us simply to respect their choices. Yet car critics, even if they refrain from condemning the foolish masses, remind us that automobility comes at a price—that stepping into a car means giving up something, which is presumably why Forster's fears have kept creeping back during the past century, like the guilt that haunts a hangover. Forster was not alone in his belief that the motorcar was uniquely suited to express the arrogance of the rich, and the democratization of driving has meant that we can all aspire to be petty tyrants of the road. In the end, the driver's sense of sovereign mastery and the bystander's perception of inhuman arrogance are two sides of the same coin. The abhorrence of cars is inseparable from their appeal.

CARS AND PRIVILEGE

One force working in the automobile's favor has always been its aura of wealth and power. That connection is less obvious in those twenty-first-century countries with a prosperous and motorized majority, but what was true there decades ago is still apparent in poorer lands. Long before motorists became a majority, their influence—reinforced by auto manufacturers, oil companies, and other powerful interests—helped them impose policies favorable to auto ownership and road construction. Those policies have of course been justified on the grounds that motorization benefits the entire society and economy, and that governments should help more people become motorists. The one-sided promotion of cars does not, however, work to the benefit of the carless minority (in wealthy countries) or majority (in poorer ones) when it weakens mass transit or forces pedestrians to negotiate high-speed roads, for example. In other words, the well-known fact that cars are status symbols as much as transportation machines has implications beyond the world of style

Figure 19. The dilemma of world motorization. Mike Luckovich cartoon, 1992. By permission of Mike Luckovich and Creators Syndicate, Inc.

and fashion. In societies that are car centered in both fashion and transportation (and few societies are not, in the early twenty-first century) motorization is tantamount to full citizenship, and a contented nonmotorist is almost a contradiction in terms.

The fact that cars can reinforce privilege has contributed to resentment of them. But those who are left on the outside are, understandably, less likely to demand that cars be taken away from the privileged than they are to want their own vehicles. And they may oppose restrictions on car use, knowing that these are likely to fall disproportionately on poorer and weaker motorists. Not only do the poor want to live like the rich, they must also negotiate cities built to accommodate the preferences of the rich—for example, with new freeways instead of sidewalks or transit systems. Prosperous Westerners who are tired of their cars often fail to understand how important personal mobility is for residents of poor countries, and how crucial the automobile is for that mobility. As long as cars seem to be essential tools of prosperity, they will probably remain symbols of it as well, and their numbers will continue to increase, especially in the burgeoning cities of the developing world, where cars are fouling the air, clogging the streets, exacting a fearful death toll, and becoming generally indispensable to a hectic modern life. It is not likely that many people will heed calls to voluntarily relinquish their mobility, nor do modest incentives seem to make much difference. Critics continue to offer alternative models of urban form and mobility, but these remain choices available to only a few. The grave crisis of civilization that some pessimists predict (whether precipitated by fuel shortages, global warming, or the collapse of urban order) may, in fact, if it arrives, be the only way to get people out of their cars—if it actually does so.

Since people see cars as liberating, and acquire them when they can, it is no surprise that automobiles are a fairly good proxy for wealth and prosperity. National rates of car ownership have tended to rise with per capita income. This leads auto proponents to describe the differences between the U.S. and the rest of the world as a simple function of wealth and time: as those other lands become more prosperous, their ownership and use of cars will follow in a kind of natural progression, unless governments impose draconian restrictions. Still, American car use exceeds that of most other wealthy countries by a far greater margin than does (by nearly any measure) American income. It is an America-centric or auto-centric view of the world that sees the U.S. as the natural model and most other wealthy countries as aberrations. Since cars are useful tools and status symbols at the same time, it is difficult to measure their practical worth or to predict how people will value them in the future. For now, their social prestige is largely unimpaired, despite all awareness of their drawbacks. But there are determined efforts afoot (by citizens and some governments) to loosen people's grip on their car keys. American mass motorization certainly did not occur in the absence of criticism, as we have seen, but unlike that of other lands, it long preceded the era of fundamental doubts about the car's sustainability. In Europe and Japan, and even in Canada and Australia, these doubts have permitted a degree of restriction on auto use, and a set of policies less wholeheartedly supportive of cars. It remains to be seen which path is followed by newly motorizing lands.

The theory of a natural progression also offers a partial explanation for the rise and fall of bicycles, which briefly ruled the road (often along with motorbikes) in many lands: in much of Europe during the middle decades of the twentieth century; in major Asian cities such as Jakarta and Seoul a little later; and in Vietnam and China still at the end of the century. People shift from bicycles to cars (often via motorcycles) because cars are more comfortable and useful, and because bicycles cease to be a respectable conveyance. The exceptions are the wealthy nations where many commuters and shoppers still travel by bicycle, notably Japan, Denmark, and the Netherlands. These are among the countries in which government policies have succeeded, at least up to the beginning of the twenty-first century, in holding car use well below the international norm and in maintaining reliance on alternative modes—walking and transit as well as bicycling. Singapore, too, has discouraged car use with heavy taxes and other restrictions since the 1970s. Car critics believe that these places can be models for our liberation from the car, while autophiles insist that such limitations on freedom are inevitably doomed, because people will insist on the irreplaceable mobility offered by their cars.

THE LIMITS OF FREEDOM

When the architectural critic Reyner Banham praised the extraordinary mobility that the drivers of Los Angeles took for granted, he also acknowledged that there was a price to be paid for freeway life. Mobility did not bring unfettered freedom; on the contrary, "what seems to be hardly noticed or commented on is that the price of rapid door-to-door transport on demand is the almost total surrender of personal freedom for most of the journey." Freeway driving, Angelinos' "most sacred ritual," required drivers to submit to the strenuous discipline of high-speed driving on crowded roads while maintaining the "illusion" that they were in charge of the situation.[5] The car does seem to feed dangerous illusions of freedom and control. As automobile advertising sustains our fantasies of the open road, a particular provocation of the freeway age has been the frustration bred by the failure of drivers' experience on clogged highways to measure up to their fantasies. In 1961, the German sociologists Wolfgang Hartenstein and Klaus Liepelt drew on survey data to conclude that this disappointment might be lethally coupled with the peculiar effect of experiencing the world from inside a car: "The auto driver does not like it when someone gets in his way. He sees his vehicle as a peaceful home, protected for his security and surrounded by 'armored' vehicles that restrict his freedom and mobility. He complains that there are too many cars, forgetting that his, too, is one of them. He objects to drivers' lack of discipline, forgetting that he moves over the pavement in a permanent state of aggression."[6]

A rush-hour commuter has plenty of opportunity to doubt that the automobile is a boon to humanity. From the beginning, as we have seen, critics and even boosters blamed cars for unleashing aggression and provoking violent behavior. An international flurry of journalistic and scholarly panic about "road rage" during the 1990s merely gave a new name to a long tradition. The U.S. led the way, partly because of its freeway-centered life, partly because of the millions of guns in the hands of its drivers. Shocking examples of violent and even lethal responses to minor altercations spawned professional as well as lay diagnoses of the breakdown of civility, along with attempts to define road rage as a medically recognized psychiatric condition, professional advice for keeping cool in the face of highway adversity, and a market for hand-held signs to compensate for drivers' inability to speak to their neighbors—signs that promoted calm and reconciliation ("Sorry!") as well as others designed to help vent the driver's rage more fully ("Learn How to Drive, Imbecile!" and "Speed It Up Already, Jackass!" being among the less offensive examples).

If car boosters have sometimes been loath to admit that the freedom offered by the automobile encourages aggression, advertisers have shown no such reticence. They appeal to the urge to dominate others in order to sell cars that are larger, faster, or flashier, if not simply to persuade people to escape the pathetic indignity of having to walk or ride a bus. These impulses are easier to justify when they are thought of as a defense against dangerous strangers. The SUV craze followed on the heels of the road-rage hysteria of the early 1990s, and Keith Bradsher's study of SUVs quotes marketers who admitted that they were appealing to insecure, vain, and selfish buyers dominated by a "reptilian desire for survival."[7]

The century-old conflict over speed limits also reveals a collective ambivalence about automotive freedom. Although many lives were probably saved by the nationwide fifty-five-mile-per-hour speed limit in the United States—which was imposed in 1974 not for safety, but rather to save fuel—support for it faded quickly (as did observance and enforcement) until it was eventually repealed. Nor have decades of effort succeeded in imposing a speed limit on Germany's legendary and crowded autobahns. The effect of such a speed limit on safety is disputed (even if the horror of a hundred-mile-per-hour crash is not), as is the degree of its potential contribution to Germany's unmet goals for energy conservation and greenhouse-gas emissions. Still, there are few practical reasons not to impose one, even if one can, by contrast, make a case for permitting fast driving across the expanses of Montana (which restored a speed limit in 1999 after only four years without one). The fact that Germans passionately defend the open autobahn as their last bastion of freedom might be a sad commentary on the state of German masculinity, but it is clear that German politicians, otherwise more ecologically minded than most, have not dared to offend their speed-loving constituents, even while the Green Party belonged to the governing coalition from 1998 to 2005. That government was headed by the Social Democrat Gerhard Schröder, whose devotion to cars and to the auto industry made him known as the "auto chancellor" and probably contributed to his popularity.

If the motorist's freedom sometimes seems illusory, the nonmotorist lacks even the illusion. The motoring majority gives little thought to the dangers and hardships that speeding cars, wide roads, and auto-fueled sprawl impose on nonmotorists, whether on foot, on bicycles, using mass transit, or stranded at home—children, the poor, the disabled, or the occasional perverse autophobe. Much-trumpeted reductions in pedestrian fatalities have often come at the cost of children's independent mobility—that is, by driving pedestrians off the streets entirely.[8]

The freedom that comes with an automobile—freedom from place, from oversight and hierarchies, from nosy neighbors, and even from family—is of course the very kind that can resemble isolation, alienation, or anomie; and one of the roots of anti-auto hostility is a nostalgia for local communities that have fallen victim to modern mobility. Critics of modern society and technology in general, and of the automobile in particular, often romanticize urban sociability and leisurely movement. The mundane reality of the bustling cities they recall—the continual jostling of a busy sidewalk or a crowded streetcar—might have invigorated the aristocratic flaneur, but it also provoked its equivalent of road rage often enough. A stroll across the countryside might make it easier to "only connect" the destinations of one's life, or it might be a journey so arduous, time consuming, and dull that it is rarely undertaken at all. Mobility has its uses as well as its abuses, and much of the easy individual mobility we take for granted has become essential to the modern city or country dweller.

For better or worse, the automobile has profoundly reshaped the times and places of human interaction. Although it shares some characteristics with its more exclusive predecessor, the private carriage, it ensures that encounters with others will occur at a different rhythm than those experienced by train passengers, pedestrians, or carriage riders. Indeed, partisans of walking—in the country or the city—lament that too few people experience the world on foot.[9] Perhaps they can be dismissed as eccentrics, and the oft-alleged links between auto use, lack of exercise, and obesity are difficult to prove, but the disappearance of walking in many places (or its failure to emerge in the typical suburb) has certainly changed the way human beings use their bodies and interact with their environment as well as their neighbors, as E. M. Forster already saw a century ago.

Even in the early days of the automobile, witnesses observed that motorists were less likely than drivers of horse-drawn wagons to stop and offer rides to hitchhikers or pedestrians. Car owners explained that the wear and tear on their brakes and gears made it inadvisable for them to stop for mere social reasons. Soon the sheer speed of the automobile ensured that motorists would be shielded from contact with others as long as they were moving, and closed cars protected them from strangers as well as weather, even when stopped. The automobile really is the futuristic pod of science fiction, indeed, increasingly so, as it is outfitted with more and more creature comforts. Within the metal cocoon, a motorist is shielded from the unpleasantness (if also the pleasures) that lurk outside, including the noise, fumes, and human occupants of everyone else's car. The outside world intrudes only when an obstruction blocks the way—and exposes the limits of automotive freedom.

NOW WHAT?

Is the automobile age coming to an end? Or does the car still have a glowing future? Plenty of people will proclaim one or the other. The prophets of doom do not have a good record of prediction so far. The automobile was not strangled in its infancy, much to their regret. It became an article of mass consumption and survived the condescension of the cognoscenti. It clogged up the old cities, but the cities did not defeat it; indeed, perhaps it defeated the cities, although that defeat is not yet final. It exacted a fearful death toll, and poisoned the air, and started a global oil addiction, but it has been made much safer, cleaner, and more efficient, permitting it to go on choking and killing and maiming at a slower rate.

Auto ownership continues to grow almost everywhere, from the newly prosperous parts of southern and eastern Europe, to the burgeoning cities of the developing world, and most spectacularly in China. The world's fleet totaled 100 million in 1956, 500 million in 1986, and 800 million in 2007; the billionth car is not far off. Growth is not at an end even in the

United States, where there are more private motor vehicles than licensed drivers. That presumably guarantees that not all are on the road at once (rush-hour grumbling to the contrary), but Americans still managed to increase their driving every year from 1980 to 2004, reaching nearly fourteen thousand miles per motorist, nearly twelve thousand per vehicle. Few other lands approach those numbers, but elsewhere, too, people are driving more and more.

For hundreds of millions of people, a car continues to be their proudest possession, their greatest symbol of success, and also a practical tool for negotiating cities. The modern city is, in fact, inconceivable without the automobile, anywhere in the world. The few car-free towns are the exceptions that prove the rule, theme parks where people take a vacation from their cars. They include thoroughly artificial towns like Disney's Main Street U.S.A.; Colonial Williamsburg, a more serious place but still a historical theme park; vacation islands like Mackinac; a remote ski resort, Zermatt, in Switzerland; and Venice, a great and glorious city that is slowly turning into a theme park because that seems to be its only economic niche. Even if we leave aside the trucks and vans that keep cities supplied and serviced, as well as the buses and taxis that offer an alternative to driving oneself, it is not only auto enthusiasts and the hopelessly car dependent who count on their private cars to enable them to work, play, and find adventure in the metropolis.

Cities that are pure creations of the automobile age—a Phoenix or a Dubai—are more auto dependent, and more rapidly growing, than their older rivals that grew up around walking, draft animals, and railways. The poor and crowded metropolises of the developing world are also increasingly organized around automotive mobility. Most are vast and sprawling, and few have extensive rail networks. Even if most residents do not own cars, they count on the mobility provided by taxis, jitneys, and buses.

Change seems both inevitable and vitally necessary. Yet it does not appear imminent. For decades, technological optimists have proclaimed that new inventions were about to solve the problems of congestion and traffic, access and parking, pollution and energy. But neither flying cars, nor minicars, nor pods on tracks, nor jetpacks have yet driven any cars off the road. Presumably some of these futuristic technologies will someday be incorporated into automobiles. Certainly the Global Positioning System makes feasible some of the decades-old proposals to increase freeway capacity and safety by having drivers temporarily relinquish control of their vehicles, with relief or reluctance, to some centralized system. Someday it may also be possible to separate the practical and recreational uses of cars. In its earliest days, the automobile was primarily a toy, and perhaps it will be again, as the media theorist Marshall McLuhan predicted already in the 1960s. He and other prophets of technological progress have long argued that in the electronic age, the physical mobility offered by cars already matters far less than it did before. So far, however, people are moving about more rather than less.

For a long time already and, it seems, for some time to come, transportation decisions and transportation policies remain a simple choice: The car or not the car? For the car or against it? And so far the choice always seems to be the car. The problems caused by automobiles have been widely acknowledged from the beginning. Since 1970 or so they have been incorporated into conventional thinking about the need for new transportation policies to reduce auto accidents, pollution, energy consumption, and urban blight. Treatises from the past four decades start from the assumption that the current level of auto use is unsustainable. For nearly as long there has been a backlash questioning the extent of the problems as well as the feasibility of all possible solutions. More important, individual decisions have consistently favored greater car use, whether in spite of public policies to discourage it or because of policies that encourage it.

There is, then, good reason to conclude that the car has triumphed, and that its opponents are spitting into the wind. Even as millions of Chinese and Indians are eager to live and drive like Americans, however, the world has scarcely begun to come to terms with the resource use and the future urban world that such habits would imply. Nothing illustrates the stalemate more than the current state of automotive polemics, if that is the word for an argument in which the two sides talk past each other. On one side we have passionate denunciations of the evil machines, along with confident predictions that the coming environmental or oil crisis will ensure their demise. The car has become the leading symbol of our "unsustainable" lives, dependent on diminishing resources while inexorably poisoning our world. Meanwhile, the other side either ridicules these premises—dismissing "sustainability" as flawed economics and global warming as an overblown scare, if not a hoax—or simply ignores them. People have made their choice, according to this way of thinking, and it is up to governments and markets to give them what they want. A philosopher argues that "automobile motoring is a good because people wish to engage in it, and they wish to engage in it because it is inherently good."[10] A more sober study concludes, "People prefer driving their cars because that is the most comfortable and convenient way for them to travel, so it makes sense to pursue public policies that enable people to enhance their quality of life."[11]

It does make sense—if we understand the automobile to be a fundamentally benign (or desirable) tool. It makes sense if we assume that the earth and the market and the cities will somehow accommodate hundreds of millions of additional cars in China and India. It makes sense if we believe that our increasingly car-centered lives are indeed the lives we want. It makes sense if we can agree that the dark side of automobility is a price worth paying for its blessings. But we have never agreed about these matters, and we never will.

Acknowledgments

Several scholars have been kind enough to share their knowledge with me. My main debts, however, are to their published works. I have used the notes to acknowledge those debts, although the notes make no pretense of completeness, just as the book does not pretend to be the last word on any of its far-flung topics.

The writing of this book has been (like most car trips) a solitary endeavor. However, I am grateful to Donna Harsch for her valuable comments on an early draft, and to the press's anonymous readers as well. I would also like to thank the many language teachers I have had (most of them very briefly) over the years. I may be barely able to stammer out my thanks, but their efforts opened up worlds to me, and made this book possible. To my steady companions, Louise and Clare, I am grateful for many, many things, including their good-humored tolerance for my occasional rants about the stupidity of something I had just read. Their willingness to dismiss my outbursts has spared readers from having to endure them.

At the University of Chicago Press, I have enjoyed Susan Bielstein's encouragement since I first broached the project. Thanks as well to the others at the press who have turned this into a book, including Anthony Burton for organizing illustrations and Kate Frentzel for judicious copyediting. For their work in digging out a photo, special thanks are also due to the kind people at the city of Luxembourg and its Tramways and Bus Museum.

Despite the topic, this has been a sedentary project. I have relied on the library of the University at Albany, especially its hardworking interlibrary loan staff. Although the project benefited from a certain amount of travel, I am not going to thank my car. (A Prius is still just a car.) Instead, I want to dedicate the book to my parents, George and Marlys Ladd. This would probably be a different book if I had grown up on the Upper West Side, thinking that the typical car was a yellow Checker. I am a child of the American car culture—but with a difference. In the heyday of mammoth Chevys and Fords, my parents reared me in the back seat of a Rambler and the front seat of a Datsun, thus (I now realize) launching me on a lifelong quest to figure out if I was missing out on something. I was, as it turns out, and I'm glad I did.

Notes

INTRODUCTION

1. "The Hooting Nuisance," *The Living Age*, no. 3502 (19 Aug. 1911): 508–9.

2. John R. Meyer and José A. Gómez-Ibáñez, *Autos, Transit, and Cities* (Cambridge, MA: Harvard University Press, 1981), 290–95, make the point that subsidies are extended not just to cars or to transit but to both, that is, to mobility in the U.S. (which is certainly not unique). The argument that a calculation of subsidies should not dictate transportation policy is made by Mark A. Delucchi, "The Annualized Social Cost of Motor-Vehicle Use in the U.S., Based on 1990–1991 Data," in *The Full Costs and Benefits of Transportation*, ed. David L. Greene, Donald W. Jones, and Mark A. Delucchi (Berlin: Springer, 1997), 27–68; and Delucchi, "Should We Try to Get the Prices Right?" *Access* 16 (Spring 2000): 10–14. In this book, I have used few statistics, avoiding many opportunities to impart an illusory precision to matters that are in dispute.

3. Among the best general works are Wolfgang Sachs, *For the Love of the Automobile: Looking Back into the History of our Desires*, trans. Don Reneau (Berkeley: University of California Press, 1992); James J. Flink, *The Automobile Age* (Cambridge, MA: MIT Press, 1988), primarily about the U.S.; Tom McCarthy, *Auto Mania: Cars, Consumers, and the Environment* (New Haven: Yale University Press, 2007), on the U.S.; Kurt Möser, *Geschichte des Autos* (Frankfurt: Campus, 2002), mainly on Germany; Federico Paolini, *Un paese a quattro ruote: Automobili e società in Italia* (Venice: Marsilio, 2005); Federico Paolini, *Storia sociale dell'automobile in Italia* (Rome: Carocci, 2007); Mathieu Flonneau, *Paris et l'automobile, un siècle de passions* (Paris: Hachette, 2005); Graeme Davison, *Car Wars: How the Car Won Our Hearts and Conquered Our Cities* (Crows Nest, NSW: Allen & Unwin, 2004), on Melbourne, Australia; and, for Britain, the more narrowly focused but indispensable William Plowden, *The Motor Car and Politics, 1896–1970* (London: Bodley Head, 1971).

1. F. A. Hyde, "Automobile Club of California," *Overland Monthly*, Aug. 1902, reprinted in *The Quotable Car: A Literary Mozaic Highlighting Changing Views of Automobility*, ed. Kenneth Schneider and Blanche Schneider (Berkeley: Continuing Education in City, Regional, and Environmental Planning, University Extension, University of California, Berkeley, 1973), 93. This chapter, far more than the others, draws on a body of solid historical scholarship. Among the most useful studies are Michael L. Berger, *The Devil Wagon in God's Country: The Automobile and Social Change in Rural America, 1893-1929* (Hamden, CT: Archon Books, 1979); Ashleigh Brilliant, *The Great Car Craze: How Southern California Collided with the Automobile in the 1920s* (Santa Barbara: Woodbridge, 1989); David Blanke, *Hell on Wheels: The Promise and Peril of America's Car Culture, 1900-1940* (Lawrence: University Press of Kansas, 2007); Sean O'Connell, *The Car and British Society: Class, Gender and Motoring, 1896-1939* (Manchester: Manchester University Press, 1998); Peter Thorold, *The Motoring Age: The Automobile and Britain, 1896-1939* (London: Profile, 2003); Christoph Maria Merki, *Der holprige Siegeszug des Automobils 1895-1930: Zur Motorisierung des Strassenverkehrs in Frankreich, Deutschland und der Schweiz* (Vienna: Böhlau, 2002); Uwe Fraunholz, *Motorphobia: Anti-automobiler Protest in Kaiserreich und Weimarer Republik* (Göttingen: Vandenhoeck und Ruprecht, 2002); Frank Uekoetter, "Stark im Ton, schwach in der Organisation: Der Protest gegen den frühen Automobilismus," *Geschichte in Wissenschaft und Unterricht* 54 (2003): 658-70; and Dorit Müller, *Gefährliche Fahrten: Das Automobil in Literatur and Film um 1900* (Würzburg: Königshausen und Neumann, 2004).

2. Aldous Huxley, "Wanted, a New Pleasure," in *Music at Night* (London: Chatto and Windus, 1949), 255.

3. Edith Wharton, *A Motor-Flight through France* (New York: Scribner, 1908), 1.

4. C. E. M. Joad, *The Babbitt Warren* (New York: Harper, 1927), 13, 16–17.

5. C. E. M. Joad, *Under the Fifth Rib: A Belligerent Autobiography* (New York: Dutton, 1933), 197–98.

6. Sombart in *Allgemeine Automobil-Zeitung*, 16 Mar. 1929, reprinted in Merki, *Der holprige Siegeszug*, 453. Earlier German examples, from the first years of the century, are found in Müller, *Gefährliche Fahrten*, 22–23.

7. Joad, *Babbitt Warren*, 15.

8. Sheila Kaye-Smith, "Laughter in the South-East," in *Britain and the Beast*, ed. Clough Williams-Ellis (London: J. M. Dent and Sons, 1937), 34.

9. Joad, *Under the Fifth Rib*, 198. On wilderness protection: Paul S. Sutter, *Driven Wild: How the Fight against Automobiles Launched the Modern Wilderness Movement* (Seattle: University of Washington Press, 2002); David Louter, *Windshield Wilderness: Cars, Roads, and Nature in Washington's National Parks* (Seattle: University of Washington Press, 2006).

10. Joad, *Babbitt Warren*, 15.

11. From *Motor*, July 1922, quoted in *Annals of the American Academy of Political and Social Science* 116 (Nov. 1924): 19.

12. Joad, *Babbitt Warren*, 18.

13. J. Walker Smith, *Dustless Roads, Tar Macadam* (London: Charles Griffin, 1909), 1, quoted in Gijs Mom, "Constructing Multifunctional Networks," in *Road History*, ed. Gijs Mom and Laurent Tissot (Neuchatel: Alphil, 2007), 40.

14. Richard Braunbeck in *Allgemeiner Schnauferl-Club, Festschrift 1900–1925* (Berlin, 1925), 63–64, quoted in Barbara Haubner, *Nervenkitzel und Freizeitvergnügen: Automobilismus in Deutschland 1886–1914* (Göttingen: Vandenhoeck und Ruprecht, 1998), 152.

15. Merki, *Der holprige Siegeszug*, 365.

16. Beverly Rae Kimes, "Willie K.: Saga of a Racing Vanderbilt," *Automobile Quarterly* 15(1977): 319, attributes this story to the *St. Louis Star*.

17. *Allgemeine Automobil-Zeitung*, no. 28 (1904): 31, quoted in Haubner, *Nervenkitzel*, 161. On prejudices against supposedly lazy carters, see Martin Scharfe, "'Ungebundene Circulation des Individuen,' Aspekte des Automobilfahrens in der Frühzeit," *Zeitschrift für Volkskunde* 86 (1990): 238–42; and Scharfe, "Pferdekutscher und Automobilist," in *Mensch und Tier: Kulturwissenschaftliche Aspekte einer Sozialbeziehung*, ed. Siegfried Becker and Andreas C. Bimmer (Marburg: Jonas, 1991), 139–62.

18. *Motori, Cicli e Sports*, 22 Sept. 1912, quoted in Sara Moscatelli, "Il veicolo della modernità: l'automobile," in *La capitale dell'automobile: Imprenditori, cultura e società a Torino*, ed. Paride Rugafiori (Venice: Marsilio, 1999), 13.

19. *Allgemeine Automobil-Zeitung*, no. 11 (1909): 27, quoted in Haubner, *Nervenkitzel*, 151.

20. Quoted in William Plowden, *The Motor Car and Politics, 1896–1970* (London: Bodley Head, 1971), 277.

21. Quoted in Uekoetter, "Stark im Ton," 659.

22. Ilya Ehrenburg, *The Life of the Automobile*, trans. Joachim Neugroschel (New York: Urizen, 1976), 135.

23. S. Daule, "Der Krieg gegen das Auto," cited in *Allgemeine Automobil-Zeitung*, no. 16 (1906): 43–44, and quoted in Haubner, *Nervenkitzel*, 160.

24. Octave Mirbeau, *Sketches of a Journey*, trans. D. B. Tubbs (London: Philip Wilson, 1989), 132.

25. O'Connell, *Car and British Society*, 164–65.

26. Quoted in Bernd Utermöhlen, "Margarete Winter—eine Automobilistin aus Buxtehude," *Technik und Gesellschaft* 10 (1999): 278.

27. James J. Flink, *America Adopts the Automobile, 1895–1910* (Cambridge, MA: MIT Press, 1970), 68; Reynold M. Wik, *Henry Ford and Grass-roots America* (Ann Arbor: University of Michigan Press, 1972), 17.

28. Haubner, *Nervenkitzel*, 159; Hans Strassl, "Das Hennigsdorfer Automobilattentat," *Kultur und Technik* 11, no. 1 (1987): 62–65.

29. Edwin P. Hoyt, *The Vanderbilts and Their Fortune* (Garden City: Doubleday, 1962), 323, 345–46; Kimes, "Willie K.," 323; Fraunholz, *Motorphobia*, 234, 251.

30. Wik, *Henry Ford*, 17; Fraunholz, *Motorphobia*, 152–53; on armed French motorists, Catherine Bertho Lavenir, *La roue et le stylo: Comment nous sommes devenue touristes* (Paris: Editions Odile Jacob, 1999), 203; on the U.S., Tom McCarthy, *Auto Mania: Cars, Consumers, and the Environment* (New Haven: Yale University Press, 2007), 11–12.

31. Merki, *Der holprige Siegeszug*, 181.

32. Philipp Köhler, quoted in Fraunholz, *Motorphobia*, 198.

33. Fraunholz, *Motorphobia*, 208.

34. Uekoetter, "Stark im Ton," 551–52.

35. Quoted in Philip Bagwell and Peter Lyth, *Transport in Britain: From Canal Lock to Gridlock* (London: Hambledon and London, 2002), 89.

36. Reproduced in *Royal Automobile Club Journal*, 20 Aug. 1908, and in Mick Hamer, *Wheels within Wheels: A Study of the Road Lobby* (London: Routledge and Kegan Paul, 1987), 26, and quoted in Plowden, *Motor Car and Politics*, 81.

37. *Dexter (MI) Leader*, 10 Sept. 1903, quoted in Lowell Juilliard Carr, "How the Devil-Wagon Came to Dexter: A Study of Diffusional Change in an American Community," *Social Forces* 11 (1932): 67.

38. Hesse, *Der Steppenwolf* (Zurich: Büchergilde Gutenberg, 1927), 239.

39. Berger, *Devil Wagon*, 25.

40. Merki, *Der holprige Siegeszug*, 147–66; Wolfgang Sachs, *For the Love of the Automobile: Looking Back into the History of Our Desires* (Berkeley: University of California Press, 1992), 18–21. On a neighboring canton where opponents were less successful, see Rolf Gisler-Jauch, *Uri und das Automobil—des Teufels späte Rache?* (Altdorf: Gisler, 1994). The same defense of tourism against automotive intrusion was used against Spain's Costa Blanca freeway in the 1970s: Mario Gaviria, *Libro negro sobre la autopista de la Costa Blanca* (Valencia: Editorial Cosmos, 1973), 354.

41. Berger, *Devil Wagon*, 25.

42. Flink, *America*, 188; Angela Zatsch, *Staatsmacht und Motorisierung am Morgen des Automobilzeitalters* (Konstanz: Hartung-Gorre, 1993), 233; Theo Gubler, *Der Kampf um die Strasse* (Bern: Verlag der ASPA, 1953), 66–69. Discontent with insufficiently militant resistance to speed traps prompted a secession from the Royal Automobile Club that led to the creation of Britain's Automobile Association in 1905. See Thorold, *Motoring Age*, 41.

43. *Horseless Age*, 30 July 1902, quoted in Flink, *America*, 188.

44. Flink, *America*, 191; Plowden, *Motor Car and Politics*, 97–106; Clive Emsley, "'Mother, What Did the Policeman Do When There Weren't Any Motors?' The Law, the Police and the Regulation of Motor Traffic in England, 1900–1939," *Historical Journal* 36 (1993): 369–70.

45. *Allgemeine Automobil-Zeitung*, e.g., 13 Oct. 1928; Mathieu Flonneau, *Paris et l'automobile, un siècle de passions* (Paris: Hachette, 2005), 47; J. S. Dean, *Murder Most Foul: A Study of the Road Deaths Problem* (London: George Allen and Unwin, 1947), 83–84.

46. Flink, *America*, 193–99.

47. "Motorists Don't Make Socialists, They Say," *New York Times*, 4 Mar. 1906, 12.

48. Virginia Scharff, *Taking the Wheel: Women and the Coming of the Motor Age* (New York: Free Press, 1991), 20–22; see also Berger, *Devil Wagon*, 140.

49. Fraunholz, *Motorphobia*, 202–3; Berger, *Devil Wagon*, 178–81.

50. H. L. Barber, *Story of the Automobile: Its History and Development from 1760 to 1917* (Chicago: A. J. Munson, 1917), 163; James Rood Doolittle, *The Romance of the Automobile*

Industry: Being the Story of its Development—its Contribution to Health and Prosperity—its Influence on Eugenics—its Effect on Personal Efficiency—and its Service and Mission to Humanity as the Latest and Greatest Phase of Transportation (New York: Klebold Press, 1916), 393–99.

51. Müller, *Gefährliche Fahrten*, 233–41, 250–65, on early films; Berger, *Devil Wagon*, 95, on the 1929 play; David R. Goldfield and Blaine A. Brownell, "The Automobile and the City in the American South," in *The Economic and Social Effects of the Spread of Motor Vehicles*, ed. Theo Barker (Basingstoke: Macmillan, 1987), 120, on 1920s Nashville; George Kennan, *Around The Cragged Hill* (New York: Norton, 1993), 163.

52. Robert S. Lynd and Helen Merrill Lynd, *Middletown: A Study in American Culture* (New York: Harcourt, Brace, 1929), 114; see also Berger, *Devil Wagon*, 139–41.

53. *Argus*, 6 Sept. 1924, quoted in Graeme Davison, *Car Wars: How the Car Won Our Hearts and Conquered Our Cities* (Crows Nest, NSW: Allen & Unwin, 2004), 49.

54. Federico Paolini, *Storia sociale dell'automobile in Italia* (Rome: Carocci, 2007), 49; Beat Hächler, *Automobilmachung: Zur Geschichte der Massenmotorisierung Spaniens (1939-1975)* (Saarbrücken: Breitenbach, 1991), 110. On French priests, see Michel Lagrée, "Le clergé automobile devant le développement de l'automobile," in *L'automobile, son monde et ses réseaux*, ed. Anne-Françoise Garçon (Rennes: Presses universitaires de Rennes, 1998), 89–100.

55. Lynd and Lynd, *Middletown: A Study*, 259; see also Berger, *Devil Wagon*, 133–37.

56. Joseph Interrante, "You Can't Go to Town in a Bathtub: Automobile Movement and the Reorganization of Rural American Space, 1900–1930," *Radical History Review* 21 (1979): 151–68.

57. Robert S. Lynd and Helen Merrill Lynd, *Middletown in Transition: A Study in Cultural Conflicts* (New York: Harcourt, Brace, 1937), 265.

58. Franklin M. Reck, *A Car Traveling People: How the Automobile Has Changed the Life of Americans—A Study of Social Effects* (Detroit: Automobile Manufacturers Association, 1945), 8. Reck insists that the story is true but gives no source. Clay McShane, *Down the Asphalt Path: The Automobile and the American City* (New York: Columbia University Press, 1994), 133, gives more examples of moralistic condemnation of spending on cars.

59. Quoted in Dietmar Fack, *Automobil, Verkehr und Erziehung: Motorisierung und Sozialisation zwischen Beschleunigung und Anpassung, 1885-1945* (Opladen: Leske + Budrich, 2000), 149.

60. Mirbeau, *Sketches*, 17, 130–32.

61. Louis Baudry de Saunier, *L'automobile: Théorique et Pratique* (Le Vallois: L. Baudry de Saunier, 1900), 2:511.

62. Adolf Schmal, writing under the name of Filius, *Ohne Chauffeur: Ein Handbuch für Besitzer von Automobilen und Motorradfahrer*, 5th ed. (1913), 22–23, quoted in Fack, *Automobil*, 149.

63. Filius, *Die Kunst des Fahrens*, rev. ed. (1922), 156, quoted in Kurt Möser, *Geschichte des Autos* (Frankfurt: Campus, 2002), 333.

64. All these phrases come from a single issue of *Car and Driver*, no. 6 (1989), as

noted by Karin Sandqvist, *The Appeal of Automobiles: Human Desires and the Proliferation of Cars* (Stockholm: KFB—The Swedish Transport and Communications Board, 1997), 38.

65. N. De Sanctis, "La corsa alla morte," *L'Auto d'Italia*, 12 Aug. 1906, quoted in Moscatelli, "Il veicolo," 101. A few years later, similar images appeared in the poetry of Filippo Marinetti and Gabriele d'Annunzio; see Müller, *Gefährliche Fahrten*, 53–61.

66. According to Gijs Mom, *The Electric Vehicle: Technology and Expectations in the Automobile Age*, trans. Jenny Wormer (Baltimore: Johns Hopkins University Press, 2004), 44. Two broadly focused articles on Germany by Kurt Möser are: "World War I and the Creation of Desire for Automobiles in Germany," in *Getting and Spending: European and American Consumer Societies in the Twentieth Century*, ed. Susan Strasser, Charles McGovern, and Matthias Judt (Cambridge: Cambridge University Press, 1998), 195–222; and "The Dark Side of 'Automobilism,' 1900–1930: Violence, War and the Motor Car," *Journal of Transport History* 24 (2003): 238–58.

67. Speech at Berlin auto show, 15 Feb. 1936, in Max Domarus, *Hitler, Speeches and Proclamations, 1932–1945*, trans. Mary Fran Gilbert and Chris Wilcox (London: Tauris, 1990–97), 2:753–54.

68. *Völkischer Beobachter*, 9 Mar. 1934, quoted in Wolfgang Sachs, *Die Liebe zum Automobil* (Reinbek: Rowohlt, 1984), 72.

69. Fraunholz, *Motorphobia*, 207.

70. Domarus, *Hitler*, 3:1477, as cited by Rudy Koshar, "Organic Machines: Cars, Drivers, and Nature from Imperial to Nazi Germany," in *Germany's Nature*, ed. Thomas Lekan and Thomas Zeller (New Brunswick: Rutgers University Press, 2005), 130.

71. Seth K. Humphrey, "Our Delightful Man-Killer," *Atlantic Monthly* 148 (Dec. 1931): 730.

72. J. C. Furnas, "And Sudden Death," *Reader's Digest*, Aug. 1935, 23. On his motives: Joel W. Eastman, *Styling vs. Safety: The American Automobile Industry and the Development of Automotive Safety, 1900–1966* (Lanham, MD: University Press of America, 1984), 181. An extended discussion of the tensions between exhilaration and anxiety is offered by Blanke, *Hell on Wheels*. Both Blanke and Peter Norton, *Fighting Traffic: The Dawn of the Motor Age in the American City* (Cambridge, MA: MIT Press, 2008) argue that, contrary to earlier scholarship, the U.S. did see a major (if thwarted) outcry against automotive carnage around 1920.

73. Quoted in Plowden, *Motor Car and Politics*, 284. On the 1930s safety campaigns, 266–85; and Thorold, *Motoring Age*, 206–9.

74. Dean, *Murder*, 7–8.

75. Dean, *Murder*, 42, 72.

76. Robert Graves and Alan Hodge, *The Long Week End: A Social History of Great Britain, 1919–1939* (London: Faber and Faber, 1940), 172.

77. Dennistoun Burney, "The Car of the Future," *Auto-Motor Journal*, 9 Jan. 1931.

78. Quoted in Blanke, *Hell on Wheels*, 113.

79. Quoted in Uekoetter, "Stark im Ton," 658.

1. John R. Griffith, "The Complete Highway: Modern Transportation in the Light of Ancient Philosophy," *Landscape Architecture* 47 (Jan. 1957): 352, 355.

2. William H. Whyte, *The Organization Man* (New York: Simon and Schuster, 1956); David Riesman, *The Lonely Crowd: A Study of the Changing American Character* (New Haven: Yale University Press, 1950).

3. This argument is made by Louis Menand, "Drive, He Said," *New Yorker*, 1 Oct. 2007, 91.

4. John Keats, *The Insolent Chariots* (Philadelphia: Lippincott, 1958), 188, 192.

5. *Die Jagd nach Liebe*, quoted in Dorit Müller, *Gefährliche Fahrten: Das Automobil in Literatur und Film um 1900* (Würzburg: Königshausen und Neumann, 2004), 24.

6. Max Frisch, *Stiller* (Frankfurt: Suhrkamp, 1954), 211–12.

7. Lewis Mumford, "The Roaring Traffic's Boom, I" *New Yorker*, 19 Mar. 1955, 121. See also Mumford, *The Culture of Cities* (New York: Harcourt, Brace, 1938), 254, on roads despoiling the countryside.

8. E. B. White, "Letter from the North," *New Yorker*, 5 Apr. 1958, 34; Raymond Loewy, "Jukebox on Wheels," *Atlantic Monthly* 195 (Apr. 1955): 36–38. On Loewy: Karal Ann Marling, "America's Love Affair with the Automobile in the Television Age," *Design Quarterly* 146 (1989): 16; in general, David Gartman, *Auto Opium: A Social History of American Automobile Design* (London: Routledge, 1994).

9. Jean Baudrillard, *The System of Objects*, trans. James Benedict (London: Verso, 1996), 59. Reyner Banham, "The Machine Aesthetic," *Architectural Review* 117, no. 700 (Apr. 1955): 225–28, attacked car designers' dishonest imitations of engineering.

10. Both essays are reprinted in S. I. Hayakawa, ed., *Our Language and Our World* (New York: Harper, 1959): "Sexual Fantasy and the 1957 Car" (1957), 237; and "Why the Edsel Laid an Egg: Motivational Research vs. the Reality Principle" (1958), 244.

11. W. Valderpoort, *De zelfzuchtige personenauto: Beschouwingen over een onderdeel van het verkeersvraagstuk, met een bijzondere toepassing op de stedebouw* (Amsterdam: G. van Saane, 1953).

12. Quoted in Jeffry M. Diefendorf, "Städtebauliche Traditionen und der Wiederaufbau von Köln vornehmlich nach 1945," *Rheinische Vierteljahrsblätter* 55 (1991): 255. Uwe Fraunholz, *Motorphobia: Anti-automobiler Protest in Kaiserreich und Weimarer Republik* (Göttingen: Vandenhoeck und Ruprecht, 2002), 208, cites a similar remark by Adenauer.

13. Quoted in Dietmar Klenke, *Bundesdeutsche Verkehrspolitik und Motorisierung* (Stuttgart: Steiner, 1993), 164.

14. Quoted in Barbara Schmucki, "Cyborgs unterwegs? Verkehrstechnik und individuelle Mobilität seit dem 19. Jahrhundert," *Technik und Gesellschaft* 10 (1999): 104–5.

15. Alfred Sauvy, *Les quatre roues de la fortune: Essai sur l'automobile* (Paris: Flammarion, 1968), 43–44; William Plowden, *The Motor Car and Politics, 1896–1970* (London: Bodley Head, 1971), 329; Federico Paolini, *Un paese a quattro ruote: Automobili e società in Italia* (Venice: Marsilio, 2005), 69–74; Bieri quoted in Jean-Daniel Blanc, *Die Stadt—*

Ein Verkehrshindernis? Leitbilder städtischer Verkehrsplanung und Verkehrspolitik in Zürich 1945-75 (Zurich: Chronos, 1993), 83.

16. Quoted in Kurt Möser, *Geschichte des Autos* (Frankfurt: Campus, 2002), 197. Similar sentiments from Italian Socialist and Communist politicians in 1958 are quoted by Federico Paolini, *Storia sociale dell'automobile in Italia* (Rome: Carocci, 2007), 69–70. Norway in the 1950s, where the governing Socialists were hostile to cars, was an exception, according to Per Østby, "Educating the Norwegian Nation: Traffic Engineering and Technological Diffusion," *Comparative Technology Transfer and Society* 2 (2004): 247–72.

17. Guy Debord, "Situationist Theses on Traffic," no. 1 (1959), trans. Ken Knabb, http://www.bopsecrets.org/SI/3.traffic.htm.

18. Henri Lefebvre, *Everyday Life in the Modern World*, trans. Sacha Rabinovitch (New York: Harper, 1971), 101. Along the same lines, see Baudrillard, *System of Objects*, 65–69.

19. Roland Barthes, "The New Citroen," in *Mythologies* (1957), trans. Annette Lavers (New York: Hill and Wang, 1972), 88.

20. Quoted in James J. Flink, *The Automobile Age* (Cambridge, MA: MIT Press, 1988), 283.

21. Vladimir Nabokov, *Lolita* (New York: Berkeley, 1966), 108. England's equivalent, the 1930s roadhouse, offered a more refined depravity, reflecting the greater exclusivity of the motoring class there. See Peter Thorold, *The Motoring Age: The Automobile and Britain, 1896-1939* (London: Profile, 2003), 138–41.

22. Alexander Spoerl, *Living with a Car*, trans. and adapted by Otto Gregory (London: Frederick Muller Ltd., 1960), 246.

23. Keats, *Insolent Chariots*, 11–13.

24. Lewis Mumford, "The Highway and the City" (1958), reprinted in Mumford, *The Urban Prospect* (New York: Harcourt Brace Jovanovich, 1969), 93.

25. Mumford, "Highway," 92; and "The Roaring Traffic's Boom, II," *New Yorker*, 2 Apr. 1955, 99.

26. Quoted in Mathieu Flonneau, *Paris et l'automobile, un siècle de passions* (Paris: Hachette, 2005), 150; Georges Portal, *Pour l'automobile* (Nancy: Berger-Levrault, 1967), 78. Jean Baudrillard analyzed the centaur imagery in *System of Objects*, 101.

27. Robert Poulet, *Contre l'automobile* (Nancy: Berger-Levrault, 1967), 76.

28. Hans F. Erb, *Auto, Auto über alles: Porträt eines neuen Menschen* (Hamburg: Hoffmann und Campe, 1966), 125, 128; Bernard Charbonneau, *L'hommauto* (Paris: Denoel, 1967).

29. Poulet, *Contre l'automobile*, 20–27, 43.

30. Erb, *Auto, Auto über alles*, 125–27.

31. Janpeter Kob, "Werkzeug, Konsumgut, Machtsymbol: Zur Soziologie des Automobils," *Hamburger Jahrbuch für Wirtschafts- und Gesellschaftspolitik* 11 (1966): 184–92.

32. Erb, *Auto, Auto über alles*, 127.

33. Tom Wolfe, *The Kandy-Kolored Tangerine Flake Streamline Baby* (1965; repr., New York: Bantam, 1999), 33.

34. Daniel P. Moynihan, "The War against the Automobile," *Public Interest* 3 (Spring 1966): 17.

35. Ronald A. Buel, *Dead End: The Automobile in Mass Transportation* (Englewood Cliffs, NJ: Prentice-Hall, 1972), 4.

36. Sauvy, *Les quatre roues*, 87, 88.

37. E. J. Mishan, *The Costs of Economic Growth* (New York: Praeger, 1967), 94.

38. Charbonneau, *L'hommauto*, 105, 107. The accident researcher Anatol Rapoport attributed the same disturbing acceptance of blood sacrifice to Americans, in "Some Comments on Accident Research," in *Accident Research—Methods and Approaches*, ed. William Haddon, Jr., Edward Suchman, and David Klein (New York: Harper and Row, 1964), 257.

39. On this and other French films, see Kristin Ross, *Fast Cars, Clean Bodies: Decolonization and the Reordering of French Culture* (Cambridge, MA: MIT Press, 1996), 29–53. More generally, see Mikita Brottman, ed., *Car Crash Culture* (New York: Palgrave, 2001).

40. Joel W. Eastman, *Styling vs. Safety: The American Automobile Industry and the Development of Automotive Safety, 1900–1966* (Lanham, MD: University Press of America, 1984), 224–32.

41. David Cort, "Our Strangling Highways: The Vicious (Traffic) Circle," *Nation* 182, no. 17 (28 Apr. 1956): 360.

42. Daniel P. Moynihan, "Epidemic on the Highways," *Reporter* 20, no. 9 (30 Apr. 1959): 16–23.

43. Eastman, *Styling vs. Safety*, 232.

44. Ralph Nader, *Unsafe at Any Speed: The Designed-In Dangers of the American Automobile* (New York: Grossman, 1965). A second major exposé was Jeffrey O'Connell and Arthur Myers, *Safety Last: An Indictment of the Auto Industry* (New York: Random House, 1966).

45. Axel Dossmann, *Begrenzte Mobilität: Eine Kulturgeschichte der Autobahnen in der DDR* (Essen: Klartext, 2003), 138; Barbara Schmucki, *Der Traum vom Verkehrsfluss: Städtische Verkehrsplanung seit 1945 im deutsch-deutschen Vergleich* (Frankfurt: Campus, 2001), 139, 141–42; Thomas Weymar, *Im Trabi zur Sonne, zur Freiheit: Entwicklung, Folgen und Ursachen des Automobilverkehrs am Beispiel der DDR* (Cologne: Verlag Wissenschaft und Politik, 1985), 17–18.

46. Kevin Riley, "Motor Vehicles in China: The Impact of Demographic and Economic Changes," *Population and Environment* 23 (2002): 491.

47. Dossmann, *Begrenzte Mobilität*, 138–39; Weymar, *Im Trabi*, 15–18.

48. Dossmann, *Begrenzte Mobilität*, 140; Weymar, *Im Trabi*, 79; Jonathan Zatlin, "The Vehicle of Desire: The Trabant, the Wartburg, and the End of the GDR," *German History* 15 (1997): 358–80.

49. Schmucki, *Der Traum*, 142; Dossmann, *Begrenzte Mobilität*, 300; Weymar, *Im Trabi*, 30–36, 64, 67–68, 73.

50. Zatlin, "The Vehicle of Desire," 358.

51. Ursula Lehner-Lierz, "The Role of Cycling for Women," in *The Greening of Urban Transport*, 2nd ed., ed. Rodney Tolley (Chichester: Wiley, 1997), 53–69; and two

essays in Die Grünen im Bundestag, ed., *Welche Freiheit brauchen wir? Zur Psychologie der AutoMobilen Gesellschaft* (Berlin: Verlag für Ausbildung und Studium, 1989): Ulrike Reuter, "Problemaufriss: zur Mobilität der Frauen," 104–13; and Ute Preis, "Lösungsansätze," 113–18.

52. Sandra Rosenbloom, "Why Working Families Need a Car," in *The Car and the City: The Automobile, the Built Environment, and Daily Urban Life*, ed. Martin Wachs and Margaret Crawford (Ann Arbor: University of Michigan Press, 1992), 39–56; an English study is Lynn Dobbs, "Wedded to the Car: Women, Employment and the Importance of Private Transport," *Transport Policy* 12 (2005): 266–78.

53. Chester Himes, *The Quality of Hurt: The Autobiography of Chester Himes* (New York: Doubleday, 1972), 78; see also Kathleen Franz, " 'The Open Road': Automobility and Racial Uplift in the Interwar Years," in *Technology and the African-American Experience*, ed. Bruce Sinclair (Cambridge, MA: MIT Press, 2004), 135–36.

54. Kathleen Franz, *Tinkering: Consumers Reinvent the Automobile* (Philadelphia: University of Pennsylvania Press, 2005), 7; Cory Lesseig, *Automobility: Social Changes in the American South, 1909–1939* (New York: Routledge, 2001), 112–14.

55. Jean-François Doulet and Mathieu Flonneau, *Paris-Pékin, civiliser l'automobile* (Paris: Descartes & Cie, 2003); Andrew H. Spencer, "Challenges to Sustainable Transport in China's Cities," in *Urban Growth and Development in Asia*, ed. Graham P. Chapman, Ashok K. Dutt, and Robert W. Bradnock (Aldershot: Ashgate, 1999), 1:426–43; on work units and urban form, Duanfang Lu, *Remaking Chinese Urban Form* (London: Routledge, 2006), 47–79.

CHAPTER THREE

1. Frank Uekoetter, "The Merits of the Precautionary Principle: Controlling Automobile Exhausts in Germany and the United States before 1945," in *Smoke and Mirrors: The Politics and Culture of Air Pollution*, ed. E. Melanie DuPuis (New York: NYU Press, 2004), 119–53; Uwe Fraunholz, *Motorphobia* (Göttingen: Vandenhoeck und Ruprecht, 2002), 203; Tom McCarthy, *Auto Mania* (New Haven: Yale University Press, 2007), 21–25.

2. Quoted in Fraunholz, *Motorphobia*, 203.

3. Theodor Lessing, *Der Lärm: Eine Kampfschrift gegen die Geräusche unseres Lebens* (Wiesbaden, 1908), http://www.salmoxisbote.de/Bote03/Lessing.htm; Lawrence Baron, "Noise and Degeneration: Theodore Lessing's Crusade for Quiet," *Journal of Contemporary History* 17 (1982): 165–78; Richard Birkefeld and Martina Jung, *Die Stadt, der Lärm und das Licht: Die Veränderung des öffentlichen Raumes durch Motorisierung und Elektrifizierung* (Seelze: Kallmeyer, 1994), 48–57; Peter Payer, "The Age of Noise: Early Reactions in Vienna, 1870–1914," *Journal of Urban History* 33 (2007): 781–83. Lessing insisted that Germany was far behind London and New York in the campaign against the deafening auto plague and other threats to the human ear and nerves. On New York's Society for the Suppression of Unnecessary Noise, established in 1906, see Raymond W. Smilor, "Toward an Environmental Perspective: The Anti-Noise Campaign, 1893–

1932," in *Pollution and Reform in American Cities, 1870–1930*, ed. Martin V. Melosi (Austin: University of Texas Press, 1980), 141–44.

4. From his diary, quoted in Peter Thorold, *The Motoring Age* (London: Profile, 2003), 259.

5. Speech of 18 Mar. 1932, in *Scritti e discursi*, 8:33–34, quoted in Spiro Kostof, *The Third Rome, 1870–1950: Traffic and Glory* (Berkeley: University Art Museum, 1973), 15.

6. Gijs Mom, *The Electric Vehicle: Technology and Expectations in the Automobile Age* (Baltimore: Johns Hopkins University Press, 2004), 173, makes this argument. On electric cars, also see Michael Brian Schiffer, *Taking Charge: The Electric Vehicle in America* (Washington: Smithsonian Institution Press, 1994); and David A. Kirsch, *The Electric Vehicle and the Burden of History* (New Brunswick: Rutgers University Press, 2000).

7. Booth Tarkington, *The Magnificent Ambersons* (Doubleday, Page & Company, 1925), 260.

8. Jeffrey T. Schnapp, "Crash (Speed as Engine of Individuality)" *Modernism/Modernity* 6, no. 1 (1999): 1–49; Christophe Studeny, *L'invention de la vitesse: France, XVIIIe–XXe siècle* (Paris: Gallimard, 1995), 67–71, 131–35.

9. Paul Barrett, *The Automobile and Urban Transit: The Formation of Public Policy in Chicago, 1900–1930* (Philadelphia: Temple University Press, 1983), 58; Clay McShane, *Down the Asphalt Path: The Automobile and the American City* (New York: Columbia University Press, 1994), 176–77, 183; James J. Flink, *America Adopts the Automobile, 1895–1910* (Cambridge, MA: MIT Press, 1970), 65–66.

10. "Time is money" is in English in the original: Guy de Charnacé, *Hommes et choses du temps présent* (1902), 1:8–9, quoted in Studeny, *L'invention*, 286.

11. Mathieu Flonneau, *L'automobile à la conquête de Paris: Chroniques illustrées* (Paris: Presses de l'école nationale des Ponts et Chaussées, 2003), 184–85; Studeny, *L'invention*, 323.

12. Fraunholz, *Motorphobia*, 66; see also Christoph Maria Merki, *Der holprige Siegeszug des Automobils 1895–1930* (Vienna: Böhlau, 2002), 172.

13. Dietmar Fack, *Automobil, Verkehr und Erziehung: Motorisierung und Sozialisation zwischen Beschleunigung und Anpassung 1885–1945* (Opladen: Leske + Budrich, 2000), 158.

14. Strosser, quoted in Frank Uekoetter, "Stark im Ton, schwach in der Organisation: Der Protest gegen den frühen Automobilismus," *Geschichte in Wissenschaft und Unterricht* 54 (2003): 658.

15. Pidoll, *Der heutige Automobilismus: Ein Protest und Weckruf*, 4, quoted in Payer, "The Age of Noise," 789.

16. Quoted in Wolfgang Sachs, *Die Liebe zum Automobil* (Reinbek: Rowohlt, 1984), 30.

17. Quoted in Sachs, *Die Liebe zum Automobil*, 27.

18. This paragraph draws mainly on Peter D. Norton, "Street Rivals: Jaywalking and the Invention of the Motor Age Street," *Technology and Culture* 48 (2007): 331–59. See also Peter D. Norton, *Fighting Traffic: The Dawn of the Motor Age in the American City* (Cambridge, MA: MIT Press, 2008). Also valuable is Ashleigh Brilliant, *The Great Car*

Craze: How Southern California Collided with the Automobile in the 1920s (Santa Barbara: Woodbridge Press, 1989), 75–90.

19. Quoted in Victor Gruen, *Centers for the Urban Environment: Survival of the Cities* (New York: Van Nostrand Reinhold, 1973), 170.

20. Reprinted in Graeme Davison, *Car Wars: How the Car Won Our Hearts and Conquered Our Cities* (Crows Nest, NSW: Allen & Unwin, 2004), 151.

21. Frederick Upham Adams, "Get Ready for 5,000,000 Automobiles," *American Magazine*, 19 Apr. 1916, reprinted in *The Quotable Car*, ed. Kenneth Schneider and Blanche Schneider (Berkeley: Continuing Education in City, Regional, and Environmental Planning, University Extension, University of California, Berkeley, 1973), 71.

22. Richard O. Bennett, "Highway Safety: The Case of the Pedestrian, Cyclist, and Horse-Drawn Vehicle," in *Highways in Our National Life*, ed. Jean Labatut and Wheaton J. Lane (Princeton: Princeton University Press, 1950), 374, 377.

23. Cited in Robert Fogelson, *Downtown: Its Rise and Fall, 1880–1950* (New Haven: Yale University Press, 2001), 253.

24. Bruce E. Seely, *Building the American Highway System: Engineers as Policy Makers* (Philadelphia: Temple University Press, 1987), 150. On early traffic jams, see McShane, *Down the Asphalt Path*, 193.

25. Norman Bel Geddes, *Magic Motorways* (New York: Random House, 1940), 12–13.

26. Clarence Stein, *Toward New Towns for America* (Liverpool: University Press of Liverpool, 1951), 41–42.

27. This was the slogan of his 1925 Voisin plan: Le Corbusier, *L'Urbanisme* (Paris: Editions Vincent, 1966), 263.

28. Francis Bello, "The City and the Car," in *The Exploding Metropolis*, editors of *Fortune* (Garden City: Doubleday, 1958), 33.

29. See Richard Longstreth, *City Center to Regional Mall: Architecture, the Automobile, and Retailing in Los Angeles, 1920–1950* (Cambridge, MA: MIT Press, 1997).

30. On Gruen, see M. Jeffrey Hardwick, *Mall Maker: Victor Gruen, Architect of an American Dream* (Philadelphia: University of Pennsylvania Press, 2004); as well as Victor Gruen, *The Heart of Our Cities: The Urban Crisis, Diagnosis and Cure* (New York: Simon and Schuster, 1964); and Gruen, *Centers*.

31. Gruen, *Centers*, 192. He was actually reviving an idea that had been proposed in many U.S. cities during the 1920s: Fogelson, *Downtown*, 254.

32. Oswald Spengler, *Man and Technics*, trans. Charles Francis Atkinson (New York: Knopf, 1932), 94.

33. W. Valderpoort, *De zelfzuchtige personenauto* (Amsterdam: G. van Saane, 1953), 40, 42.

34. Hans Bernhard Reichow, *Die autogerechte Stadt* (Ravensburg: Otto Maier, 1959). See also Barbara Schmucki, *Der Traum vom Verkehrsfluss: Städtische Verkehrsplanung seit 1945 im deutsch-deutschen Vergleich* (Frankfurt: Campus, 2001); and Schmucki, "Cities as Traffic Machines: Urban Transport Planning in East and West Germany," in *Suburbanizing the Masses: Public Transport and Urban Development in Historical Perspective*, ed. Colin Divall and Winstan Bond (Aldershot: Ashgate, 2003), 149–70.

35. Quoted in Schmucki, *Der Traum*, 123.

36. Quoted in Harald Bodenschatz, "Berlin West: Abschied von der steinernen Stadt," in *Neue Städte aus Ruinen*, ed. Klaus von Beyme et al. (Munich: Prestel, 1992), 74.

37. Colin Buchanan, *Mixed Blessing: The Motor in Britain* (London: Leonard Hill, 1958), 190.

38. Ministry of Transport, *Traffic in Towns: A Study of the Long Term Problems of Traffic in Urban Areas* (London: Her Majesty's Stationery Office, 1963).

39. Quoted in William Plowden, *The Motor Car and Politics, 1896–1970* (London: Bodley Head, 1971), 401.

40. Werner Zellner, in *Münchner Merkur*, 8 Apr. 1961, quoted in Walter Först, *Chaos oder Ordnung auf unseren Strassen?* (Cologne: Deutscher Städtetag, 1962), 14.

41. Heinz Kleppe, in Deutscher Städtetag, *Erneuerung unserer Städte* (Stuttgart: Kohlhammer, 1960), 124. The sociologist Hans Paul Bahrdt, *Die moderne Grossstadt: Soziologische Überlegungen zum Städtebau* (Reinbek: Rowohlt, 1961), 112, objected to the use of organic metaphors by planners like Hans Bernhard Reichow.

42. For example: Kleppe, in *Erneuerung*, 122–23; Bahrdt, *Die moderne Grossstadt*, 97; Lucius Burckhardt, "Die Krise der Stadt," *Werk* 48 (1961): 336–37. Influential German books included Wolf Jobst Siedler, Elisabeth Niggemeyer, and Gina Angress, *Die gemordete Stadt* (Berlin: Herbig, 1964); and Alexander Mitscherlich, *Die Unwirtlichkeit unserer Städte* (Frankfurt: Suhrkamp, 1965). A German counterpart to the Buchanan report was the *Bericht der Sachverständigenkommission über eine Untersuchung von Massnahmen zur Verbesserung der Verkehrsverhältnisse der Gemeinden* (Bonn: Federal Parliament, 1964).

43. Leonardo Borgese, 1959 article reprinted in *L'Italia rovinata dagli Italiani* (Milan: Rizzoli, 2005), 226; Valderpoort, *De zelfzuchtige personenauto*.

44. The group was founded in 1968. Kimmo Antila, "Actors, Factors, and Foreign Influences in the Finnish Highway Building from the 1930s to the 1960s" (paper presented at Ester advanced seminar, University of Tampere, 12–15 November 2003), 14, http://www.uta.fi/laitokset/historia/ester/papers/Paper_Antila.pdf.

45. Enrique Barón, *La civilización del automóvil* (Madrid: Cuadernos para el Diálogo, 1971), 36.

46. Bernard Charbonneau, *L'hommauto* (Paris: Denoel, 1967), 74.

47. Michel Ragon, *Paris hier, aujourd'hui, demain* (Paris: Hachette, 1965), 67.

48. M. E. Beesley and J. F. Kain, "Urban Form, Car Ownership and Public Policy: An Appraisal of Traffic in Towns," *Urban Studies* 1 (1964): 174–203; D. J. Reynolds, *Economics, Town Planning and Traffic* (London: Institute of Economic Affairs, 1966).

49. Ministry of Transport, *Traffic in Towns*, 183; C. D. Buchanan, "Traffic in Towns: The Critics Answered," *Traffic Engineering and Control* 6, no. 1 (May 1964): 41–42; Stephen V. Ward, "Cross-national Learning in the Formation of British Planning Policies 1940–99. A Comparison of the Barlow, Buchanan and Rogers Reports," *Town Planning Review* 78 (2007): 378–84.

50. Mario Gaviria, *Libro negro sobre la autopista de la Costa Blanca* (Valencia: Editorial Cosmos, 1973), 354.

51. P. H. Randle, *Buenos Aires, burocracia y urbanismo: Mas allá de las autopistas* (Buenos Aires: Oikos, 1979), 33.

52. Hans-Jochen Vogel, "Das Auto mordet unsere Städte," *Stern*, no. 19 (27 Apr. 1971): 15–17, quoted in Hans Dollinger, *Die totale Autogesellschaft* (Munich: Carl Hanser, 1972), 22.

53. Reyner Banham, *Los Angeles: The Architecture of Four Ecologies* (London: Penguin, 1971). More thoughts along the same lines are offered by David Brodsly, *L.A. Freeway: An Appreciative Essay* (Berkeley: University of California Press, 1981).

54. Dan Jacobson, "Cars, Cars, Cars, Roads, Roads, Roads: A South African Looks at California," *Reporter* 18, no. 4 (21 Feb. 1957): 19–20.

55. Much earlier, Jan Gordon and Cora Gordon, *Star-Dust in Hollywood* (London: Harrap, 1930), 143–44, offered an apocryphal tale of a similar incident.

56. Melvin Webber, "Order in Diversity: Community without Propinquity," in *Cities and Space*, ed. Lowdon Wingo, Jr. (Baltimore: Johns Hopkins University Press, 1963), 23–54. Gabriel Dupuy's apt French term is "habitation multilocale": Dupuy, *L'auto et la ville* (Paris: Flammarion, 1995), 104–5.

57. The latter view is a commonplace of preservationists and "smart growth" advocates. The former is the argument of Robert Bruegmann, *Sprawl: A Compact History* (Chicago: University of Chicago Press, 2005).

58. Some theorists since Webber argue that the information economy still promotes the growth of megacities, for example Manuel Castells, *The Rise of the Network Society*, 2nd ed. (Oxford: Blackwell, 2000), 429–40.

59. Joan Didion, *Play It As It Lays* (New York: Farrar, Straus and Giroux, 1970), 13–16. Heinrich Böll does something similar with the title character of his *Lost Honor of Katharina Blum*: Böll, *Die verlorene Ehre der Katharina Blum* (Cologne: Kiepenheuer und Witsch, 1974), 65–67.

60. Chris Mosey, *Car Wars: Battles on the Road to Nowhere* (London: Vision Paperbacks, 2000), 177.

61. See Joe Moran, "Early Cultures of Gentrification in London, 1955–1980," *Journal of Urban History* 34 (2007): 101–21.

62. Richard Sennett, *The Fall of Public Man* (New York: Knopf, 1977), 14.

63. Bahrdt, *Die moderne Grossstadt*, 118.

64. 1957 lecture quoted in Fogelson, *Downtown*, 316.

65. Jane Jacobs, *The Death and Life of Great American Cities* (New York: Vintage, 1961), 370.

CHAPTER FOUR

1. André Gorz, "The Social Ideology of the Motorcar" (1973) in *Ecology as Politics*, trans. Patsy Vigderman and Jonathan Cloud (Boston: South End Press, 1980), 74, and at http://rts.gn.apc.org/socid.htm.

2. Robert Fogelson, *Downtown: Its Rise and Fall, 1880–1950* (New Haven: Yale University Press, 2001), 280.

3. On highway engineers and their influence in the U.S., see Bruce E. Seely, *Building the American Highway System: Engineers as Policy Makers* (Philadelphia: Temple University Press, 1987); Paul Barrett and Mark H. Rose, "Street Smarts: The Politics of Transportation Statistics in the American City, 1900–1990," *Journal of Urban History* 25 (1999): 405–33; Mark H. Rose and Bruce E. Seely, "Getting the Interstate System Built: Road Engineers and the Implementation of Public Policy, 1955–1985," *Journal of Policy History* 2 (1990): 23–55; Louis Ward Kemp, "Aesthetes and Engineers: The Occupational Ideology of Highway Design," *Technology and Culture* 27 (1986): 759–97; Alan A. Altshuler, *The City Planning Process: A Political Analysis* (Ithaca: Cornell University Press, 1965). On the interstate program, Mark H. Rose, *Interstate: Express Highway Politics, 1939–1989*, 2nd ed. (Knoxville: University of Tennessee Press, 1990) and Owen D. Gutfreund, *Twentieth-Century Sprawl: Highways and the Reshaping of the American Landscape* (New York: Oxford University Press, 2004), 37–59.

4. John F. Bauman, "The Expressway 'Motorists Loved to Hate': Philadelphia and the First Era of Postwar Highway Planning, 1943–1956," *Pennsylvania Magazine of History and Biography* 115 (1991): 503–33.

5. Ronald Bayor, "Roads to Racial Segregation: Atlanta in the Twentieth Century," *Journal of Urban History* 15 (1988): 3–21.

6. Raymond A. Mohl, "The Interstates and the Cities: Highways, Housing, and the Freeway Revolt" (research report, Poverty and Race Research Action Council, 2002), http://www.prrac.org/pdf/mohl.pdf; Charles E. Connerly, *"The Most Segregated City in America": City Planning and Civil Rights in Birmingham, 1920–1980* (Charlottesville: University of Virginia Press, 2005), 129–66; Ben Kelley, *The Pavers and the Paved* (New York: Donald W. Brown, 1971), 97–107, on Nashville. On Mexican-Americans in Los Angeles, see Matthew W. Roth, "Whittier Boulevard, Sixth Street Bridge, and the Origin of Transportation Exploitation in East Los Angeles," *Journal of Urban History* 30 (2004): 729–48.

7. Richard Thruelsen, "Coast to Coast without a Stoplight," *Saturday Evening Post*, 20 Oct. 1956, 64. This was more or less the conventional view of planning professionals as well.

8. Homar Bigart, "U.S. Road Plans Periled by Urban Hostility," *New York Times*, 13 Nov. 1967, 50.

9. Raymond A. Mohl, "Stop the Road: Freeway Revolts in American Cities," *Journal of Urban History* 30 (2004): 674–706. There is nothing approaching a general history of freeway revolts in the U.S. (or, for that matter, in any other country); Mohl's is the closest thing.

10. Zachary M. Schrag, *The Great Society Subway: A History of the Washington Metro* (Baltimore: Johns Hopkins University Press, 2006), 41, 119–21; Schrag, "The Freeway Fight in Washington, D.C.: The Three Sisters Bridge in Three Administrations," *Journal of Urban History* 30 (2004): 648–73; Helen Leavitt, *Superhighway—Superhoax* (Garden City, NY: Doubleday, 1970), 91–109.

11. On Chicago, William Barry Furlong, "Profile of an Alienated Voter," *Saturday Review* 55, no. 31 (29 July 1972): 48–51; on Philadelphia, Christopher Klemek, "Urbanism

as Reform: Modernist Planning and the Crisis of Urban Liberalism in Europe and North America" (Ph.D. diss., University of Pennsylvania, 2004), 227–39; on Boston, Alan Lupo et al., *Rites of Way: The Politics of Transportation in Boston and the U.S. City* (Boston: Little, Brown, 1971), 9–111; Gordon Fellman and Barbara Brandt, *The Deceived Majority: Politics and Protest in Middle America* (New Brunswick: Transaction, 1973), 57–90. On a similar case in Minneapolis, see Patricia Cavanaugh, "Politics and Freeways: Building the Twin Cities Interstate System," University of Minnesota, Center for Transportation Studies and Center for Urban and Regional Affairs, Oct. 2006, 29–34, http://www.cura.umn.edu/publications/Freeways.pdf.

12. This argument was made by the Swiss architect Jean Robert, *Le temps qu'on nous vole: Contre la société chronophage* (Paris: Seuil, 1980), 44–51.

13. Richard O. Baumbach, Jr, and William E. Borah, *The Second Battle of New Orleans: A History of the Vieux Carré Riverfront-Expressway Controversy* (University, AL: University of Alabama Press, 1981).

14. William H. Lathrop, "San Francisco Freeway Revolt," *Transportation Engineering Journal of ASCE* 97 (Feb. 1971): 133–44; David W. Jones, Jr., *California's Freeway Era in Historical Perspective* (Berkeley: University of California Institute of Transportation Studies, 1989), 256–308; Joseph A. Rodriguez, *City Against Suburb: The Culture Wars in an American Metropolis* (Westport: Praeger, 1999), 21–46.

15. Quoted in Alice Sparberg Alexiou, *Jane Jacobs: Urban Visionary* (New Brunswick: Rutgers University Press, 2006), 110. See also Leavitt, *Superhighway—Superhoax*, 58–73.

16. Robert A. Caro, *The Power Broker: Robert Moses and the Fall of New York* (New York: Random House, 1974), 849. A more balanced take on Moses appears in Hilary Ballon and Kenneth T. Jackson, eds., *Robert Moses and the Modern City* (New York: Norton, 2007).

17. David Louter, *Windshield Wilderness: Cars, Roads, and Nature in Washington's National Parks* (Seattle: University of Washington Press, 2006); Gabrielle Barnett, "Drive-By Viewing: Visual Consciousness and Forest Preservation in the Automobile Age," *Technology and Culture* 45 (2004): 30–54.

18. Lewis Mumford, "The Roaring Traffic's Boom, I" *New Yorker*, 19 Mar. 1955, 121.

19. Quoted in William Plowden, *The Motor Car and Politics, 1896–1970* (London: Bodley Head, 1971), 199–200. A few years later, John Maynard Keynes offered an ironic view of highway finance: "Our grandest exercises to-day in the arts of public construction are the arterial roads, which, however, creep into existence under a cloak of economic necessity and by the accident that a special tax earmarked for them brings in returns of unexpected size, not all of which can be decently diverted to other purposes." Keynes, "Art and the State," in *Britain and the Beast*, ed. Clough Williams-Ellis (London: J. M. Dent and Sons, 1937), 3.

20. Quoted in Leonie Sandercock, *Cities for Sale: Property, Politics and Urban Planning in Australia* (Carlton, Victoria: Melbourne University Press, 1975), 133. On freeway debates in Adelaide, ibid., 121–35; as well as Hugh Stretton, *Ideas for Australian Cities* (North Adelaide: Hugh Stretton, 1970), 183–87; on Melbourne, Graeme Davison,

Car Wars: How the Car Won Our Hearts and Conquered Our Cities (Crows Nest, NSW: Allen & Unwin, 2004), 168–238; on Sydney, David Ball, *Urban Freeway Planning in Sydney to 1977 and in the Present Day* (Canberra: Urban Research Program, Research School of Social Sciences, Australian National University, 1996); in general, Ian Manning, *The Open Street: Public Transport, Motor Cars and Politics in Australian Cities* (Sydney: Transit Australia, 1991), 68–87.

21. Sandercock, *Cities for Sale*, 194; Davison, *Car Wars*, 185, 252.

22. David and Nadine Nowlan, *The Bad Trip: The Untold Story of the Spadina Expressway* (Toronto: New Press/House of Anansi, 1970); V. Setty Pendakur, *Cities, Citizens and Freeways* (Vancouver, 1972); Donald Gutstein, *Vancouver Ltd.* (Toronto: James Lorimer and Company, 1975), 152–66; Mike Harcourt and Ken Cameron with Sean Rossiter, *City Making in Paradise: Nine Decisions That Saved Vancouver* (Vancouver: Douglas & McIntyre, 2007), 31–55; Christopher Leo, *The Politics of Urban Development: Canadian Urban Expressway Disputes* (Toronto: Institute of Public Administration of Canada, 1977). Davis quoted in Robert Dunphy et al., *Moving Beyond Gridlock: Traffic and Development* (Washington, DC: Urban Land Institute, 1997), 114. In a different context, an argument that the nature of German planning partly explains lower transit use in a German city compared to a Swiss one is presented by Ueli Haefeli, "Public Transport Can Pay: A Historical Analysis of Transport Policies in Bern (Switzerland) and Bielefeld (Germany) since 1950," First Swiss Transport Research Conference, 2001, http://www.strc.ch/haefeli.pdf.

23. On London: J. Michael Thomson, *Motorways in London* (London: Gerald Duckworth, 1969); Simon Jenkins, "The Politics of London Motorways," *Political Quarterly* 44 (1973): 257–70; Douglas A. Hart, *Strategic Planning in London: The Rise and Fall of the Primary Road Network* (Oxford: Pergamon, 1976), 159–73; George Charlesworth, *A History of British Motorways* (London: Thomas Telford, 1984), 194–99; Peter Hall, *Great Planning Disasters* (Berkeley: University of California Press, 1980), 56–86.

24. Mathieu Flonneau, *Paris et l'automobile, un siècle de passions* (Paris: Hachette, 2005), 225–35, 320–21; Flonneau, "Notre Dame of Paris Challenged by the Car: Between the 'Secular' and the 'Sacred,'" in *Road History*, ed. Gijs Mom and Laurent Tissot (Neuchatel: Alphil, 2007), 133–61; Louis Fougère, "La voie-express rive gauche," *La nouvelle Revue des Deux Mondes*, June 1976, 628–43.

25. On highway plans: Jeffry M. Diefendorf, "Motor Vehicles and the Inner City," in *Urban Planning in a Changing World*, ed. Robert Freestone (London: Spon, 2000), 175–93; Barbara Schmucki, "Schneisen durch die Stadt—Sinnbild der 'modernen' Stadt: Stadtautobahnen und amerikanisches Vorbild in Ost- und Westdeutschland, 1925–1975," *WerkstattGeschichte* 21, no. 7 (1998): 43–64. On Berlin opposition: Barma von Sartory, Georg Kohlmaier, and Jürgen Allesch, "Verkehrspolitik als politisches Handeln: Zum Stadtautobahn-System Berlin," *Baumeister* 67 (1970): 1466–69; Bürgerinitiative Westtangente, ed., *Stadtautobahnen: Ein Schwarzbuch zur Verkehrsplanung* (Berlin: BIW, 1976); Michael Busse, *Die Auto-Dämmerung: Sachzwänge für eine neue Verkehrspolitik* (Frankfurt: Fischer, 1980). Also Jürgen Roth, *Z. B. Frankfurt: Die Zerstörung einer Stadt* (Munich: Bertelsmann, 1975), 158–63; and Barbara Schmucki, *Der Traum vom Verkehrsfluss:*

Städtische Verkehrsplanung seit 1945 im deutsch-deutschen Vergleich (Frankfurt: Campus, 2001), 343–45, on Munich.

26. Quoted in Jean-Daniel Blanc, *Die Stadt—Ein Verkehrshindernis? Leitbilder städtischer Verkehrsplanung und Verkehrspolitik in Zürich 1945-75* (Zurich: Chronos, 1993), 228–29. On Switzerland, in addition to Blanc, see Michael Ackermann, *Konzepte und Entscheidungen in der Planung der schweizerischen Nationalstrassen von 1927 bis 1961* (Bern: Peter Lang, 1992); George Kammann, *Mit Autobahnen die Städte retten? Städtebauliche Ideen der Expressstrassen-Planung in der Schweiz 1954-1964* (Zurich: Chronos, 1990); Michel Bassand et al., *Politique des routes nationales: Acteurs et mise en oeuvre* (Lausanne: Presses Polytechniques Romandes, 1986), 117–31; Ueli Haefeli, "Stadt und Autobahn— eine Neuinterpretation," *Schweizerische Zeitschrift für Geschichte* 51 (2001): 181–202; and Matthias Hehl, "Die Stadt Bern in der Automobilisierungseuphorie—Schnellstrassenprojekte 1950-1970," in *Bern—eine Stadt bricht auf: Schauplätze und Geschichten der Berner Stadtentwicklung zwischen 1798 und 1998*, ed. Christian Lüthi and Bernhard Meier (Bern: Paul Haupt, 1998), 69–83.

27. Quoted in Gordon Fellman, Barbara Brandt, and Roger Rosenblatt, "Dagger in the Heart of Town: Mass. Planners and Cambridge Workers," *Transaction* 7, no. 11 (Sept. 1970): 46; and A. Q. Mowbray, *Road to Ruin* (Philadelphia: Lippincott, 1969), 142, respectively.

28. Robert Ruckli, 1962, quoted in Stefan Studer, *Nationalstrasse—Nationalstrafe oder die Demokratie bleibt auf der Strecke* (Zurich: Rotpunktverlag, 1985), 111.

29. Thruelsen, "Coast to Coast without a Stoplight," 65.

30. *Life*, 14 Apr. 1967, 4.

31. Quoted in Mohl, "Stop the Road," 696.

32. British broadsides include J. S. Dean, *Murder Most Foul* (London: George Allen and Unwin, 1947), 34–71; John Tyme, *Motorways versus Democracy* (London: Macmillan, 1978); and Mick Hamer, *Wheels within Wheels: A Study of the Road Lobby* (London: Routledge and Kegan Paul, 1987); on Switzerland, Studer, *Nationalstrasse—Nationalstrafe*.

33. Federico Paolini, *Un paese a quattro ruote: Automobili e società in Italia* (Venice: Marsilio, 2005), 21–24.

34. *Cassier's Magazine* 31 (Feb. 1907): 456, quoted in Paul Barrett, *The Automobile and Urban Transit* (Philadelphia: Temple University Press, 1983), 46.

35. Miller McClintock, *Street Traffic Control* (New York: McGraw-Hill, 1925), 4. On McClintock: Peter D. Norton, *Fighting Traffic* (Cambridge, MA: MIT Press, 2008), 163–69. Other examples from the era are cited in Fogelson, *Downtown*, 260, 268; Ashleigh Brilliant, *The Great Car Craze* (Santa Barbara: Woodbridge Press, 1989), 144; and Mark S. Foster, *From Streetcar to Superhighway: American City Planners and Urban Transportation, 1900-1940* (Philadelphia: Temple University Press, 1981), 44, 174.

36. Stephen Plowden, *Taming Traffic* (London: Andre Deutsch, 1980), 50, cites a similar 1937 example from London, an expert who, like McClintock, did not let this realization stop him from recommending more roads.

37. Quoted in Mark H. Rose, *Interstate: Express Highway Politics, 1941-1956* (Lawrence: Regents Press of Kansas, 1979), 58.

38. Walter H. Blucher, "Moving People," *Virginia Law Review* 35 (1950): 849.

39. Daniel P. Moynihan, "New Roads and Urban Chaos," *Reporter* 22, no. 8 (14 Apr. 1960): 19.

40. Anthony Downs, "The Law of Peak-Hour Express-Way Congestion," *Traffic Quarterly* 16 (1962): 393–409; Downs, *Still Stuck in Traffic* (Washington: Brookings Institution Press, 2004), 82–86.

41. *Asphalt* 17, no. 4 (Oct. 1965): 2; *Asphalt* 18, no. 2 (Apr. 1966): 1; Gabriel Dupuy, "From the Magic Circle to Automobile Dependence," *Transport Policy* 6 (1999): 1–17.

42. Quoted in Jeffrey Brown, "From Traffic Regulation to Limited Ways: The Effort to Build a Science of Transportation Planning," *Journal of Planning History* 5 (2006): 27.

43. Baumbach and Borah, *Second Battle of New Orleans*, 230–34.

44. Ford speech reprinted in Richard O. Davies, *The Age of Asphalt* (Philadelphia: Lippincott, 1975), 74; Jenkins, "The Politics of London Motorways," 261.

45. Recent U.S. and UK research includes Mark Hansen and Yuanlin Huang, "Road Supply and Traffic in California Urban Areas," *Transportation Research A* 31 (1997): 205–18; Mark Hansen, "Do New Highways Generate Traffic?" *Access* 7 (Fall 1995): 16–22; Robert Cervero, "Road Expansion, Urban Growth, and Induced Travel: A Path Analysis," *Journal of the American Planning Association* 69 (2003): 145–65; Robert Cervero, "Are Induced-Travel Studies Inducing Bad Investments?" *Access* 22 (Spring 2003): 22–27; Robert B. Noland, "Relationships between Highway Capacity and Induced Vehicle Travel," *Transportation Research A* 35 (2001): 47–72; and a special issue of *Transportation* 23, no. 1 (1996). A good overview is Todd Litman, "Generated Travel and Induced Travel: Implications for Transport Planning," Victoria Transport Policy Institute, 2007, http://www.vtpi.org/gentraf.pdf. Robert Bruegmann, *Sprawl: A Compact History* (Chicago: University of Chicago Press, 2005), 130–32, downplays the problem; Dunphy et al., *Moving Beyond Gridlock*, 88, 149–50, cites evidence that massive freeway-building in 1980s Phoenix and Houston successfully reduced congestion; Ted Balaker and Sam Staley, *The Road More Traveled: Why the Congestion Crisis Matters More Than You Think, and What We Can Do about It* (Lanham: Rowman and Littlefield, 2006), 64–65, 125–38, also trumpet the Houston example. More generally, for the UK, A. B. Prakash, E. H. D'A. Oliver, and K. Balcombe, "Does Building New Roads Really Create Extra Traffic? Some New Evidence," *Applied Economics* 33 (2001): 579–85, offer statistics to deny the existence of induced traffic; Phil Goodwin and Robert A. Noland, "Building New Roads Really Does Create Extra Traffic: A Response to Prakash et al.," *Applied Economics* 35 (2003): 1451–57, convincingly demonstrate the shortcomings of those statistics.

46. Randal O'Toole, *The Vanishing Automobile and Other Urban Myths* (Bandon, OR: Thoreau Institute, 2001), 398.

47. Valeda von Steinberg, "No Parking," *New York Times Magazine*, 10 Jul. 1955, 42.

48. The seminal work on the perverse economics of parking is Donald C. Shoup, *The High Cost of Free Parking* (Chicago: Planners Press, 2005).

49. Jane Jacobs, *The Death and Life of Great American Cities* (New York: Vintage, 1961), 360–63; Alexiou, *Jane Jacobs*, 55–6; Robert Fishman, "Revolt of the Urbs: Robert Moses and His Critics," in Ballon and Jackson, *Robert Moses*, 122–29.

50. Sally Cairns, Carmen Hass-Klau, and Phil Goodwin, *Traffic Impact of Highway Capacity Reductions: Assessment of the Evidence* (London: Landor, 1998).

51. Cited in Alan Altshuler and David Luberoff, *Mega-Projects: The Changing Politics of Urban Public Investment* (Washington: Brookings Institution, 2003), 182. Allen presumably intended the image of a twenty-eight-lane road to illustrate the absurdity of endless highway construction, yet roads of nearly that width were being proposed amid a pro-highway backlash in the early twenty-first century, including a plan to widen one of Atlanta's radial highways to twenty-three lanes.

52. The most thorough study is of France: Gabriel Dupuy, *Une technique de planification au service de l'automobile: Les modèles de trafic urbain* (Paris: Action concertée de recherches urbaines, 1975). Similar evidence for Britain comes from Stephen Plowden, *Towns Against Traffic* (London: Andre Deutsch, 1972), 41–56; for Norway and Sweden, from a series of articles in *Comparative Technology Transfer and Society* 2, no. 3 (2004): Bruce E. Seely, "'Push' and 'Pull' Factors in Technology Transfer: Moving American-Style Highway Engineering to Europe, 1945–1965," 229–46; Per Østby, "Educating the Norwegian Nation: Traffic Engineering and Technological Diffusion," 247–72; Rär Blomkvist, "Transferring Technology—Shaping Ideology: American Traffic Engineering and Commercial Interests in the Establishment of a Swedish Car Society, 1945–1965," 273–302; Per Lundin, "American Numbers Copied! Shaping the Postwar Swedish Car Society," 303–34. Yale University in particular attracted highway engineers from many lands, and the New Haven–based consultant Wilbur Smith drew up plans for cities across Europe, Australia, and Asia.

53. Quotations from Thomas Südbeck, *Motorisierung, Verkehrsentwicklung und Verkehrspolitik in der Bundesrepublik Deutschland der 1950er Jahre: Umrisse der allgemeinen Entwicklung und zwei Beispiele: Hamburg und das Emsland* (Stuttgart: Steiner, 1994), 187–88.

54. Stuart Hart, unpublished paper quoted in Sandercock, *Cities for Sale*, 127. The head of Sydney's regional government, Rod Fraser, made much the same point at the same time: see Ball, *Urban Freeway Planning*, 15.

55. 6 Apr. 1972, quoted in Sandercock, *Cities for Sale*, 194.

56. *San Francisco Chronicle*, 24 Sept. 1956, quoted in Jones, *California's Freeway Era*, 296.

57. Quoted in *Smithsonian* 3, no. 1 (Apr. 1972): 24.

58. Lewis Mumford, "The Highway and the City" (1958), reprinted in Mumford, *The Urban Prospect* (New York: Harcourt Brace Jovanovich, 1969), 92.

59. Moynihan, "New Roads and Urban Chaos," 19.

60. Gorz, "Social Ideology," 73–74.

61. Wolf Linder, Ulrich Maurer, and Hubert Resch, *Erzwungene Mobilität: Alternativen zur Raumordnung, Stadtentwicklung und Verkehrspolitik* (Cologne: Europäische Verlagsanstalt, 1975).

62. Gorz, "Social Ideology," 76.

63. Quoted in Moynihan, "New Roads and Urban Chaos," 17. McCarthy was probably inspired by the reflections on private splendor and public squalor in John Kenneth Galbraith's *The Affluent Society* (Boston: Houghton Mifflin, 1958), esp. 253.

64. Fogelson, *Downtown*, 44–111, on rail plans; on Los Angeles, Scott L. Bottles, *Los Angeles and the Automobile: The Making of the Modern City* (Berkeley: University of California Press, 1987), 158–74; and Jeremiah B. C. Axelrod, "'Keep the "L" out of Los Angeles': Race, Discourse, and Urban Modernity in 1920s Southern California," *Journal of Urban History* 34 (2007): 3–37.

65. Leavitt, *Superhighway—Superhoax*, 291.

66. Quoted in Lupo et al., *Rites of Way*, 106.

67. Moynihan, "New Roads and Urban Chaos," 19.

68. Raymond A. Mohl, "The Interstate and the Cities: The U.S. Department of Transportation and the Freeway Revolt, 1966–1973," *Journal of Policy History* 20, no. 2 (Spring 2008). An insider's account is John Burby, *The Great American Motion Sickness or Why You Can't Get There from Here* (Boston: Little, Brown, 1971).

69. Robert C. Post, "Urban Railway Redivivus: Image and Ideology in Los Angeles, California," in *Suburbanizing the Masses*, ed. Colin Divall and Winstan Bond (Aldershot: Ashgate, 2003), 187–209; Jonathan Richmond, *Transport of Delight: The Mythical Conception of Rail Transit in Los Angeles* (Akron: University of Akron Press, 2005).

70. Altshuler and Luberoff, *Mega-Projects*, 88–120. According to Brian D. Taylor, "Public Perceptions, Fiscal Realities, and Freeway Planning: The California Case," *Journal of the American Planning Association* 61 (1995): 43–56; and Jones, *California's Freeway Era*, 26, 309–21, the primary reason for the curtailment of California freeway construction in the 1970s was not opposition but spiraling costs. Altshuler and Luberoff, *Mega-Projects*, 253–54, disagree. The nearly simultaneous cancellation of freeways in many lands suggests that tight budgets were usually not the primary cause, although the widespread inflation of the 1970s undoubtedly aided the cause of freeway opponents in some places, as opponents questioned whether scarce resources were well spent. Also, as Jones observes, part of the cost increase was a result of mitigating measures intended to placate opponents. On Boston's Big Dig, for example, see Nicole Gelinas, "Lessons of Boston's Big Dig," *City Journal*, Autumn 2007.

71. *New York Times*, 18 Dec. 2006.

72. Peter Sloterdijk, *Eurotaoismus: Zur Kritik der politischen Kinetik* (Frankfurt: Suhrkamp, 1989), 42–43.

73. Edward Dimendberg, "The Will to Motorization: Cinema, Highways, and Modernity," *October* 73 (1995): 135; and Dimendberg, *Film Noir and the Spaces of Modernity* (Cambridge, MA: Harvard University Press, 2004), 204.

CHAPTER FIVE

1. Quoted in John Jerome, *The Death of the Automobile: The Fatal Effect of the Golden Era, 1955–1970* (New York: Norton, 1972), 241.

2. Jerome, *Death of the Automobile*, 14. Other notable anti-auto works from this era include, from the U.S., A. Q. Mowbray, *Road to Ruin* (Philadelphia: Lippincott, 1969); Helen Leavitt, *Superhighway—Superhoax* (Garden City, NY: Doubleday, 1970); Ben Kelley, *The Pavers and the Paved* (New York: Donald W. Brown, 1971); Kenneth R. Schneider,

Autokind vs. Mankind: An Analysis of Tyranny, A Proposal for Rebellion, A Plan for Reconstruction (New York: Norton, 1971); Tabor R. Stone, Beyond the Automobile: Reshaping the Transportation Environment (Englewood Cliffs, NJ: Prentice-Hall, 1971); Ronald A. Buel, Dead End: The Automobile in Mass Transportation (Englewood Cliffs, NJ: Prentice-Hall, 1972); Emma Rothschild, Paradise Lost: The Decline of the Auto-Industrial Age (New York: Random House, 1973); from Britain and Europe, Alistair Aird, The Automotive Nightmare (London: Hutchinson, 1972); Terence Bendixson, Without Wheels: Alternatives to the Private Car (Bloomington: Indiana University Press, 1974); Thomas Krämer-Badoni, Herbert Grymer, and Marianne Rodenstein, Zur sozio-ökonomischen Bedeutung des Automobils (Frankfurt: Suhrkamp, 1971); Hans Dollinger, Die totale Autogesellschaft (Munich: Carl Hanser, 1972); Catherine Dreyfus and Jean-Paul Pigeat, Les maladies de l'environnement: La France en saccage (Paris: Editions E. P., 1971); André Gorz, "L'ideologie sociale de la bagnole," Le sauvage, Sept.–Oct. 1973; Ivan Illich, Energy and Equity (New York: Harper, 1974); Enrique Barón, La civilización del automóvil (Madrid: Cuadernos para el Diálogo, 1971).

3. Catherine Marshall, "The Obsolescent Auto," Michigan Quarterly Review 19, no. 4 / 20, no. 1 (Fall 1980/Winter 1981): 752.

4. Peter M. Bode, Sylvia Hamberger, and Wolfgang Zängl, eds., Alptraum Auto: Eine hundertjährige Erfindung und ihre Folgen (Munich: Raben, 1986).

5. Among the many anti-car books of the era are: Wolfgang Zuckermann, End of the Road: From World Car Crisis to Sustainable Transportation (Post Mills, VT: Chelsea Green, 1992); Steve Nadis and James J. MacKenzie, Car Trouble (Boston: Beacon, 1993); Stanley I. Hart and Alvin L. Spivak, Automobile Dependence and Denial: The Elephant in the Bedroom (Pasadena: New Paradigm, 1993); James Howard Kunstler, The Geography of Nowhere (New York: Simon and Schuster, 1993); Stephen P. Goddard, Getting There: The Epic Struggle between Road and Rail in the American Century (New York: Basic, 1994); Jane Holtz Kay, Asphalt Nation (New York: Crown, 1997); Katie Alvord, Divorce Your Car! Ending the Love Affair with the Automobile (Gabriola Island, BC: New Society, 2000); J. H. Crawford, Carfree Cities (Utrecht: International Books, 2000); Sue Zielinski and Gordon Laird, eds., Beyond the Car (Toronto: Steel Rail, 1995); Moshe Safdie with Wendy Kohn, The City after the Automobile (New York: Basic, 1997); David Engwicht, Towards an Eco-City: Calming the Traffic (Sydney: envirobook, 1992); Colin Ward, Freedom to Go: After the Motor Age (London: Freedom Press, 1991); Nicola Baird, The Estate We're In: Who's Driving Car Culture? (London: Indigo, 1998); Chris Mosey, Car Wars: Battles on the Road to Nowhere (London: Vision Paperbacks, 2000); Die Grünen im Bundestag, ed., Welche Freiheit brauchen wir? Zur Psychologie der AutoMobilen Gesellschaft (Berlin: Verlag für Ausbildung und Studium, 1989); Till Bastian and Harald Theml, Unsere wahnsinnige Liebe zum Auto (Weinheim: Beltz, 1990); Tom Koenigs and Roland Schaeffer, eds., Fortschritt vom Auto? Umwelt und Verkehr in den 90er Jahren (Munich: Raben, 1991); Klaus Kuhm, Das eilige Jahrhundert: Einblicke in die automobile Gesellschaft (Hamburg: Junius, 1995); Winfried Wolf, Car Mania, trans. Gus Fagan (London: Pluto, 1996); Christian Zeller, Mobilität für alle! Umrisse einer Verkehrswende zu einem autofreien Basel (Basel: Birkhäuser, 1992); Guido Viale, Tutti in taxi: Demonologia dell'automobile (Milan: Feltrinelli, 1996).

6. B. Bruce-Briggs, *The War against the Automobile* (New York: Dutton, 1977), 101, 75.

7. Keith Bradsher, *High and Mighty: SUVs—the World's Most Dangerous Vehicles and How They Got That Way* (New York: PublicAffairs, 2002). Also see Tom McCarthy, *Auto Mania* (New Haven: Yale University Press, 2007), 231–52. Perhaps the fundamental difference between Nader's and Bradsher's revelations was the fact that Nader's accompanied legislative hearings. In the 1990s and 2000s, few American politicians dared say a word against SUVs or their manufacturers.

8. Colin Buchanan, "Some Thoughts about the Motor Car," *Traffic Engineering and Control* 15, no. 3 (July 1973): 134–35.

9. J. B. Jackson in *Landscape* 17, no. 3 (Spring 1968): 2.

10. Bruce-Briggs, *War against the Automobile*, 188–89.

11. Ibid., 189.

12. Ibid., 128.

13. James Rood Doolittle, *The Romance of the Automobile Industry* (New York: Klebold Press, 1916), 440.

14. Erik d'Ornhjelm, quoted in Mathieu Flonneau, *Paris et l'automobile, un siècle de passions* (Paris: Hachette, 2005), 236.

15. Gianni Mazzocchi, "L'automobile per vivere meglio" (1956), reprinted in *Dalla parte dell'auto* (Milan: Editoriale Domus, 1980), 18.

16. Flonneau, *Paris*, 109.

17. Urs Altermatt and Markus Furrer, "Die Autopartei: Protest für Freiheit, Wohlstand und das Auto," in *Rechte und Linke Fundamentalopposition: Studien zur Schweizer Politik 1965-1990*, ed. Urs Altermatt et al. (Basel: Helbing und Lichterhahn, 1994), 135–53.

18. Bruce-Briggs, *War against the Automobile*, 176.

19. P. G. M. Gregory, *The Plight of the Motorist* (London: Conservative Political Centre, 1968), 3.

20. Quoted in William Plowden, *The Motor Car and Politics* (London: Bodley Head, 1971), 386.

21. Bretz, in *ADAC-Motorwelt*, no. 2 (1967): 30, quoted in Krämer-Badoni, *Zur sozioökonomischen Bedeutung*, 237.

22. *ADAC-Motorwelt*, no. 3 (1967): 25, cited in Krämer-Badoni, *Zur sozioökonomischen Bedeutung*, 236.

23. Reprinted in Wolfgang Sachs, *Die Liebe zum Automobil* (Reinbek: Rowohlt, 1984), 94.

24. Peter Boenisch, in *Bild am Sonntag*, 10 Feb. 1974, quoted in Siegfried Reinecke, "Das Mass aller Dinge: Autokultur und Mediendiskurse," in Die Grünen, *Welche Freiheit*, 46.

25. Derek Wall, *Earth First! and the Anti-Roads Movement* (London: Routledge, 1999); Mosey, *Car Wars*, 97–112; Matthew Paterson, *Understanding Global Environmental Politics* (Houndmills: Macmillan, 2000), 95–117; Benjamin Seel, Matthew Paterson, and Brian Doherty, eds., *Direct Action in British Environmentalism* (London: Routledge, 2000).

26. James Q. Wilson, "Cars and Their Enemies," *Commentary* 104, no. 1 (July 1997): 17–23; James A. Dunn, Jr., *Driving Forces: The Automobile, Its Enemies, and the Politics of Mobility* (Washington: Brookings Institution Press, 1998), 4. An auto lobbyist's brief is James D. Johnson, *Driving America: Your Car, Your Government, Your Choice* (Washington: AEI Press, 1997). A French counterpart to Wilson is Henri Vagnon, *La chasse à la bagnole: Refléxions sur le rejet de l'automobile en milieu urbain* (Paris: L'Harmattan, 2000).

27. Randal O'Toole, *The Greatest Invention: How Automobiles Made America Great* (Bandon, OR: American Dream Coalition, 2006), 28, http://americandreamcoalition .org/Greatest.pdf.

28. Bruce-Briggs, *War against the Automobile*, 109–10.

29. *Wall Street Journal*, 11 Nov. 2005.

30. This is the argument presented in Ted Balaker and Sam Staley, *The Road More Traveled: Why the Congestion Crisis Matters More Than You Think, and What We Can Do about It* (Lanham: Rowman and Littlefield, 2006).

31. Jim Klein and Martha Olson, *Taken for a Ride* (1996); Bradford C. Snell, *American Ground Transport* (Washington, D.C.: U.S. Government Printing Office, 1974). Other substantial defenses of the conspiracy theory include David St. Clair, *The Motorization of American Cities* (New York: Praeger, 1986); and Edwin Black, *Internal Combustion: How Corporations and Governments Addicted the World to Oil and Derailed the Alternatives* (New York: St. Martin's, 2006), 193–260. Debunkings and a wider context are offered in Sy Adler, "The Transformation of the Pacific Electric Railway: Bradford Snell, Roger Rabbit, and the Politics of Transportation in Los Angeles," *Urban Affairs Quarterly* 27 (Sept. 1991): 51–86; Martha J. Bianco, "The Decline of Transit: A Corporate Conspiracy or Failure of Public Policy? The Case of Portland, Oregon," *Journal of Policy History* 9 (1997): 450–74; Martha J. Bianco, "Kennedy, *60 Minutes*, and Roger Rabbit: Understanding Conspiracy-Theory Explanations of The Decline of Urban Mass Transit," 1998, http://www .upa.pdx.edu/CUS/publications/docs/DP98-11.pdf; Cliff Slater, "General Motors and the Demise of Streetcars" *Transportation Quarterly* 51, no. 3 (Summer 1997): 45–66, www.lava.net/cslater/TQOrigin.pdf; and Zachary M. Schrag, "'The Bus is Young and Honest': Transportation Politics, Technical Choice, and the Motorization of Manhattan Surface Transit, 1919–1936," *Technology and Culture* 41 (2000): 51–79.

32. Quoted in Mark S. Foster, *A Nation on Wheels: The Automobile Culture in America since 1945* (Belmont, CA: Wadsworth/Thomson, 2003), 18.

33. Examples of demands to remove the trams in 1920s Paris are cited in André Guillerme, "La congestion urbaine: Problèmes et solutions dans l'entre-deux-guerres," in *L'automobile, son monde et ses réseaux*, ed. Anne-Françoise Garçon (Rennes: Presses universitaires de Rennes, 1998), 125; also Albert Guérard, *L'Avenir de Paris* (Paris: Payot, 1929), 210–11.

34. Flonneau, *Paris*, 224–25; Flonneau, "City Infrastructures and City Dwellers: Accommodating the Automobile in Twentieth-Century Paris," *Journal of Transport History* 27 (2006): 93–114. James A. Dunn, Jr., argues that the French highway lobby was weak in "The French Highway Lobby: A Case Study in State-Society Relations and Policymaking," *Comparative Politics* 27 (1995): 275–95.

35. Reprinted in Flonneau, *Paris*, 327–28, see also 195; and Flonneau, "Georges Pompidou Président conducteur et la première crise urbaine de l'automobile," *Vingtième siècle, Revue d'histoire* 61 (Jan.–Mar. 1999): 30–43.

36. Lewis Mumford, *The City in History* (New York: Harcourt, Brace, 1961), 508.

37. Peter Newman and Jeffrey Kenworthy, *Sustainability and Cities: Overcoming Automobile Dependence* (Washington, D.C.: Island Press, 1999), 60. Their data can be found in Peter W. G. Newman and Jeffrey R. Kenworthy, *Cities and Automobile Dependence: A Sourcebook* (Aldershot: Gower, 1989); Jeffrey R. Kenworthy, Felix B. Laube, and Peter Newman, *An International Sourcebook of Automobile Dependence in Cities, 1960–1990* (Boulder: University Press of Colorado, 1999); and Jeffrey R. Kenworthy, Felix B. Laube, and Jean Vivier, *Millennium Cities Database for Sustainable Transport* (Murdoch, Australia: ISTP, 2001).

38. Gabriel Dupuy, "From the Magic Circle to Automobile Dependence," *Transport Policy* 6 (1999): 12; also Dupuy, *La dépendance automobile: Symptomes, analyses, diagnostic, traitements* (Paris: Anthropos, 1999), 29–42. Also see Roger Gorham, "Car Dependence as a Social Problem: A Critical Essay on the Existing Literature and Future Needs," in *Social Change and Sustainable Transport*, ed. William R. Black and Peter Nijkamp (Bloomington: Indiana University Press, 2002), 107–15.

39. Quoted in *Globe and Mail*, 23 Jan. 2007.

40. Jeffrey Rose, introduction to *Car Dependence*, ed. Phil Goodwin (London: RAC Foundation for Motoring and the Environment, 1995), 4.

41. Hartwig Heine, Rüdiger Mautz, and Wolf Rosenbaum, *Mobilität im Alltag: Warum wir nicht vom Auto lassen* (Frankfurt: Campus, 2001), 23; Goodwin, *Car Dependence*, 39–41.

42. Heine, *Mobilität*, esp. 125–46; and Goodwin, *Car Dependence*, 43.

43. Goodwin, *Car Dependence*, 52.

44. Cited in Viale, *Tutti in taxi*, 220–21.

45. Projektgruppe Mobilität, *Die Mobilitätsmaschine: Versuche zur Umdeutung des Autos* (Berlin: edition sigma, 2004), 122–23.

46. Gerard Tertoolen, Dik van Kreveld, and Ben Verstraten, "Psychological Resistance against Attempts to Reduce Private Car Use," *Transportation Research A* 32 (1998): 171–82; L. Steg, "Car Use: Lust and Must. Instrumental, Symbolic and Affective Motives for Car Use," *Transportation Research A* 39 (2005): 147–62; as well as two articles in Rodney Tolley, ed., *The Greening of Urban Transport*, 2nd ed. (Chichester: Wiley, 1997): Rodney Tolley and Alan Hallsworth, "'I'd walk there, but . . .': Thoughts on the Attitude-Behavior Gap," 129–45; and René Diekstra and Martin Kroon, "Cars and Behavior: Psychological Barriers to Car Restraint and Sustainable Urban Transport," 147–57. A study of German youth that found contradictory attitudes toward driving and the environment is Claus J. Tully, *Rot, cool und was unter der Haube: Jugendliche und ihr Verhältnis zu Auto und Umwelt* (Munich: Aktuell, 1998), 176–200. On conflicted and guilty feelings in an English survey, see Simon Maxwell, "Negotiating Car Use in Everyday Life," in *Car Cultures*, ed. Daniel Miller (Oxford: Berg, 2001), 203–22.

47. Projektgruppe Mobilität, *Die Mobilitätsmaschine*. However, since 2004 other car-sharing businesses in Berlin have grown rapidly. Similar thinking prompted Guido Viale's proposal for universal taxi service: Viale, *Tutti in taxi*.

48. Two vivid examples, one rural, one urban, are presented in Miller, *Car Cultures*: Diana Young, "The Life and Death of Cars: Private Vehicles on the Pitjanjatjara Lands, South Australia," 35–57; and Jojada Verrips and Birgit Meyer, "Kwaku's Car: The Struggles and Stories of a Ghanaian Long-Distance Taxi-Driver," 153–84. One might also point to Indian reservations in the United States, as discussed by Philip J. Deloria, *Indians in Unexpected Places* (Lawrence: University Press of Kansas, 2004), 136–82, and as portrayed in the fiction of Louise Erdrich, Sherman Alexie, and Leslie Marmon Silko.

49. Kurt Leibbrand, *Transportation and Town Planning*, trans. Nigel Seymer (Cambridge, MA: MIT Press, 1970), 87.

50. Federico Paolini, *Un paese a quattro ruote: Automobili e società in Italia* (Venice: Marsilio, 2005), 197–98, 205.

51. Leibbrand, *Transportation*, 87–88.

52. Randal O'Toole, *The Vanishing Automobile and Other Urban Myths* (Bandon, OR: Thoreau Institute, 2001), 349–50.

53. David Riesman and Eric Larrabee, "Autos in America," in Riesman, *Abundance for What? And Other Essays* (Garden City, NY: Doubleday, 1964), 292.

54. *Neue Zürcher Zeitung*, 11 Nov. 1956, quoted in Jean-Daniel Blanc, *Die Stadt—Ein Verkehrshindernis?* (Zurich: Chronos, 1993), 67, 216n.

CONCLUSION

1. Robert Musil, *Der Mann ohne Eigenschaften* (Hamburg: Rowohlt, 1952), 11.

2. Maurice Maeterlinck, "En Automobile," in *Le Double Jardin* (Paris: Bibliothèque-Charpentier, 1904), 51–65. Maeterlinck expressed his enthusiasm already in "Motor-Car Impressions," *Harper's*, Feb. 1902, 397–99.

3. On Matisse and on Proust and other writers, see Sara Danius, *The Senses of Modernism: Technology, Perception, and Aesthetics* (Ithaca: Cornell University Press, 2002), 124–40; and Danius, "The Aesthetics of the Windshield: Proust and the Modernist Rhetoric of Speed," *Modernism/Modernity* 8, no. 1 (2001): 99–126.

4. The early directors Cecil B. DeMille, in the U.S., and Max Mack, in Germany, both declared that cars were essential elements of film. Mack quoted in Dorit Müller, *Gefährliche Fahrten* (Würzburg: Königshausen und Neumann, 2004), 261–62; DeMille in Kenneth Hey, "Cars and Films in American Culture, 1929–1959," *Michigan Quarterly Review* 19, no. 4 / 20, no. 1 (Fall 1980/Winter 1981): 588.

5. Reyner Banham, *Los Angeles: The Architecture of Four Ecologies* (London: Penguin, 1971), 217, 221, 220.

6. Wolfgang Hartenstein and Klaus Liepelt, *Man auf der Strasse: Eine verkehrssoziologische Untersuchung* (Frankfurt: Europäische Verlagsanstalt, 1961), 104.

7. Keith Bradsher, *High and Mighty: SUVs—the World's Most Dangerous Vehicles and How They Got That Way* (New York: PublicAffairs, 2002), 93–101, 106.

8. A study of English and German children is Mayer Hillman, John Adams, and John Whitelegg, *One False Move: A Study of Children's Independent Mobility* (London: PSI, 1990).

9. Rebecca Solnit, *Wanderlust: A History of Walking* (New York: Penguin, 2000); Joseph A. Amato, *On Foot* (New York: NYU Press, 2004); Dietrich Garbrecht, *Gehen: Plädoyer für das Leben in der Stadt* (Weinheim: Beltz, 1981); David Le Breton, *Eloge de la marche* (Paris: Métailié, 2000); Loren Demerath and David Levinger, "The Social Qualities of Being on Foot: A Theoretical Analysis of Pedestrian Activity, Community, and Culture," *City and Community* 2 (Sept. 2003): 217–37.

10. Loren Lomasky, "Autonomy and Automobility," *Independent Review* 2, no. 1 (Summer 1997), http://www.independent.org/pdf/tir/tir_02_1_lomasky.pdf.

11. Randall G. Holcombe and Samuel R. Staley, "Policy Implications," in *Smarter Growth: Market-Based Strategies for Land-Use Planning in the 21st Century* (Westport, CT: Greenwood, 2001), 262.

Index

Ehrenburg, Ilya, 22–23
Eisenhower, Dwight, 61, 103
electric automobiles: early, 9, 15, 70–71; recent, 10, 143, 152
Eliot, T. S., 45
Embarcadero Freeway, 109
emissions controls. *See* air pollution
Empire State Building, 109
energy conservation, 129, 143, 151–52. *See also* oil
enforced mobility, 128, 161
engineers: and highway construction, 104, 118, 119, 120–21, 123, 125, 127, 137; international influence of, 112, 116, 126; and traffic regulation, 74, 76, 77, 79, 172
England. *See* Great Britain
environmental movement, 129, 140–42, 143, 145, 165
Erb, Hans F., 54
Essen, Germany, 168, 169
eugenics, 30
Europe: automobile ownership and use, 28, 49, 83, 141; car-free days, 171; cities, 83–89, 129; dependence on automobiles, 162–66; eastern, 61–63, 77, 135, 141; environmental regulations, 142; freeway revolts, 113–14; Green hostility to cars, 140, 148, 150, 165, 172; mass transit, 134, 135, 157; pedestrian zones, 167–70; postwar, 48–50, 53–56; pro-automobile backlash, 148–50; rural tensions, 17, 28; sport utility vehicles, 145. *See also individual countries and cities*
exhaust, automotive. *See* air pollution
Explosion of a Motor Car, 32
Eynatten, Baron von, 25–26

Falling Down, 94
Fall of Public Man, The, 96
families, 29, 31, 44, 93
Fascist party, 35. *See also* Italy; Mussolini, Benito

Faulkner, William, 29
Feux rouges, 56
Figaro, Le, 20, 176
film and automobiles, 32, 56, 57, 177
fins, tail, 47
Firestone Tire, 155
Fitzgerald, F. Scott, 56
Flensburg, Germany, 68
Flonneau, Mathieu, 158
Ford, Henry, 34, 36, 61, 71
Ford, Henry, II, 122
Ford Motor Company, 34, 44, 48, 57; Edsel, 5, 48; Model T, 28, 48
Forster, E. M., 175, 177, 183
Fort Worth, Texas, 82, 169
France, 28, 143, 157; highway construction, 112, 115, 137; pro-auto attitudes, 15, 37, 49, 148, 157, 169. *See also* Paris
Franco, Francisco, 61
Frank, Lawrence, 163
freedom: ambivalence about automobiles and, 2, 36, 64–68, 93, 180–83; rhetoric of, 1, 61, 86–87, 127, 149
Freeway (film), 94
freeways, 78, 100, 103; opposition to, 99, 104–10, 111–29, 134, 136, 150; urban, 81, 82, 87, 93–94, 103–10, 112–17, 136–38
Freiburg, Germany, 172
Frisch, Max, 45
Furnas, J. C., 37–38
Futurama, 78, 101
futurists, Italian, 34, 35, 176

Galbraith, John Kenneth, 208n63
gated communities, 162
gender, 29, 50–51, 64–65
General Motors, 44, 58, 61, 78, 144; alleged conspiracy involving, 153–54, 155, 157, 159
Geneva, 116, 117
gentrification, 95
German parliament, 22, 25, 32–33, 73

noise, 17–18, 70
NOPE (Not On Planet Earth), 150
Norway, 125, 196n16, 208n52
Notre Dame cathedral (Paris), 115

oil: industry, 119, 142, 143, 151; supplies and shortages of, 3, 4, 143–45, 150–51
Oldfield, Barney, 65
Olmsted, Frederick Law, 110
On the Road, 45
OPEC, 143
Orlando, 176
Orlando, Florida, 106
O'Toole, Randal, 150
Ottawa, 135
Otto, Nicolaus, 15

Packard, Vance, 47–48
Panhard & Levassor, 15
Paris, 71, 75, 77, 89, 148; early fashion for cars, 15, 35, 72–73; highway construction, 115–16, 138; mass transit, 134, 157–58
parking, 76, 81, 85–86, 125, 136; induced demand for, 124
Parks, Rosa, 66
parks, urban, 104–5, 107
parkways, 101, 104, 110. *See also* freeways
Pasadena, California, 106
Pasadena Freeway, 104
path dependence, 8, 10, 158, 163, 166
Pau, France, 25
pedestrian paradises, 171
pedestrians, 90, 182–83; driven from city streets, 73, 74, 85, 182; ignored by planners, 79, 121, 162; threatened by automobiles, 21, 38–39, 48, 60, 75
Pedestrians' Association, 38
Pedestrians' Rights Association (Paris), 148
pedestrian zones, 82, 167–71
Pennsylvania, University of, 106
Pennsylvania Turnpike, 101
Pensacola, Florida, 106

Peters, Mary, 79
petroleum. *See* oil
Philadelphia, 105, 106, 107
Phillips Petroleum, 155
physicians, 29–30, 33
Pidoll, Baron Michael von, 73
Play It As It Lays, 93–94
Plunder Road, 138
police, 27, 67–68
Pollock, Jackson, 53
Pompidou, Georges, 115, 157–58
Porsche, Ferdinand, 36
Portal, Georges, 53
Portland, Oregon, 129
Portugal, 50
Posadowky-Wehner, Arthur von, 33
Poulet, Robert, 53, 54
preservation, historic, 95
progress, 23, 34, 40–41
Proust, Marcel, 176
Provos, 88
Prussian parliament, 25, 40, 73
Pygmalion, 30

race relations, 65–66, 105–7
racing, automobile, 15, 16, 52–53, 56, 65, 100
Radburn, New Jersey, 78, 79
Radiant City, 77, 79, 167
Ragon, Michel, 89
railways, 14, 16, 50, 97, 130, 131; street (*see* streetcars); suburban, 92, 97, 134; underground (subways), 81, 113, 131–32, 134, 136
Rambler, 48
Ravaillac, François, 75
Reader's Digest, 37, 119
Red Cars (Los Angeles), 154–55
Red Flag law, 27
Red Hook (Brooklyn), 107
refrigerators, 160–61
Reichow, Hans Bernhard, 83, 85
Reivers, The, 29

St. Louis, Missouri, 105
Stockholm, 125
stone throwing, 24, 71
St. Paul, Minnesota, 106
St. Petersburg, Florida, 106
streetcars, 14, 73–74, 92, 97; removal of, 85, 132, 134, 136, 153–59
streets, city, 69–74, 77, 78, 85, 171–72. *See also* freeways; pedestrians; pedestrian zones
Studebaker, 47
subsidies, 6–7
suburbs, 78–82, 91, 97, 98, 123, 137
subways. *See* railways: underground (subways)
Sunday driving, 27, 31
sustainability 3, 145, 151, 161, 185
Sweden, 208n52
Switzerland: early opposition to cars, 24, 25, 27; freeway revolts, 116–17; highway construction, 100, 112, 116, 118, 137; recent polarization, 148, 172
Sydney, 74, 112, 137

Taconic State Parkway, 110
Taken for a Ride, 154
Takoma Park, Maryland, 106
Tale of Two Cities, A, 71
Tampa, 106
Tarkington, Booth, 71
Tata Nano, 166
taxes, automotive and fuel, 6–7, 36, 40, 100, 111–12, 134, 148
taxis, 9, 35, 184
Thailand, 142
Toad, Mr., 17
Tokyo, 135, 167
Toronto, 113, 135
Trabant, 63
traffic calming, 170–71
traffic jams, 67, 76, 81, 83, 85, 88
trams. *See* streetcars
transit, mass, 130–36, 153–59. *See also* buses; railways; streetcars

transport clubs, 172
trucks, 40, 50, 82, 184. *See also* sport utility vehicles (SUVs)
Tuscany, 25

United Auto Workers, 44, 119
United Kingdom (UK). *See* Great Britain
United States: automobile manufacturing (*see* Detroit auto manufacturers); automobile ownership and use, 28, 43, 83–85, 142, 184; as center of car culture, 10, 43; cities, 79–82 (*see also* downtown); City Beautiful, 75–76; contribution to global warming, 3; Department of Transportation, 133; dependence on automobiles, 161–62, 179; drivers' licenses, 68; environmental movement, 140, 141; freeway revolts, 104–11, 119; highway construction, 100–101, 102–4, 137; highway finance, 111–12; influence of highway planners, 112, 116, 125; mass transit, 131–34, 155–57; NIMBY influence on land-use planning, 98; 1950s car culture, 4–5, 43–48; pedestrian zones, 169–70; pollution regulations, 142; race relations, 65–66, 105–7; road rage, 181; rural tensions, 24, 26–28; safety initiatives, 37–38, 57–60; speed limits, 24–25, 181; suburbs, 78, 80–82, 98, 107, 123, 137
Unsafe at Any Speed, 58

Valderpoort, W., 48, 83, 88
Vancouver, 113, 135
Vanderbilt, William K., II, 21, 24–25, 100
Venice, 184
Vermont, 27
Vienna, 73, 82, 175
Vietnam, 179
violence. *See* accidents, traffic; aggression; deaths
Vogel, Hans-Jochen, 49, 89–90

Voisin plan, 77
Volkswagen, 35–36, 48, 49, 54, 59

Wacker Drive, 104
walking, 18, 72, 182–83. *See also* pedestrians
Warhol, Andy, 56
Washington, DC, 101, 106, 134
Washington Square (New York), 124
Webber, Melvin, 92
Weekend, 56
Wellington, Duke of, 23
West Side Highway (New York), 104, 124, 138
West Virginia, 26
West Virginia University, 131
Westway (London), 94, 114–15
Wharton, Edith, 17
whips, 25
White, E. B., 47
Who Framed Roger Rabbit?, 154–55
wilderness, 18, 66, 110, 172
Williamsburg, Virginia, 184
Wilshire Boulevard, 81, 90

Wilson, Charles, 61, 149
Wilson, James Q., 150
Wilson, Woodrow, 28
Wind in the Willows, The, 17
Wolfe, Tom, 54–55
Wolverhampton, England, 94
women: as bicyclists and pedestrians, 29, 64–65; as motorists, 29, 51, 52, 64–65, 66
Woolf, Virginia, 176
World Bank, 61
World War I, 35
World War II, 43, 101–2, 103
Wright, Frank Lloyd, 91
Wright, Henry, 78

Yale University, 208n52
Yellow Truck and Coach, 155

Zemeckis, Robert, 154
Zermatt, Switzerland, 184
Zurich, 49, 116, 117, 137, 169